DISCRIMINATION IN THE NHL

Bob Sirois

DISCRIMINATION IN THE NHL

Quebec Hockey Players Sidelined

Baraka
Books

Montreal

Published by Baraka Books

6977, rue Lacroix
Montréal, Québec H4E 2V4
Telephone: 514-808-8504
info@barakabooks.com
www.barakabooks.com

Translation © 2010, Baraka Books

Published originally under the title: *Le Québec mis en échec*
© 2009, Les Éditions de L'Homme, division du Goupe Sogides inc., filiale du Groupe
Livre Quebecor Media inc. (Montreal, Québec)

Avec le soutien financier de la SODEC pour la traduction.

Cover and book design by Folio infographie
Translation by Jacqueline Snider and Robin Philpot

Printed and bound in Quebec

Library and Archives Canada Cataloguing in Publication

Sirois, Bob, 1954-

    Discrimination in the NHL: Quebec hockey players sidelined / Bob Sirois.

    Translation of: Le Québec mis en échec.

    ISBN 978-1-926824-01-7

    1. National Hockey League. 2. Discrimination in sports. 3. Hockey players—
Québec (Province). I. Title.

GV847.8.N3S5713 2010   796.962'64   C2010-906190-X

Legal Deposit, 4th quarter, 2010
Bibliothèque et Archives nationales du Québec
Library and Archives Canada

Trade Distribution & Returns

Canada:
LitDistCo
1-800-591-6250; orders@litdistco.ca

United States:
Independent Publishers Group
1-800-888-4741 (IPG1);
orders@ipgbook.com

"French-speaking hockey players are clearly disadvantaged
and must be better than the others to succeed
in the National Hockey League."

Maurice Richard, *La Presse*, 28 September 1986.

Contents

Acknowledgements 11

Preface 13

CHAPTER 1
Introduction 19

CHAPTER 2
Quebec Hockey Players Drafted by the NHL 29

CHAPTER 3
NHL Teams and Their Use of Quebec Hockey Players 77

CHAPTER 4
Quebecers in the NHL 161

CHAPTER 5
Coaches 195

CHAPTER 6
Conclusion 199

Epilogue 215

Appendix 217

List of Tables and List of Abbreviations 221

Acknowledgements

This book would not have appeared in English without the enthusiastic support of Baraka Books and Publisher Robin Philpot. I want to thank my son Shawn for the essay *The French Blue Line*, which has continually inspired me. Marc Lavoie, Professor of Economics at the University of Ottawa, has provided advice and insight based on the two books he had already published. His expertise has been vital in developing many tables. Sincere thanks go to my great friend, André Matteau. Our common friend, the late François Vinet, would be proud of us. Thanks also to my business partner Neil Haché: yes, the book is finally finished! During the two years it took to write this book, my partner Suzanne wrote another one entitled, *The Jobs Bob Didn't Do at Home for the Past Two Years*. Maybe I should write another one...

Preface

It is often said that sports fans are fanatical about statistics, they always want more. Bob Sirois has not disappointed those fans! He undertook the massive task of compiling all significant statistics for French and English-speaking Quebec hockey players who were drafted by National Hockey League teams or who played in the NHL over the past forty years,. When he first showed me the results of his research, I was astonished by both the minute details and the scope of his work. What's more, Bob Sirois did the research in his spare time. He also manages a very busy company in the aviation industry, which I can vouch for since in each of our meetings he had to field a record number of calls.

Bob Sirois has an advantage over academics like me who have looked into the situation of French Canadians and French-speaking Quebecers in the National Hockey League. He played in the NHL for several seasons, he was deputy administrator of the NHL Veterans Association for the transfer of the Chevaliers de Longueuil to Victoriaville and, two years later, he was responsible for the sale of the Tigres of the Quebec Major Junior Hockey League to a group of businessmen in that region. For five years he was as an agent for hockey players, partnering with Gilles Lupien. He is much more familiar than any academic with the origins and background of the different hockey players. Moreover, he has experienced from within the way in which amateur hockey players are drafted, how teams make their draft picks, and how information circulates throughout the network of scouts, coaches, and managers in the league.

People closely involved with the NHL rarely dare to address the question of discrimination against French-speaking hockey players, because they fear reprisals. To his credit, Bob Sirois has defied that trend by speaking out. In earlier studies I have shown that French-speaking defencemen have been underpaid compared to English-Canadian defencemen and that French-speaking players have been underrated during the draft. The proof of this latter point is the fact that French-speaking players drafted at the same rank as English-speaking players performed better, gathering an average of ten more points for each full season played while maintaining an equivalent level of defensive play. At that time I attributed the situation to a myth, which was also repeated in Quebec, to the effect that French-speaking players were poor in defensive hockey, but also to the crucial role of largely English-speaking old-boy network during the Entry Draft.

Bob Sirois clearly shows that French-speaking hockey players who were drafted by the NHL teams or who played in the NHL are not evenly or randomly distributed throughout the league. The Montreal Canadiens and the Quebec Nordiques are known to have recruited many French-speaking hockey players, but Bob Sirois' research shows that although some other teams have recruited French-speaking players, several teams seem to be allergic to players who speak French. He shows how friendship networks help explain why French-speaking players are so unequally distributed throughout the NHL.

Bob Sirois also breaks new ground with his study of the evolution of midget hockey players in Quebec and the percentage of players who end up being drafted by NHL teams. He discovers another facet of the open, veiled or unwitting Francophobia that appears to reign in the NHL. Based on the number of French and English-speaking midget hockey players between 1968 and 2006, Bob Sirois observes that between 1970 and 2009 English-speaking Quebec hockey players were almost twice as likely as French-speaking Quebec hockey players to be drafted by an NHL team. He also notes that an English-speaking Quebec hockey player who is drafted is more likely to play in the NHL than a French-speaking player who was drafted. This occurs even though all Quebec hockey players up to age sixteen enjoy the same training and hockey development framework in the same leagues and organization. The hypothesis that prejudice and old-boy networks in the NHL are detrimental to French-speaking hockey players is thus reinforced.

On another plane, when I studied the lists of Quebec hockey players in the NHL, I realized that very few of the few Quebec hockey players who make it in the NHL manage to stay there. Whereas the average career length for hockey players in the NHL is five seasons, half of the French-speaking Quebec players play fewer than one hundred games in the NHL and more than a quarter of them never play more than thirty games. These figures are food for thought for junior hockey players and for their parents...

Marc LAVOIE
Professor of Economics, University of Ottawa
Author of
Avantage numérique: l'argent et la Ligue nationale de Hockey,
Vents d'ouest (1997)
Désavantage numérique: les francophones dans la LNH,
Vents d'ouest (1998)

Foreword

I was nine years old on December 18, 1963, a time when all French Canadian kids wanted to be Maurice Richard. I was getting ready to play hockey at one of many Montreal outdoor hockey rinks at Ahuntsic Park in the north end of Montreal. After clearing the snow from the ice and warming up in the change room in front of a wood-burning fire, we were finally ready to begin the game of the year. We all dreamed of being the Rocket and, in fact, we all believed we were.

My team was the Loisirs Saint-Alphonse in the Petite-Patrie district. We were up against the Ahuntsic Braves with the Rocket's son André Richard on it. André's father was everyone's hero, but he was there simply as a spectator. The pressure in the change room was unbelievable because deep down we thought we were about to play our own Stanley Cup. For the first time in my hockey career I had butterflies in my stomach and sweaty palms. I just wanted the game to start.

My teammates were as nervous as I was and some of us had to make unscheduled trips to the washroom just like in the National Hockey League. I don't even remember who won, but I do remember very clearly how Maurice Richard cheered for us just as much as he did for his son's team. We were all his children. For Maurice we were all children of the Montreal Canadiens, all nine and ten-year-old kids secretly hoping to be like him.

When I got home I'd made my decision. I wanted to play in the National Hockey League and of course it had to be for Montreal Canadiens. It was simply *the* dream of all kids my age, children who belonged to what is now known as the Quebec nation.

I am a very lucky man because just ten years later, in 1973, I had become a Montreal Junior playing at the Forum. I wore number nine on my hockey sweater and was captain of the team. All other comparisons with Maurice Richard end there, but what more could I have asked for?

My luck continued. Just four years later, in 1978, I played in the National Hockey League All-Star game in Buffalo. What surprised me then was that thirty-six of the forty players on the Campbell and Prince of Wales teams were Canadian. Thirteen of those thirty-six Canadian players were Quebecers, an impressive thirty-six percent in a league in which only fifteen percent of the Canadian players were from Quebec.

What has happened to all those French-speaking Quebecers in the National Hockey League? What became of all the talented young Quebecers who hoped to have a hockey career and follow in the footsteps of the Montreal Canadiens, the team that the Quebec nation has called its own? Have they been treated fairly, justly, equitably? Are they treated differently in 2010?

The debate has gone on in Quebec ever since French-speaking Quebecer Maurice Richard was suspended by English-speaking National Hockey League President Clarence Campbell. Nobody will forget that his suspension degenerated into a terrible riot. The debate continues and is very much on the sports agenda, and those who want to understand it will have no trouble doing so. People are invited to judge for themselves!

Chapter 1

Introduction

The prime minister of Canada, Stephen Harper, declared that Quebec was a nation on November 22, 2006. One week later the House of Commons approved a motion to that effect. The prime minister also stated that Canada had been founded by two nations. Although the National Hockey League was created by a group of English-Canadian business men in 1917, the pioneers of the NHL belonged to both of Canada's founding nations.

Montreal Canadiens are the pride of a nation

In the early 1900s Montreal had two large French-Canadian hockey teams: Le National and Le Montagnard. These two teams recruited their players from well-known Montreal classical colleges. They were big rivals fighting for supremacy in French-Canadian hockey. In 1907 however, the Montagnard team was dissolved, and in 1908 Le National pulled out of the professional circuit. This left the major leagues without a single French-Canadian team.

In 1909 a new league was created, the National Hockey Association, and four of the five teams in that new league belonged to John Ambrose O'Brien. This Ontario entrepreneur firmly believed that hockey in Montreal would profit financially from an English-French rivalry, and that a patriotic face-off of that nature would enhance French Canadian interest in the sport. Montreal had two teams then and one of them was called Le Club de hockey canadien. French-speaking hockey fans quickly identified with the players on the new team and soon developed into a large group of faithful supporters. People ended up calling the players *Les Habitants* or even *The Flying Frenchmen* because of their ties to French-Canadian society. Hockey was one of the rare domains in which the French and English would compete and sometimes, if not often, the French would win. It was clear that the local team inspired great pride throughout French Canada.

Hockey also became a distinctive identity factor for both Canadians and Quebecers since the passion for hockey was then one of the rare things that united the two nations whose relations were strained. The same can be said one hundred years later.

Until the mid-1970s the majority of National Hockey League players were Canadians or Quebecers. With the globalization of the League and the arrival of many European and American hockey players, the Montreal Canadiens slowly lost their French identity, but that did not mean that young Quebecers would not stop dreaming of wearing the tri-coloured uniform that represented their nation. The Montreal Canadiens' centennial was also the hundredth anniversary of French Canadian participation in professional hockey.

This book documents the experience of the Quebec nation in the National Hockey League from the 1970-71 season until the 2008-2009 season.

Many books have been published about the Montreal Canadiens and many biographies have been written about all the legendary hockey players but no one has established as comprehensive a study as this one on Quebec hockey players in the NHL. Statistics are provided on the NHL Entry Draft since 1970, along with an exhaustive study of Quebecers who have played on NHL teams, including players who might have played only a single match over the last forty years. A whole chapter deals with Quebec coaches who led NHL teams during that period. Although many serious studies have been conducted on the specific situation of French-speaking Quebecers in professional hockey, the media have largely ignored them. Their silence is surprising. Personally, I find them very useful and refer to them often.

Censored!

If you think I'm going to talk about that eccentric who rants and raves on the very English national television network, the CBC, the man who enjoys dumping on French-speaking and European hockey players, then you've got the wrong book. I'd rather not even mention him. Why promote someone who means absolutely nothing on the Quebec side of the Ottawa River?

If you think I am going to comment on the Shane Doan affair and specifically on the foul language he used with four French-speaking referees at the Bell Centre in December 2006, rest assured, I'll pass on it. If you believe I am going to lose sleep on the Sean Avery-Denis Gauthier incident about how French-speaking hockey players are supposed to be wimps because they wear visors, again I hope you'll understand that I really don't give a damn. I won't say anything more about the Patrice Brisebois incident where he was called a "Fucking Frog." I don't plan on wasting my time, or yours, on the Gilles Gratton affair in which he accused his St. Louis Blues coach of being racist. I won't bore you with the case of Robert Picard who settled one incident with a teammate who had used a racial slur…and I will also remain silent about a similar event that pitted Alain Langlais and Bill Goldsworthy of the Minnesota North Stars against each other.

And if you thought that you might learn about how speaking French is actually forbidden in some NHL locker rooms, while other languages like Russian, Swedish, and Finish are allowed, well, you will be disappointed. It is perfectly obvious that French, unlike other languages, tends to rub some English-speaking people the wrong way and make them feel vulnerable. As former NHL referee Ron Fournier says on French-language television, "That's official." I won't talk about it at all. I won't write anything on those contentious issues because I might make Quebecers sound like whiners again, and that is certainly not the aim of this book.

I have therefore decided to censor myself, however only after this short essay entitled *The French Blue Line*.

The French Blue Line

Imagine for a moment, after a hard bodycheck from Jarome Iginla or another homerun by Barry Bonds, a frustrated player from the opposing team yelled out, "Go take a hike, filthy Nigger!" Such comments, and especially those that include specific words, stir up anger in the popular media machine, and rightly so. There's no doubt that, as the *La Presse* columnist Patrick Lagacé pointed out, the frustrated person in question would suffer "the wrath of God and then some."

The targeted player's community, whether their skin was black, yellow, white or red, would fittingly storm the media and the hot-lines. The political and pressure groups, buffeted by popular outrage, would seize on the story and the commissioner responsible for the professional sports league would most likely impose exemplary sanctions on the person who made the racial slur. That would happen if we were dealing with skin colour. Imagine what would happen if the insults were of a religious nature! That would create a real commotion, if not civil war...

What is racism? It occurs when an individual shows scorn or contempt for another group with a different skin colour, a different culture or a different religion. Language, which is the heart of culture, can also become the source of racism. In short, it's a vicious attack aimed at injuring the pride people have in their origins, their beliefs or their sense of belonging. Being able to nurture and value one's particular roots, origins, and history, without falling into chauvinism, is a human right. Simply put, it's a question of live and let live.

Quebec is the only jurisdiction north of the Rio Grande where the majority speak a language other than English. The people of Quebec have been struggling for centuries to preserve their identity. The French-speaking citizens of Quebec are particularly attached to the French language and to their history, just as they are emotionally attached to their national sport of hockey.

For Quebecers speaking French and playing hockey in the twentieth century hasn't always been an easy mix. Hockey rinks have often been venues for very unsportsmanlike confrontations between English and French, up to and including professional hockey in the NHL. Physical barriers were known to be used to separate hockey fans from the two groups who had come out to support their team at the Montreal Forum.

With time and the arrival European players as hockey went global, one might have expected the situation to change and that offensive and disgraceful comments or acts relating to cultural differences would be prohibited. Great strides have been made in this area, but it seems that certain differences take longer to accept and appreciate than others. In Canada, a supposedly bilingual country, hateful remarks can still be heard in 2010 from a clown cum sports commentator dressed in red who gets his thrills insulting French-speaking players on a government-owned national TV network. The National Hockey League has remained silent all too often or has studiously ignored racial slurs about "Frogs," especially when they are made by star players. Even when politicians of all political stripes get involved, Quebecers rarely get more than a friendly pat on the back, while the problem is conveniently swept under the rug.

In many other professional sports, racial slurs are not tolerated. Rule-breakers are punished immediately. Why does the NHL still operate with a 1950s mindset?

Hockey fans and professional hockey players from Quebec don't want to be considered different and don't want by-laws tailored for them. They simply want the same rules to apply to everyone. The question isn't whether the French or the English are more racist, both are known to take cheap shots. The real problem is that when a player crosses the *French Blue Line*, even if the referee blows his whistle the player is never called offside.

Uncensored

These questions are constantly addressed in the French-language media but rarely an echo is heard in the English media, unless it is to shoot the messenger. Here is a sampling of comments made by respected columnists and reporters from a broad selection of Quebec's mainstream media.

On Don Cherry

Don Cherry enjoys controversy. The most recent dates back to last January 24 [2004] when a crew from the CBC television program *Enjeux* was accompanying him while doing a feature on him. During his comment on Hockey Night in Canada, he claimed that French-speaking and European hockey players were wimps because, according to him, they were mainly the ones who wore visors.
— Alain Gravel speaking on *Enjeux*, February 17, 2004.

Letter to a Distinguished Colleague, Shane Doan

Why is it that racist slurs directed towards the "frogs" or the "fucking Frenchmen" continue to be tolerated in a professional sports league and that those who make them are not reprimanded?
— Vincent Marissal, *La Presse*, May 5, 2007.

The Disappearance of Quebecers

Are Quebecers playing in the National Hockey League to be considered as a threatened or disappearing species? It seems to be true.
— Martin Leclerc, *Le Journal de Montréal*, September 4, 2006.

The Annual Nose Thumbing (Selection of Junior Team Canada)

That's about enough! Only one Quebec hockey player picked this year, two in 2007, three in 2006, one in 2005, and two in 2004. What is holding back the people in positions of authority and keeping them from denouncing it publicly?
— Maurice Dumas, *Le Soleil*, Québec, December 15, 2007

We are to blame too

We have not insisted enough on being respected. I'm talking mainly about the players who, after being on the receiving end [of racist slurs], have often tried to trivialize it. Maybe they thought that they would be called whiners. A "frog" has always been a "frog," whether it was Maurice Richard, Jean Béliveau or Guy Lafleur.
— Bertrand Raymond, *Le Journal de Montréal*, April 3, 2007.

Éric Desjardins: "Racism" on the Ice

I often got called "frog" or "fucking Frenchman," but I didn't let it get to me. I knew that they were just trying to make me lose my concentration, which meant that I was doing my job well or that I really was bothering the guy who was making the remark.
— Comments made to Mathias Brunet for *www.cyberpresse.ca*
May 5, 2007.

What cannot be censored are the facts documented in the many essays, research papers, and articles written by Canadian and American academics on the subject of discrimination against French-speaking Quebecers in the National Hockey League.[1]

Economics and sociology professors have revealed some surprising and troubling indicators. After their studies were published, critics and opponents in English Canada challenged their research saying that the sample used was too small and that the results could be attributed to factors other than discrimination. With this book, the sample used is now complete. Those other factors raised are also addressed throughout this book.

"Hockey is all messed up in Quebec," reported the *Journal de Montréal* on June 26, 2008, quoting New Jersey Devils scout Claude Carrier. The statement was made a few days after the "annual slap in the face" that the majority of Quebec hockey players have to endure when National Hockey League holds its annual draft. In fact Claude Carrier's statement is a striking example of the so-called "other factors." It is just another one of those myths, stereotypes, prejudice, and pseudo-scientific explanations that some hockey personalities, both French and English, have tried to make people swallow for decades.

In another article in the *Journal de Montréal* in September 2008, San Jose Sharks' scout Gilles Côté suggested a way to straighten out minor hockey in Quebec. He ventured his own diagnosis on the health of Hockey Quebec, supposedly to improve minor hockey throughout Quebec. Another scout, Mario Saraceno from the New York Islanders, also spoke out in the *Journal de Montréal* on September 2006, and offered his recommendations on solving the problem of underrepresentation of Quebecers in the NHL.

Claude Carrier, Gilles Côté, and Mario Saraceno should first answer the nagging question as to how long Quebec hockey has been in such bad shape? One year, ten years, forty years, or always? Chapter 2 on the NHL Draft provides answers as to whether minor hockey in Quebec is ravaged by some unknown cancer or whether

---

1. Neil Longley, "The underrepresentation of French Canadians on English Canadian NHL Teams: Evidence from 1943 to 1998," in *Journal of Sports Economics*, Vol. 1, No. 3, pp. 236-256, March 2001.

an anti-French virus has attacked certain NHL teams. If a virus has in fact infected some teams, then I hope the right antiviral medication will be found. The three NHL scouts mentioned above have screamed at the top of their lungs that hockey is all messed up in Quebec and that Hockey Quebec has always been at fault for the underrepresentation of Quebec hockey players in the NHL. Although all three are experienced hockey scouts, their suggestions sound like shameless simplistic clichés. The chapter below on the NHL Entry Draft provides more accurate and enlightened grounds for a diagnosis of the problem. It is hoped that scouts will then understand that other very real factors are at play, but unfortunately they are taboo.

The three NHL scouts are cited as examples, but they are not alone. Several other gratuitous comments made by supposedly serious hockey people also appear in this book. Readers may be asking questions such as: do any NHL teams completely and intentionally ignore French-speaking Quebec hockey players during the draft? This leads to the obvious question as to whether reference to Quebecers in hockey encompasses all Quebecers or just those whose mother tongue is French, and to the question who is a Quebecer? Although politically correct sports fans might want to lynch me in front of the Bell Centre, this book makes a distinction between French-speaking and English-speaking Quebecers. Not to worry, however, all sports fans will find reason to unite once again by the end of my book.

To complete this study, it was necessary to identify the hockey players' birthplaces. That was easy enough for those born in Quebec. However, many players were born in other provinces or other countries, their parents having immigrated here for work or other reasons. Francis Bouillon, André Roy, Donald Brashear, Jere Gillis, and Scott Garland are hockey players in this group. The research was complicated and possibly some players have been missed.

The next step was certainly the most delicate and difficult. A French-speaking Quebecer is someone whose mother tongue is French, while an English-speaking Quebecer is someone whose mother tongue is English. The major problem in making this distinction was in classifying new Quebecers in one group or another.

The solution was to base it on the school they attended, and on the French-English ratio in Quebec, which is ninety percent French-speaking and ten percent English-speaking.

Though I said that I might be lynched, perhaps I may even run the risk of being drawn and quartered because I have also distinguished between the sons of first and second-generation immigrants. Since I'm discussing immigration, before being drawn and quartered, it's important to mention that I too am the son of a first generation immigrant. My father was born on June 19, 1927, in Saint-David, Maine, United States. Being the son of a Franco-American, I always needed more free tickets for family members when I was playing in Boston than in Montreal. My father's entire family is American and they live in the greater Boston area. The United States and the English language were therefore not new to me when I started playing in the NHL. I have made all these distinctions somewhat against my will, but felt that it was necessary in order to verify certain facts that are presented throughout the book.

Tackling the issue of discrimination is very sensitive. The big question is: why does it still go on in the very serious National Hockey League? The Webster dictionary defines *to discriminate* as making a distinction in favour of or against a person on a categorical basis rather than according to actual merit. Economists and jurists often consider that discrimination occurs when, all things being equal, access to a position is not equal for everybody. In everyday language, we talk about double standards. In the sports world, and more specifically in hockey, we talk about equal talent meeting with unequal treatment.

Discrimination is rarely mentioned in the NHL unless there's a debate over which racial slur encouraged certain players to battle it out on the ice. How is discrimination practiced in hockey? This book addresses two types: discrimination during the draft and discrimination when contracts are signed. The first type takes place when players are being selected at the NHL Entry Draft, which will be referred to as "entry discrimination." The other type occurs when team managers decide to sign a player for their team or demote him to their farm team, which will be referred to as "contract discrimination."

In order to have a better idea of how many Québec hockey players really had an NHL career in the last forty years, all the tables are based on two hundred games played in regular season play, which represents a minimum of three seasons in the NHL. After perusing these tables, readers will definitely understand why it was important to go into such detail.

Chapter 2 on the NHL Entry Draft provides answers to many questions. It even answers questions you might never have asked. That's what happened to me when I gathered this data from a variety of tables on the NHL draft.

Chapter 2

Quebec Hockey Players Drafted by the NHL

In 1963, in a move to prevent NHL teams from controlling amateur hockey teams and players, National Hockey League administrators instituted a system that gave each team an equal chance to draft amateur hockey players. The first NHL amateur draft was held at the Queen Elizabeth Hotel in Montreal on June 5, 1963. All hockey players seventeen or older who were not already sponsored by an NHL team could hope to be drafted. Until the 1969 draft, the Montreal Canadiens had the right to draft two Quebec players at the beginning of each draft.

Marc Tardif and Réjean Houle were the last two players drafted under that arrangement which automatically gave the Montreal Canadiens the rights over Quebec's best hockey players. Thus the first real draft in modern hockey began in 1970 and that is why this chapter on the NHL Entry Draft covers the last forty years (1970-2009).

NHL Central Scouting

Before the 1975-76 season, the National Hockey League created the Central Scouting to provide NHL teams with scouting and evaluation services for amateur hockey talent. Central Scouting employs nine full-time and six part-time scouts for North America as well as five full-time scouts in Europe. Every year Central Scouting provides two lists in which the best players in North America and Europe are classed.

The first list is released in January and the final one in May. NHL teams also have their own scouting services that use the Central Scouting lists and classifications as a reference.

The NHL Draft is a media show

The big National Hockey League media event is held every year in June. It is the one time that all NHL hockey and marketing personnel meet in one of the league's cities. The goal of the event is to show the hockey world to what extent the National Hockey League is a serious and professional operation. Journalists from all over the world attend. Hockey fans attending the NHL draft might believe that they are witnessing a very scientific and rigorously accurate assessment of the young talented hockey players for which the different NHL teams are vying. In my opinion, the opposite is true. Talent scouting is much more a question of intuition, feeling or even gut instinct. Myths, prejudice, stereotypes, and favouritism are an integral part of each National Hockey League Draft.

Myths, prejudice, stereotypes, and favouritism in the NHL Draft

As general manager of the Montreal Canadiens, Serge Savard unabashedly showed favouritism towards Quebec players during the NHL Draft. He would say, "At equal talent, I will always choose a Quebec hockey player."[2] The Quebec Nordiques definitely acted in the same way. If the Calgary Flames and the Edmonton Oilers do the same thing and choose local talent, it is unlikely that anybody would complain about discrimination since it is only normal to do so in the National Hockey League. So if all NHL teams are acting the same way then they are all showing favouritism by choosing local players when the talent is equal. What happens, however, when there is little or no local amateur talent? It might be possible to answer that question but first the myths, prejudice, and stereotypes have to be put aside.

In 1971 the Quebec Remparts in the Quebec Major Junior Hockey League with players like Guy Lafleur, André Savard, and Pierre Roy won the Memorial Cup in a virtual bloodbath against the St. Catharines Black Hawks of the Ontario Hockey League. Marcel Dionne led the Ontario team, with Pierre Guité as their enforcer, both of whom hailed from Quebec.[3] Already in 1971 the experts, analysts, media pundits, and a certain petty English hockey world claimed that the Quebec Remparts would never be able to hold out very long against the Canadian-style hockey played by the Ontario

---

2. Albert Ladouceur, "Les Nordiques aidaient la cause des Québécois," *Le Journal de Québec*, November 16, 2006.
3. "Que les champions se lèvent," www.remparts.qc.ca.

champions. Things change, often for the worse. Even today the same song is sung at every Memorial Cup tournament. Yet in the last ten years, Quebec reached the Memorial Cup finals eight times, western Canada seven times, and Ontario five times. It seems to me that the Quebec Major Junior Hockey League is perfectly capable of competing against the best teams in the Canadian Junior Hockey Leagues.

The same old song can also be heard every year when it's time to make the final picks for Junior Team Canada. Unfortunately, English-speaking commentators are not the only ones who try to make us swallow that strange old myth about the English-Canadian style of play. Some of the token NHL scouts and coaches from Quebec spread the same clichés that would have it that French-speaking players from Quebec just can't seem to adapt to that Canadian style. Here are some direct quotes: "Francophones don't like the rough play." "They are too small." "Francophones only think offensively and don't know how to play defence." But the best quote is, "Francophones have shortcomings that cannot be measured statistically." Fortunately all of these stereotypes have been analysed over the years by a number Canadian and American academics.

Some of their findings are presented in the Conclusion. The following tables and results spanning the last forty years are based on the NHL draft.

NHL draft of Quebec players from 1970 to 2009: results and facts

During the forty NHL drafts between the 1970 NHL draft in Montreal and the draft show held again in Montreal on June 27, 2009, NHL teams selected 9,253 hockey players of different nationalities. Of that total, 920 hockey players or 9.94 percent were from Quebec. The following pages provide all the results of the drafts as they concern Quebec hockey players.

Draft results for French-speaking Quebecers

Table 2.17 lists all French-speaking Quebec hockey players drafted by different NHL teams from 1970 through the 2009 draft. The players' main NHL career statistics are also provided along with the league they came from. For goaltenders the only statistic in the table is the number of games played in the NHL.

Table 2.18 provides the results for French-speaking Quebecers in the last forty NHL drafts. These include the number of players drafted per year and per decade, the league they played in, the number of players who played at least one game, and the number who played more than two hundred NHL games between 1970 and 2009.

Of the 920 Quebec players drafted between 1970 and 2009:

- · 763 were French-speaking Quebecers.
- · 693 played in the Quebec Major Junior Hockey League.
- · 26 played in different Ontario hockey leagues.
- · 37 played in the United States for the NCAA or other leagues.
- · 7 played in other Quebec or Canadian leagues.
- · 323 were French-speaking players who played in the NHL.
- · 177 played between one and 199 games.
- · 146 played more then two hundred games.

Draft results for English-speaking Quebecers

Table 2.19 lists all the English-speaking Quebec hockey players who were picked by NHL teams since 1970. This list also includes the 2009 draft. The players' main NHL career statistics are provided along with the league they came from.

Table 2.20 lists the results for English-speaking Quebec hockey players in the last forty NHL drafts. These include the number of players drafted per year and per decade, the league they played in, the number of players who played at least one game, and the number who played more than two hundred NHL games between 1970 and 2009.

Of the 920 Quebec players picked between 1970 and 2009:

- · 157 were English-speaking Quebecers.
- · 78 played in the Quebec Major Junior Hockey League.
- · 24 played in different Ontario hockey leagues.
- · 41 played in the United States for the NCAA or other leagues.
- · 5 played for Canadian universities.
- · 9 played in other Quebec or Canadian leagues.
- · 79 were English-speaking Quebecers who played in the NHL.
- · 40 played between one and 199 games.
- · 39 played more than two hundred games.

TABLE 2.1

French-speaking Quebec hockey players drafted (1970-2009)

DECADE	PLAYERS DRAFTED	ORIGIN					PLAYERS WHO PLAYED	GAMES PLAYED	
		LHJMQ	ONT.	US	C.U.	OTHER		1 to 199	200 +
1970-79	203	176	18	5	–	4	85	37	48
1980-89	165	153	2	8	–	2	91	54	37
1990-99	234	212	6	16	–	–	107	57	50
2000-08	161	152	–	8	–	1	40	29	11
TOTAL	763	693	26	37	–	7	323	177	146

TABLE 2.2

English-speaking Quebec hockey players drafted (1970-2009)

DECADE	PLAYERS DRAFTED	ORIGIN					PLAYERS WHO PLAYED	GAMES PLAYED	
		LHJMQ	ONT.	US	C.U.	OTHER		1 to 199	200 +
1970-79	54	33	13	3	3	2	30	13	17
1980-89	54	22	5	23	2	2	31	13	18
1990-99	26	11	4	8	–	3	10	7	3
2000-08	23	12	2	7	–	2	8	7	1
TOTAL	157	78	24	41	5	9	79	40	39

TABLE 2.3

Comparison of Quebecers drafted (1970-2009)*

	FRENCH-SPEAKING	ENGLISH-SPEAKING	TOTAL
1970-79	203	54	257
1980-89	165	54	219
1990-99	234	26	260
2000-08	161	23	184
TOTAL	763	157	920

* Based on Tables 2.1 and 2.2.

TABLE 2.4

Hockey background of all Quebec hockey players drafted (1970-2009)

QUEBECERS	PLAYERS DRAFTED	ORIGIN					PLAYERS WHO PLAYED	GAMES PLAYED	
		LHJMQ	ONT.	US	C.U.	OTHER		1 to 199	200 +
FRENCH-SPEAKING	763	693	26	37	–	7	323	177	146
ENGLISH-SPEAKING	157	78	24	41	5	9	79	40	39
GRAND TOTAL	920	771	50	78	5	16	402	217	185
% ENGLISH-SPEAKING	17.06%	10.11%	48%	52.56%	100%	56.25%	19.65%	18.43%	21.08%

Of the 920 Quebec players drafted between 1970 and 2009:

· 763 were French-speaking, or 82.94 percent.
· 157 were English-speaking, or 17.06 percent.

TABLE 2.5

Percentage of English-speaking hockey players drafted per decade

QUEBECERS	1970-79	1980-89	1990-99	2000-2009	GRAND TOTAL
FRENCH-SPEAKING	203	165	234	161	763
ENGLISH-SPEAKING	54	54	26	23	157
GRAND TOTAL	257	219	260	184	920
% ENGLISH-SPEAKING	21.01%	24.66%	10%	12.50%	17.06%

· Between 1970 and 1979, 21.01 percent of those drafted were English-speaking Quebecers.

· Between 1980 and 1989, 24.66 of those drafted were English-speaking Quebecers.

· Between 1990 and 1999, 10 percent those drafted were English-speaking Quebecers.

· Between 2000 and 2009, 12.5 percent of those drafted were English-speaking Quebecers.

The English-speaking population in Quebec in 2001 accounted for 8.5 percent of the total population of Quebec (Institut de la statistique, Quebec population, stat.gouv.qc.ca).

TABLE 2.6

Comparison of Quebec hockey players drafted by decade

QUEBEC PLAYERS	DECADE 1970-79	PLAYERS DRAFTED	PLAYERS WHO PLAYED	% OF PLAYERS WHO PLAYED	GAMES PLAYED 200 ET +	% OF PLAYERS WHO PLAYED
FRENCH-SPEAKING		203	85	41.87%	48	23.65%
ENGLISH-SPEAKING		54	30	55.55%	17	31.48%
TOTAL		257	115	44.75%		
	1980-89					
FRENCH-SPEAKING		165	91	55.15%	37	22.42%
ENGLISH-SPEAKING		54	31	57.40%	18	33.33%
TOTAL		219	122	55.70%		
	1990-99					
FRENCH-SPEAKING		234	107	45.73%	50	21.37%
ENGLISH-SPEAKING		26	10	38.46%	3	11.54%
TOTAL		260	117	45.00%		
	2000-05					
FRENCH-SPEAKING		98	37	37.75%	11	11.22%
ENGLISH-SPEAKING		15	8	53.33%	1	6.7%
TOTAL		113	45	39.83%		

TABLE 2.7

Comparison of Quebec hockey players drafted (1970- 2005)

QUEBEC PLAYERS	1970-2005	PLAYERS DRAFTED	PLAYERS WHO PLAYED	% OF PLAYERS WHO PLAYED	GAMES PLAYED 200 ET +	% OF PLAYERS WHO PLAYED
FRENCH–SPEAKING		700	320	45.71%	146	20.85%
ENGLISH–SPEAKING		149	79	53.02%	39	26.17%
GRAND TOTAL		849	399	46.99%	185	21.79%

Conclusions from Table 2.6

Between 1970 and 1979:

· 203 French-speaking players were drafted and eighty-five played in at least one game, or 41.87 percent. Of those eighty-five hockey players, forty-eight played more than two hundred games.

· Fifty-four English-speaking hockey players were drafted and thirty of them played in at least one game, or 55.55 percent. Of those thirty hockey players, seventeen played more than two hundred games.

· 41.87 percent of the French-speaking players drafted played at least one game.

· 55.55 percent of the English-speaking players drafted played at least one game.

· The percentage of English-speaking Quebec hockey players who were drafted and who played at least one game is 14 percent higher than for French-speaking players.

· 23.65 percent of French-speaking hockey players drafted played more than two hundred games.

· 31.48 percent of English-speaking players drafted played more than two hundred games.

· Of the 115 Quebecers who played at least one game, 26.09 percent were English-speaking hockey players.

· Of the sixty-five Quebecers who played more than two hundred games, 26.15 percent were English-speaking

· Compared to the French-speaking players, the percentage of English-speaking Quebec hockey players drafted who played more than two hundred NHL games slightly exceeds 26 percent, which is three times higher than the percentage of English-speaking people in the Quebec population.

Between 1980 and 1989:

- 165 French-speaking hockey players were drafted and ninety-one, or 55.15 percent, played in at least one game. Of those ninety-one hockey players, thirty-seven played more than two hundred games.
- Fifty-four English-speaking Quebec hockey players were drafted and thirty-one, or 57.40 percent, played at least one game. Of those thirty-one hockey players, eighteen played more than two hundred games.
- 55.15 percent of the French-speaking players drafted played at least one game.
- 57.40 percent of the English-speaking players drafted played at least one game.
- 22.42 percent of the French-speaking players drafted played more than two hundred games.
- 33.73 percent of the English-speaking players drafted played more than two hundred games.
- The percentage of English-speaking Quebec hockey players who were drafted and who played more than two hundred games is 11 percent higher than for French-speaking players.
- Of the 122 Quebecers who played at least one game, 25.41 percent were English.
- Of the fifty-five Quebecers who played at least two hundred games, 32.73 percent were English. This number is equivalent to almost four times their representation in the Quebec population.

Between 1990 and 1999:

- 260 Quebecers were drafted: 234 were French-speaking players and twenty-six English-speaking player, or about 10 percent, which is close to the percentage of English-speaking people in the Quebec population (8.5 percent).
- 234 French-speaking players were drafted and 107 of them, or 45.72 percent, played at least one game. Of those 107 hockey players, fifty ended up playing two hundred games or more.
- Twenty-six English-speaking players were drafted and ten of them ended up playing at least one game, or 38.46 percent. Of

those ten hockey players, three ended up playing more than two hundred games.

- 45.73 percent of French-speaking hockey players played at least one game.
- 38.46 percent of English-speaking players played at least one game.
- 21.37 percent of French-speaking hockey players drafted played more than two hundred games.
- 11.54 percent of English-speaking hockey players drafted played more than two hundred games.
- Of the 117 Quebecers who played at least one game, 91.45 percent were French-speaking players and 8.55 percent were English-speaking. These levels closely follow the linguistic breakdown in the Quebec population.

Between 2000 and 2009:

- 161 French-speaking players were drafted, but it is too early to have the exact number of players who will play in the NHL. However, between 2000 and 2005, ninety-eight French-speaking players were drafted and thirty-seven played in at least one game, or 37.75 percent. Of the thirty-seven who played between 2000 and 2005, eleven ended up playing two hundred games or more.
- Between 2000 and 2009, twenty-three English-speaking players were drafted and, similarly, it is too early to have any accurate statistics on the number of players who will play in the NHL. However, between 2000 and 2005, fifteen English-speaking players were drafted and eight ended up playing at least one game, or 53.33 percent. Of the eight players who played, only one ended up playing two hundred games or more until 2009.
- 37.75 percent of French-speaking players played at least one game.
- 53.33 percent of English-speaking players played at least one game.
- 11.22 percent of French-speaking players played more than two hundred games.
- 6.7 percent of English-speaking players played more than two hundred games.

· Of the forty-five hockey players who played between 2000 and 2009, 82.22 percent were French-speaking and 17.78 percent were English-speaking.

TABLE 2.8

**Comparison of Quebec hockey players
who were drafted and who played (by decade)**

QUEBEC PLAYERS	DECADE 1970-79	GAMES PLAYED 1 AND +	AVERAGE	GAMES PLAYED 200 AND +	AVERAGE
FRENCH–SPEAKING		85	73.91%	48	73.85%
ENGLISH–SPEAKING		30	26.09%	17	26.15%
TOTAL		115	100%	65	100%
	1980-89				
FRENCH–SPEAKING		91	74.59%	37	67.27%
ENGLISH–SPEAKING		31	25.41%	18	32.73%
TOTAL		122	100%	55	100%
	1990-99				
FRENCH–SPEAKING		107	91.45%	50	94.33%
ENGLISH–SPEAKING		10	8.55%	3	5.67%
TOTAL		117	100%	53	100%
	2000-05				
FRENCH–SPEAKING		37	82.22%	11	91.67%
ENGLISH–SPEAKING		8	17.78%	1	8.33%
TOTAL		45	100%	12	100%

TABLE 2.9

**Comparison of Quebec hockey players who were drafted
and who played between 1970 and 2005**

QUEBEC PLAYERS	1970-2005	GAMES PLAYED 1 AND +	AVERAGE	GAMES PLAYED 200 AND +	AVERAGE
FRENCH–SPEAKING		320	20.85%	146	78.92%
ENGLISH–SPEAKING		79	26.17%	39	21.08%
GRAND TOTAL		399	100%	185	100%

Conclusion from Tables 2.6 to 2.9

· Between 1970 and 2005, a thirty-six-year period, 700 French-speaking Quebec hockey players were drafted by NHL teams. Of the 700 players, 320 played in at least one game, or 45.71 percent. Of those 320, 146 played more than two hundred games (three years). This means that of the 700 French-speaking players drafted over thirty-six years, 20.85 percent ended up having a career of more than three years in the National Hockey League.

- During the same time period, 149 English-speaking Quebec hockey players were drafted by different NHL teams. Of those 149 players, seventy-nine played in at least one game, or 53.02 percent. Of the seventy-nine who played, thirty-nine ended up having a career of more than three years in the National Hockey League. This means that of the 149 English-speaking Quebec hockey players drafted over thirty-six years, 26.17 percent ended up having a career of more than three years in the National Hockey League.
- Between 1970 and 2005, a total of 849 Quebecers were drafted by different NHL teams, and of this number, 185 enjoyed careers of more than two hundred games in the NHL. Thirty-nine of them, or 21.08 percent, were English, whereas the English-speaking population in Quebec represents 8.5 percent of the total population!

The NHL draft of Quebec hockey players by their rankings

At the beginning of this chapter, it was pointed out that the NHL draft works much like a lottery. Other than identifying the top NHL draft picks, scouts are simply unable to accurately identify the hockey players who will really succeed in the NHL. Table 2.12 shows the success rate of the scouts who often underestimate the French-speaking Quebec hockey players and the likelihood that French-speaking Quebec hockey players might play in the NHL, according to their rank.

TABLE 2.10

The number of French-speaking Quebec hockey players drafted (by rank, 1970-2005)

DECADE	1970-79	1980-89	1990-99	2000-05	GRAND TOTAL
1 to 50	60	53	61	14	188
51 to 100	54	35	49	26	164
101 +	89	77	124	58	348
TOTAL	203	165	234	98	700

Of the 700 French-speaking Quebec hockey players drafted between 1970 and 2005:

· 188 were ranked between 1 and 50
· 164 were ranked between 51 and 100
· 348 were ranked from 101 and up.

TABLE 2.11

The number of players who played one or more games (by rank, 1970-2005)

DECADE	1970-79	1980-89	1990-99	2000-05	GRAND TOTAL
1 to 50	49	46	52	12	149
51 to 100	21	20	23	10	84
101 +	15	25	32	15	87
TOTAL	85	91	107	37	320

TABLE 2.12

Summary table (1970-2005)

DRAFT RANK	PLAYERS WHO PLAYED AT LEAST ONE GAME	NUMBER OF PLAYERS DRAFTED	LIKELIHOOD OF PLAYING 1 GAME% DE JOUER 1 MATCH
1 to 50	149	188	79.25%
51 to 100	84	164	51.22%
101 +	87	348	25.00%
TOTAL	320	700	45.71%

Conclusion from tables 2.11 and 2.12

· Of the 700 French-speaking Quebec hockey players who were drafted between 1970 and 2005, 320 played at least one game in the NHL.
· Of the 188 players who were ranked among the first fifty players, 149 played, or 79.25 percent.
· Of the 164 players who were ranked between 51 and 100, eighty-four played, or 51.22 percent.
· Of the 348 players ranked 101st and higher, eighty-seven played, or 25 percent.
· These results show that more than 53 percent of the 171 French-speaking Quebec hockey players who played for the NHL were ranked after the fiftieth choice. A large number of them went on to enjoy long productive careers in the NHL. Everybody knows the story of Luc Robitaille who was ranked 171 for the 1984

screening. He was not the only one: Maxime Talbot (264) in 2002; Bruno Gervais (182) in 2003; Stéphane Robidas (164) in 1995; Patrick Lalime (156) in 1993; Ian Laperrière (158) in 1992; Donald Audette (183) in 1989; and Claude Lapointe (234) in 1988. They are some examples that clearly show that French-speaking Quebec hockey players are underrated by NHL scouts.

French-speaking Quebec hockey players are underrated

· About ten percent of NHL players are never drafted because they aren't considered to be talented enough. Many of them go on never-theless to have brilliant careers in the NHL. Ed Belfour, Joel Otto, Mike Keane, Martin St-Louis, Marc Bureau, Éric Messier, and Steve Duschesne are included in this group. If ten percent of NHL hockey players are never drafted, why is it that 19.06 percent of French-speaking Quebec hockey players in the NHL were never drafted?

· Between 1970 and 2005, ninety-four Quebecers who were not drafted ended up playing in the NHL. Seventy-two were French-speaking, twenty-two English-speaking.

· Between 1970 and 2005, 320 French-speaking Quebec hockey players were drafted by the NHL and played in the league. Another seventy-two French-speaking players who were not drafted also played in the NHL, making a total of 392. In other words, 18.37 percent of the French-speaking Quebecers who played in the NHL between 1970 and 2005 were never drafted.

· Between 1970 and 2005, seventy-nine English-speaking Quebec hockey players who were drafted by the NHL played in the league. Another twenty-two English-speaking players who were not drafted ended up playing in the NHL, making a total of 101. In other words, 21.78 percent of the English-speaking Quebecers who played in the NHL were not drafted.

· Therefore, 493 Quebec hockey players played in the NHL between 1970 and 2005. Ninety-four of them were never drafted, which represents 19.06 percent of all those who played in the NHL, whereas the average in the NHL is ten percent.

· These figures leave no doubt: Quebec hockey players are under-rated and undervalued by NHL scouts!

The Alexandre Burrows effect

Alexandre Burrows is one of the most recent cases of a Quebec hockey player who was ignored by the NHL Entry Draft. He quickly became a first-line player with the Vancouver Canucks.

Some NHL General Managers suddenly woke up and ordered their scouts to monitor Quebec hockey players who are not up for the draft just in case there are more Alexandre Burrows out there. In April 2009, six Quebec juniors signed contracts with NHL teams. The Boston Bruins started the ball rolling by signing Yannick Riendeau and the Montreal Canadiens concluded it a few days later, signing a contract with Dany Massé. Riendeau and Massé were teammates on the Drummondville Voltigeurs in the Quebec Major Junior Hockey League.

TABLE 2.13

French-speaking Quebec players not drafted (by decade)

	YEAR	TEAM	SURNAME	FIRST NAME	P	GP	G	A	PTS	PIM
1970-79										
1	1973	MINNESOTA	Langlais	Alain	W	25	4	4	8	10
2	1974	ST. LOUIS	Bélanger	Yves	G	78				
3	1974	TORONTO	Hamel	Pierre	G	69				
4	1975	OAKLAND	Girard	Robert	W	305	45	69	114	140
5	1978	PHILADELPHIA	Preston	Yves	W	28	7	3	10	4
6	1979	MINNESOTA	Levasseur	Jean-Louis	G	1				
7	1979	BUFFALO	Sauvé	J.-François	C	290	65	138	203	114
8	1979	PHILADELPHIA	St-Laurent	Sam	G	34				
9	1979	QUÉBEC	Bilodeau	Gilles	W	9	0	1	1	25
10	1979	DETROIT	Cloutier	Réjean	D	5	0	2	2	2
11	1979	BUFFALO	Mongrain	Robert	C	81	13	14	27	14
12	1979	QUÉBEC	Dion	Michel	G	227				
1980-89										
1	1980	LOS ANGELES	Pageau	Paul	G	1				
2	1980	QUÉBEC	Mailhot	Jacques	W	5	0	0	0	33
3	1981	QUÉBEC	Aubry	Pierre	W	202	24	26	50	133
4	1981	MONTRÉAL	Daoust	Dan	C	522	87	167	254	544
5	1982	CALGARY	Rioux	Pierre	W	14	1	2	3	4
6	1982	PITTSBURGH	Romano	Roberto	G	126				
7	1983	BUFFALO	Langevin	Chris	W	22	3	1	4	22
8	1983	MONTRÉAL	Baron	Normand	W	27	2	0	2	51
9	1983	TORONTO	Boisvert	Serge	W	46	5	7	12	8

	YEAR	TEAM	SURNAME	FIRST NAME	P	GP	G	A	PTS	PIM
10	1984	LOS ANGELES	Duschesne	Steve	D	1113	227	525	752	824
11	1984	MONTRÉAL	Thibodeau	Gilles	C	119	25	37	62	40
12	1985	MONTRÉAL	Riendeau	Vincent	G	184				
13	1986	ST. LOUIS	Lavoie	Dominic	D	38	5	8	13	32
14	1986	MONTRÉAL	Gauthier	Luc	D	3	0	0	0	2
15	1986	MONTRÉAL	Lebeau	Stéphane	C	373	118	159	277	105
16	1986	MONTRÉAL	Lefebvre	Sylvain	D	945	30	154	184	674
17	1987	QUÉBEC	Richard	J.-Marc	D	5	2	1	3	2
18	1987	CALGARY	Simard	Martin	W	44	1	5	6	183
19	1987	LOS ANGELES	Germain	Éric	D	4	0	1	1	13
20	1987	QUÉBEC	Fortier	Marc	C	212	42	60	102	135
21	1988	MONTRÉAL	Richer	Stéphane	D	27	1	5	6	20
22	1988	MONTRÉAL	Roberge	Mario	W	112	7	7	14	314
23	1988	MONTRÉAL	Roberge	Serge	W	9	0	0	0	24
1980-89										
24	1989	CALGARY	Bureau	Marc	C	567	55	83	138	327
25	1989	ST. LOUIS	Mongeau	Michel	C	54	6	19	25	10
26	1989	DETROIT	Shank	Daniel	W	77	13	14	27	175
27	1989	MINNESOTA	Thyer	Mario	C	5	0	0	0	0
1990-99										
1	1991	MONTRÉAL	Bélanger	Jesse	C	246	59	76	135	56
2	1991	LOS ANGELES	Bréault	François	W	27	2	4	6	42
3	1991	QUÉBEC	Charbonneau	Stéphane	W	2	0	0	0	0
4	1991	QUÉBEC	Chassé	Denis	W	132	11	14	25	292
5	1991	MONTRÉAL	Labelle	Marc	W	9	0	0	0	46
6	1992	MONTRÉAL	Brashear	Donald	W	989	85	119	204	2561
7	1992	NY Rangers	Roy	Jean-Yves	W	61	12	16	28	26
8	1993	CHICAGO	Soucy	Christian	G	1				
9	1993	ANAHEIM	Jomphe	J.-François	C	111	10	29	39	102
10	1993	NEW JERSEY	Rhéaume	Pascal	C	318	39	52	91	144
11	1994	CALGARY	Royer	Gaétan	W	3	0	0	0	2
12	1994	OTTAWA	Labbé	J.-François	G	15				
13	1994	MONTRÉAL	Labrecque	Patrick	G	2				
14	1995	COLORADO	Messier	Éric	D	406	25	50	75	146
15	1995	COLORADO	Trépanier	Pascal	D	229	12	22	34	252
16	1997	CALGARY	Landry	Éric	C	68	5	9	14	47
17	1998	MONTRÉAL	Bouillon	Francis	D	485	21	81	102	371
18	1998	WASHINGTON	Lefebvre	Patrice	W	3	0	0	0	2
19	1998	CALGARY	St-Louis	Martin	W	690	238	347	585	226
2000-2009										
1	2000	COLUMBUS	Darche	Mathieu	W	101	8	16	24	26
2	2000	MINNESOTA	Dupuis	Pascal	W	506	95	107	202	228

►

	YEAR	TEAM	SURNAME	FIRST NAME	P	GP	G	A	PTS	PIM
3	2001	TORONTO	Centomo	Sébastien	G	92				
4	2001	MONTRÉAL	Michaud	Olivier	G	1				
5	2002	EDMONTON	Bergeron	Marc-André	D	339	62	98	160	161
6	2003	NY Rangers	Dusablon	Benoit	C	3	0	0	0	2
7	2003	TAMPA BAY	Perrin	Éric	C	245	32	72	104	92
8	2004	MONTRÉAL	Côté	J.-Philippe	D	8	0	0	0	4
9	2004	DALLAS	Lessard	Junior	W	27	3	1	4	23
10	2004	WASHINGTON	Robitaille	Louis	W	2	0	0	0	5
11	2005	VANCOUVER	Burrows	Alexandre	W	288	50	53	103	483
12	2006	EDMONTON	Bisaillon	Sébastien	D	2	0	0	0	0
13	2006	VANCOUVER	Coulombe	Patrick	D	7	0	1	1	4
14	2006	MONTRÉAL	Dannis	Yann	G	37				

TABLE 2.14

English-speaking Quebec players not drafted
(1970 to 2009)

	YEAR	TEAM	SURNAME	FIRST NAME	P	GP	G	A	PTS	PIM
1	1971	TORONTO	Mcrae	Gord	G	71				
2	1973	BOSTON	Forbes	Dave	W	363	64	64	128	341
3	1973	TORONTO	Garland	Scott	W	91	13	24	37	115
4	1974	WASHINGTON	Wolfe	Bernie	G	120				
5	1975	PHILADELPHIA	Boland	Mike	W	2	0	0	0	0
6	1979	EDMONTON	Corsi	Jim	G	26				
7	1979	DETROIT	Johnson	Brian	W	3	0	0	0	5
8	1979	WINNIPEG	Maciver	Don	D	6	0	0	0	2
9	1979	QUÉBEC	Saunders	Bernie	W	10	0	1	1	8
10	1979	WINNIPEG	Tomalty	Greg	W	1	0	0	0	0
11	1979	QUÉBEC	Weir	Wally	D	320	21	45	66	625
12	1981	HARTFORD	Yates	Ross	C	7	1	1	2	4
13	1989	MINNESOTA	Courteney	Ed	W	44	7	13	20	10
14	1990	CALGARY	Sharples	Scott	G	1				
15	1992	MONTRÉAL	Fleming	Gerry	W	11	0	0	0	42
16	1993	ST. LOUIS	Montgomery	Jim	C	122	9	25	34	80
17	1995	BOSTON	Cornforth	Mark	D	6	0	0	0	4
18	1996	BOSTON	Drouin	P.C.	W	3	0	0	0	0
19	1997	ST. LOUIS	Parent	Rich	G	32				
20	1997	NY Rangers	Stock	P.J.	W	235	5	21	26	523
21	1998	DETROIT	Rodgers	Marc	W	21	1	1	2	10
22	2006	PHOENIX	Tordjman	Josh	G	2				

Quebec minor hockey is bottlenecked

Many Quebecers wonder what the likelihood is that their sons who play midget hockey in Quebec will be drafted by an NHL team. The fact is that their chances of playing in the NHL, or at least of being drafted during the NHL Entry Draft, are very slim.

Table 2.15 provides the number of young Quebecers who played midget hockey per year over the past forty years. Hockey Quebec provided the statistics for players registered in midget hockey since 1968.

In Quebec the likelihood that a midget player would be drafted three years later by an NHL team differed depending on the language they spoke. For French-speaking midgets in the past forty years, the ratio was one person drafted for every 618 young hockey players, whereas for English-speaking midgets it was one for 334.

A French-speaking Quebecer can thus double the chances of seeing his talented young drafted by an NHL team by changing his name for an English one. For example, Dubois would become Wood.

Up to the age of about sixteen, young Quebec hockey players enjoy the same training and the same programs provided by Quebec minor hockey leagues. These results confirm the existence of prejudice against French-speaking hockey players.

Table 2.15 also shows that during the decade 1980-89 approximately the same number of French-speaking Quebecers (165) were drafted as during the most recent decade of 2000-09 (161 players). The significant difference between the two decades is that 60,000 fewer people played midget hockey in Quebec during the 2000-09 decade than in the 1980s, yet approximately the same number of French-speaking players were drafted by the NHL. Therefore, the accusation that Hockey Quebec or the Quebec Major Junior Hockey League are responsible for the fact that fewer Quebecers were drafted is totally off the mark

TABLE 2.15

Midget by year (1970- 2009)

DRAFT YEAR	YEAR MIDGET	TOTAL MIDGET	MIDGET FR.	FR. DRA.	RATIO FR.	MIDGET ENG.	ENG. DRA.	RATIO ENG.
1970	1968	9945	8950	17	526	995	7	142
1971	1968	9945	8950	17	526	995	5	199
1972	1969	12648	11383	29	393	1265	5	253
1973	1970	12733	11460	22	521	1273	4	318
1974	1971	14841	13357	31	431	1484	5	297
1975	1972	16694	15025	21	795	1669	4	417
1976	1973	19057	17152	9	1906	1905	3	635
1977	1974	20774	18697	28	668	2077	11	189
1978	1975	21301	19171	15	1278	2130	6	355
1979	1976	22117	19905	14	1422	2212	4	553
TOTAL	**1968-76**	**160055**	**144050**	**203**	**1 out of 710**	**16055**	**54**	**1 out of 297**
1980	1977	21845	19660	14	1404	2185	6	364
1981	1978	20842	18758	20	938	2084	4	521
1982	1979	20315	18284	14	1306	2031	8	254
1983	1980	19482	17534	21	835	1948	6	325
1984	1981	18224	16402	11	1491	1822	6	304
1985	1982	17204	15484	15	1032	1720	6	287
1986	1983	16541	14887	17	876	1654	9	184
1987	1984	15725	14152	13	1087	1573	3	524
1988	1985	10965	9869	24	411	1096	2	548
1989	1986	9554	8598	16	537	956	4	239
TOTAL	**1977-86**	**170697**	**153628**	**165**	**1 out of 931**	**17069**	**54**	**1 out of 316**
1990	1987	9299	8369	23	364	930	3	310
1991	1988	8245	7421	21	353	824	4	206
1992	1989	8517	7665	20	383	852	3	284
1993	1990	8228	7405	24	309	823	1	823
1994	1991	8908	8017	28	286	891	4	223
1995	1992	8857	7971	31	257	886	2	443
1996	1993	9350	8415	30	281	935	1	935
1997	1994	9775	8798	17	518	977	3	326
1998	1995	9486	8537	26	328	949	3	316
1999	1996	9537	8583	14	613	954	2	477
TOTAL	**1987-96**	**90202**	**81181**	**234**	**1 out of 347**	**9021**	**26**	**1 out of 347**
2000	1997	9163	8246	15	550	917	3	306
2001	1998	8500	7650	13	588	850	2	425
2002	1999	7854	7068	14	505	786	3	262

DRAFT YEAR	YEAR MIDGET	TOTAL MIDGET	MIDGET FR.	FR. DRA.	RATIO FR.	MIDGET ENG.	ENG. DRA.	RATIO ENG.
2003	2000	7089	6380	24	266	709	3	236
2004	2001	7684	6916	15	461	768	3	256
2005	2002	11135	10022	17	590	1113	1	1113
2006	2003	11492	10343	15	690	1149	2	575
2007	2004	12359	11123	10	1112	1236	2	618
2008	2005	13192	11873	19	625	1319	2	660
2009	2006	14195	12776	19	672	1419	2	709
TOTAL	1997-06	102663	92397	161	1 out of 577	10266	23	1 out of 446
40-YEAR TOTAL		523617	471256	763	1 out of 618	52361	157	1 out of 334

Legend:

Midget Fr: French-speaking midget players, at the rate of 90 percent of total midget players, which is equivalent to the percentage of French-speaking people in the Quebec population.

Fr. Dra.: French-speaking players drafted.

Ratio Fr: The number of French-speaking midget-age hockey players necessary for at least one to be drafted.

Midget Eng.: English-speaking midget players, at the rate of 10 percent of total midget players, which is equivalent to the percentage of English-speaking people in the Quebec population.

Dra. En: English-speaking players drafted.

Ratio Eng.: The number of English-speaking midget-age hockey players necessary for at least one to be drafted.

Quebecers drafted by NHL Teams (1970- 2009)

How do each of the National Hockey League teams treat Quebec hockey players? What was the breakdown by team for the 763 French-speaking hockey players who were drafted between 1970 and 2009? NHL teams are ranked according to the average number of Quebecers picked during entry drafts since 1970. The team with the highest average is highest, while the team with the lowest average is last.

TABLE 2.16

Ranking of NHL teams by the number of French-speaking Quebec hockey players drafted

TEAM	1970-79	1980-89	1990-99	2000-2009	TOTAL	NO. YEARS AT DRAFT	AVERAGE PER YEAR
Montréal	32	31	27	15	105	40	2.63
Buffalo	20	11	8	9	48	40	1.20
PHILADELPHIA	16	5	11	13	45	40	1.13
NY Rangers	21	6	6	3	36	40	.90
Columbus	–	–	–	9	9	10	.90
Ottawa	–	–	13	3	16	18	.89
Washington	9	7	12	5	32	36	.89
Toronto	11	7	12	5	35	40	.88
Détroit	15	6	9	4	34	40	.85
Chicago	9	9	11	3	32	40	.80
NY Islanders	12	5	8	4	29	38	.76
Boston	9	8	7	5	29	40	.73
New Jersey	–	2	12	5	19	28	.68
Los Angeles	8	5	8	6	27	40	.68
Florida	–	–	9	2	11	17	.65
Pittsburgh	7	3	7	9	26	40	.65
Edmonton	–	3	9	8	20	31	.65
Tampa Bay	–	–	9	2	11	18	.61
St. Louis	7	5	8	4	24	40	.60
Anaheim	–	–	2	8	10	17	.59
San Jose	–	–	6	5	11	19	.58
Calgary	–	5	10	2	17	30	.57
Colorado	–	–	5	3	8	15	.53
Minnesota	–	–	–	5	5	10	.50
Vancouver	5	6	2	7	20	40	.50
Caroline	–	–	1	5	6	13	.46
Atlanta	–	–	0	5	5	11	.45
Phoenix	–	–	2	3	5	14	.36
Nashville	–	–	1	3	4	12	.33
Dallas	–	–	2	1	3	17	.18
TOTAL					682		

NHL teams no longer operating

Québec	2	26	10	–	38	16	2.38
Atlanta	9	–	–	–	9	9	1.00
Cleveland	1	–	–	–	1	1	1.00
Oakland	5	–	–	–	5	7	.71
Hartford	0	7	3	–	10	16	.63
Winnipeg	1	5	3	–	9	17	.59
Minnesota	5	2	1	–	8	23	.35
Kansas City	1	–	–	–	1	3	.33
Colorado	0	0	–	–	0	5	.00
TOTAL					81		
GRAND TOTAL					763		

Conclusions from Table 2.16

The Montreal Canadiens led the League with 105 French-speaking Quebec players drafted over the last forty years, for an average of 2.63 players per year.

- The Dallas Stars are at the bottom of the pack. They were only able to draft three French-speaking Quebec hockey players in the last seventeen years, for an average of 0.18 player per year. On average, the Stars draft one French-speaking hockey player every 5.5 years. What's surprising is that Bob Gainey was the team's General Manager for eight years. They are in the cellar!

- Since Bob Gainey arrived in Montreal in 2003, his annual average improved slightly: 1.57 player per year, for a total of eleven French-speaking Quebec hockey players selected in seven drafts.

- The Buffalo Sabres are runners-up in the League with forty-eight French-speaking Quebec hockey players drafted in the last forty years, for an average of 1.20 player per year.

- Philadelphia is third with a total of forty-five players in the last forty years for an average of 1.13 player per year.

- Since 2000 Philadelphia has led the pack with a total of thirteen French-speaking Quebecers and three English-speaking Quebecers for a total of sixteen, topping even the Montreal Canadiens (15) by one player. The Philadelphia Flyers are today's *Habs*.

- The Quebec Nordiques would be second if they still existed. Between 1979 and 1994, they drafted a total of thirty-eight French-speaking players in sixteen drafts for an average of 2.38 players per year.

- However, the *Nordicks* of Colorado (Avalanche), with the same managers as in Quebec, drafted a grand total of eight French-speaking Quebec hockey players over fifteen years, for an average of 0.53 player per year, which relegates them to twenty-third place. That is a drop of almost two players a year, or thirty fewer French-speaking hockey players than when the team was located in Quebec City. It begs the question to ask whether a Quebec City team would draft so few French-speaking players.

- During the sixteen-year rivalry between the Montreal Canadiens and the Quebec Nordiques, a total of eighty-four French-speaking Quebec hockey players were drafted by the two teams. The

Nordiques drafted thirty-eight, for an average of 2.38 players per year, while the Canadiens picked forty-six, for an average of 2.88 players per year.

· Between the time when the Nordiques left for Colorado in 1995 and when the Timmins-Gainey duo arrived in Montreal in 2003, the Montreal Canadiens drafted eighteen French-speaking Quebec hockey players, for an average of 2.25 per year for that eight-year period. During the seven-year Bob Gainey era, eleven players were drafted, for an average of 1.57 player per year. That average of 1.57 player per year is a drop of one less French-speaking Quebec hockey player per year in comparison to the years of the Montreal-Quebec rivalry.

· The Montreal Canadiens drafted ninety French-speaking hockey players between 1970 and 1999, for an average of thirty per decade. In the past decade (2000-09), the same team drafted fifteen French-speaking Quebec hockey players, or half as many as in the three previous decades, a 50 percent drop! That is why the team was left with only two when the 2010-11 season began.

· During the last ten drafts (2000-09), Pittsburgh and Columbus drafted nine French-speaking Quebec hockey players each, for an average of 0.90 player per year. These results put them in third place with the Buffalo Sabres for that period.

· The surprise for many people is to see the Toronto Maple Leafs in eighth position. The Leafs drafted thirty-five French-speaking Quebec hockey players over the last forty years, for an average of 0.88 player per year.

· Over the past forty years, 763 French-speaking Quebec hockey players have been drafted. Of that number, the Canadiens, Nordiques, Sabres, and Flyers drafted a total of 236 players, or thirty-one percent of all French-speaking Quebec hockey players drafted by NHL teams.

TABLE 2.17

Draft of French-speaking Quebecers 1970-2009

RANK	TEAM	SURNAME	FIRST NAME	P	LEAGUE	GP	G	A	PTS	PIM
1970										
1	BUFFALO	Perreault	Gilbert	C	ONT	1191	512	814	1326	500
11	NY RANGERS	Gratton	Normand	W	ONT	201	39	45	84	64
12	DETROIT	Lajeunesse	Serge	D	ONT	103	1	4	5	103
18	PHILADELPHIA	Clément	Bill	C	ONT	719	148	208	356	383
26	DETROIT	Guindon	Bob	W	ONT	6	0	1	1	0
27	BOSTON	Bouchard	Dan	G	ONT	655				
28	CHICAGO	Archambault	Michel	C	LHJMQ	3	0	0	0	0
40	DETROIT	Lambert	Yvon	W	LHJMQ	683	206	273	479	340
46	PHILADELPHIA	Lapierre	Jacques	W	LHJMQ	0	0	0	0	0
53	NY RANGERS	St-Pierre	André	D	LHJMQ	0	0	0	0	0
64	TORONTO	Simard	Luc	W	LHJMQ	0	0	0	0	0
70	CHICAGO	Meloche	Gilles	G	LHJMQ	788				
79	ST. LOUIS	Moreau	Claude	D	ONT	0	0	0	0	0
91	TORONTO	Larose	Paul	W	LHJMQ	0	0	0	0	0
106	NY RANGERS	Brindamour	Pierre	W	ONT	0	0	0	0	0
107	BUFFALO	Nadeau	Luc	C	LHJMQ	0	0	0	0	0
109	PHILADELPHIA	Daigle	Jean	C	LHJMQ	0	0	0	0	0
1971										
1	MONTRÉAL	Lafleur	Guy	W	LHJMQ	1127	560	793	1352	399
2	DETROIT	Dionne	Marcel	C	ONT	1348	731	1040	1771	600
3	VANCOUVER	Guèvremont	Jocelyn	D	ONT	571	84	223	307	319
5	BUFFALO	Martin	Rick	W	ONT	685	384	317	701	477
9	PHILADELPHIA	Plante	Pierre	W	LHJMQ	599	125	172	297	599
24	MONTRÉAL	Deguise	Michel	G	LHJMQ	0	0	0	0	0
29	CALIFORNIA	Leduc	Richard	W	LHJMQ	130	28	38	66	69
39	VANCOUVER	Lemieux	Richard	C	ONT	274	39	82	121	132
47	BUFFALO	Richer	Bob	D	LHJMQ	3	0	0	0	0
57	CALIFORNIA	Bélanger	Reynald	G	LHJMQ	0				
75	BUFFALO	Duguay	Pierre	C	LHJMQ	0	0	0	0	0
76	LOS ANGELES	Lapierre	Camille	W	ONT	0	0	0	0	0
90	LOS ANGELES	Dubé	Norm	W	LHJMQ	57	8	10	18	54
97	NY RANGERS	Royal	Jean-Denis	D	LHJMQ	0	0	0	0	0
111	NY RANGERS	Peloffy	André	C	LHJMQ	9	0	0	0	0
114	NY RANGERS	Lecomte	Gérald	D	LHJMQ	0	0	0	0	0
117	MINNESOTA	Coutu	Richard	G	LHJMQ	0				
1972										
2	ATLANTA	Richard	Jacques	C	LHJMQ	556	160	187	347	307
6	MONTRÉAL	Larocque	Michel	G	ONT	308				
26	DETROIT	Guité	Pierre	W	ONT	0	0	0	0	0
31	NY RANGERS	Villemure	René	W	LHJMQ	0	0	0	0	0
34	ATLANTA	Lemieux	Jean	D	LHJMQ	204	23	63	86	39

* Hockey players who played more than one game in the NHL are in bold. ➤

RANK	TEAM	SURNAME	FIRST NAME	P	LEAGUE	GP	G	A	PTS	PIM
40	PITTSBURGH	Herron	Denis	G	LHJMQ	462				
41	ST. LOUIS	Hamel	Jean	D	LHJMQ	699	26	95	121	766
43	TORONTO	Deslauriers	Denis	D	LHJMQ	0	0	0	0	0
48	BOSTON	Boudreau	Michel	W	LHJMQ	0	0	0	0	0
53	BUFFALO	Campeau	Richard	D	LHJMQ	0	0	0	0	0
54	CALIFORNIA	St-Sauveur	Claude	C	LHJMQ	79	24	24	48	23
65	NY ISLANDERS	Grenier	Richard	C	LHJMQ	10	1	1	2	2
69	BUFFALO	Gratton	Gilles	G	ONT	47				
75	TORONTO	Plante	Michel	W	LHJMQ	0	0	0	0	0
77	CHICAGO	Giroux	Réjean	W	LHJMQ	0	0	0	0	0
86	CALIFORNIA	Lefebvre	Jacques	G	LHJMQ	0				
97	NY ISLANDERS	Brodeur	Richard	G	LHJMQ	385				
103	PHILADELPHIA	Beaudoin	Serge	D	LHJMQ	3	0	0	0	0
110	MONTRÉAL	Archambault	Yves	G	LHJMQ	0				
117	NY ISLANDERS	Levasseur	René	D	LHJMQ	0	0	0	0	0
120	PITTSBURGH	Bergeron	Yves	W	LHJMQ	3	0	0	0	0
127	NY RANGERS	Blais	Yvon	D	LHJMQ	0	0	0	0	0
129	NY ISLANDERS	Rolando	Yvan	W	LHJMQ	0	0	0	0	0
130	ATLANTA	Roy	Pierre	D	LHJMQ	0	0	0	0	0
132	ATLANTA	Lamarre	Jean	W	LHJMQ	0	0	0	0	0
134	CALIFORNIA	Meloche	Denis	W	LHJMQ	0	0	0	0	0
135	PHILADELPHIA	Boutin	Raymond	G	LHJMQ	0				
137	NY RANGERS	Archambault	Pierre	D	LHJMQ	0	0	0	0	0
146	NY ISLANDERS	Lambert	René	W	LHJMQ	0	0	0	0	0
1973										
1	NY ISLANDERS	Potvin	Denis	D	ONT	1060	310	742	1052	1356
6	BOSTON	Savard	André	C	LHJMQ	790	211	271	482	411
19	VANCOUVER	Bordeleau	Paulin	C	ONT	183	33	56	89	47
28	BUFFALO	Landry	Jean	D	LHJMQ	0	0	0	0	0
44	BUFFALO	Deschamps	André	W	LHJMQ	0	0	0	0	0
49	NY ISLANDERS	St-Laurent	André	C	LHJMQ	644	129	187	316	749
52	TORONTO	Rochon	François	W	LHJMQ	0	0	0	0	0
60	BUFFALO	Dupuis	Yvon	W	LHJMQ	0	0	0	0	0
64	MONTRÉAL	Latulipe	Richard	W	LHJMQ	0	0	0	0	0
74	PHILADELPHIA	Latreille	Michel	D	LHJMQ	0	0	0	0	0
78	NY RANGERS	Laganiere	Pierre	W	LHJMQ	0	0	0	0	0
95	BOSTON	Bourgouyne	J.-P.	D	LHJMQ	0	0	0	0	0
96	MONTRÉAL	Patry	Denis	W	LHJMQ	0	0	0	0	0
112	MONTRÉAL	Belisle	Michel	W	LHJMQ	0	0	0	0	0
120	ST. LOUIS	Tétreault	Jean	W	LHJMQ	0	0	0	0	0
126	NY ISLANDERS	Desgagnés	Denis	C	LHJMQ	0	0	0	0	0
128	MONTRÉAL	Desjardins	Mario	W	LHJMQ	0	0	0	0	0
139	DETROIT	Bibeau	Raymond	D	LHJMQ	0	0	0	0	0
149	ATLANTA	Ross	Guy	D	LHJMQ	0	0	0	0	0
157	BOSTON	Bouillon	Yvan	W	LHJMQ	0	0	0	0	0

RANK	TEAM	SURNAME	FIRST NAME	P	LEAGUE	GP	G	A	PTS	PIM
158	MONTRÉAL	Labrecque	Alain	W	LHJMQ	0	0	0	0	0
168	MONTRÉAL	Chiasson	Louis	W	LHJMQ	0	0	0	0	0
1974										
8	PITTSBURGH	Larouche	Pierre	C	LHJMQ	812	395	427	822	237
12	MONTRÉAL	Tremblay	Mario	W	LHJMQ	852	258	326	584	·1043
24	MINNESOTA	Nantais	Richard	W	LHJMQ	53	5	4	9	79
27	PITTSBURGH	Cossette	Jacques	W	LHJMQ	64	8	6	14	29
28	ATLANTA	Chouinard	Guy	C	LHJMQ	578	205	370	575	120
33	MONTRÉAL	Lupien	Gilles	D	LHJMQ	226	5	25	30	416
34	CHICAGO	Daigle	Alain	W	LHJMQ	389	56	50	106	122
47	BUFFALO	Deziel	Michel	W	LHJMQ	0	0	0	0	0
53	PHILADELPHIA	Sirois	Bob	W	LHJMQ	286	92	120	212	42
62	PITTSBURGH	Faubert	Mario	D	US	231	21	90	111	222
63	DETROIT	Bergeron	Michel	W	LHJMQ	229	80	58	138	165
76	NY ISLANDERS	Toressan	Carlo	D	LHJMQ	0	0	0	0	0
119	BUFFALO	Noreau	Bernard	W	LHJMQ	0	0	0	0	0
125	PHILADELPHIA	Lemelin	Réjean	G	LHJMQ	507				
136	BUFFALO	Constantin	Charles	W	LHJMQ	0	0	0	0	0
147	VANCOUVER	Gaudreault	Marc	D	US	0	0	0	0	0
149	ST. LOUIS	Touzin	Paul	G	LHJMQ	0	·			
154	LOS ANGELES	Lessard	Mario	G	LHJMQ	240				
156	NY RANGERS	Arvisais	Claude	C	LHJMQ	0	0	0	0	· 0
162	KANSAS CITY	Carufel	Denis	W	LHJMQ	0	0	0	0	0
167	ATLANTA	Loranger	Louis	W	LHJMQ	0	0	0	0	0
174	PHILADELPHIA	Labrosse	Marcel	C	LHJMQ	0	0	0	0	0
181	PITTSBURGH	Gamelin	Serge	W	LHJMQ	0	0	0	0	0
184	LOS ANGELES	Locas	Jacques	C	LHJMQ	0	0	0	0	0
188	CHICAGO	Bernier	Jean	D	LHJMQ	0	0	0	0	0
195	PITTSBURGH	Perron	Richard	D	LHJMQ	0	0	0	0	0
196	BUFFALO	Geoffrion	Bob	W	LHJMQ	0	0	0	0	0
201	PHILADELPHIA	Guay	Richard	G	LHJMQ	0				
212	WASHINGTON	Plante	Bernard	W	LHJMQ	0	0	0	0	0
220	WASHINGTON	Chiasson	Jacques	W	LHJMQ	0	0	0	0	0
234	WASHINGTON	Plouffe	Yves	D	LHJMQ	0	0	0	0	0
1975										
15	MONTRÉAL	Mondou	Pierre	W	LHJMQ	548	194	262	456	179
17	BUFFALO	Sauvé	Robert	G	LHJMQ	420				
46	VANCOUVER	Lapointe	Normand	G	LHJMQ	0				
54	PHILADELPHIA	Ritchie	Robert	W	LHJMQ	29	8	4	12	10
61	CHICAGO	Giroux	Pierre	W	LHJMQ	6	·1	0	1	17
65	NY ISLANDERS	Lepage	André	G	LHJMQ	0				
68	BOSTON	Daigle	Denis	W	LHJMQ	0	0	0	0	0
69	LOS ANGELES	Leduc	André	D	LHJMQ	0	0	0	0	0
106	MONTRÉAL	Lachance	Michel	D	LHJMQ	21	0	4	4	22

➤

RANK	TEAM	SURNAME	FIRST NAME	P	LEAGUE	GP	G	A	PTS	PIM
112	MINNESOTA	Robert	François	D	LHJMQ	0	0	0	0	0
113	DETROIT	Phaneuf	Jean-Luc	C	LHJMQ	0	0	0	0	0
114	TORONTO	Rouillard	Mario	W	LHJMQ	0	0	0	0	0
120	Rangers	Larose	Claude	W	LHJMQ	25	4	7	11	2
150	ATLANTA	Sanza	Nick	G	LHJMQ	0				
164	DETROIT	Thibodeau	Jean-Luc	C	LHJMQ	0	0	0	0	0
165	TORONTO	Latendresse	Jean	D	LHJMQ	0	0	0	0	0
169	RANGERS	Beaulieu	Daniel	W	LHJMQ	0	0	0	0	0
190	MINNESOTA	Cloutier	Gilles	G	LHJMQ	0				
197	LOS ANGELES	Viens	Mario	G	LHJMQ	0				
201	NY RANGERS	Dionne	Paul	W	US	0	0	0	0	0
204	MONTRÉAL	Brisebois	Michel	C	LHJMQ	0	0	0	0	0
1976										
9	CHICAGO	Cloutier	Réal	W	LHJMQ	317	146	198	344	119
48	TORONTO	Bélanger	Alain	W	LHJMQ	9	0	1	1	6
60	NY RANGERS	Périard	Claude	W	LHJMQ	0	0	0	0	0
90	MONTRÉAL	Barette	Maurice	G	LHJMQ	0				
105	BUFFALO	Lemieux	Donald	D	LHJMQ	0	0	0	0	0
108	MONTRÉAL	Brassard	Pierre	W	LHJMQ	0	0	0	0	0
111	DETROIT	Leblanc	Fernand	W	LHJMQ	34	5	6	11	0
112	NY RANGERS	Lévesque	Rémi	C	LHJMQ	0	0	0	0	0
120	DETROIT	Legris	Claude	G	LHJMQ	4				
1977										
3	WASHINGTON	Picard	Robert	D	LHJMQ	899	104	319	423	1025
8	NY Rangers	Deblois	Lucien	W	LHJMQ	993	249	276	525	814
18	MONTRÉAL	Dupont	Normand	W	LHJMQ	256	55	85	140	52
19	CHICAGO	Savard	Jean	C	LHJMQ	43	7	12	19	29
23	CLEVELAND	Chicoine	Daniel	W	LHJMQ	31	1	2	3	12
39	WASHINGTON	Godin	Eddy	W	LHJMQ	27	3	6	9	12
43	MONTRÉAL	Côté	Alain	W	LHJMQ	696	103	190	293	383
46	MONTRÉAL	Lagacé	Pierre	C	LHJMQ	0	0	0	0	0
62	NY Rangers	Marois	Mario	D	LHJMQ	955	76	357	433	1746
67	PHILADELPHIA	Guillemette	Yves	G	LHJMQ	0				
71	PHILADELPHIA	Hamelin	René	W	LHJMQ	0	0	0	0	0
75	WASHINGTON	Turcotte	Denis	C	LHJMQ	0	0	0	0	0
80	NY Rangers	Gosselin	Benoit	W	LHJMQ	7	0	0	0	33
86	BUFFALO	Sirois	Richard	G	LHJMQ	VOIR 1978				
90	MONTRÉAL	Rochette	Gaetan	D	LHJMQ	0	0	0	0	0
100	ATLANTA	Harbec	Bernard	C	LHJMQ	0	0	0	0	0
107	PHILADELPHIA	Chaput	Alain	C	LHJMQ	0	0	0	0	0
115	MINNESOTA	Sanvido	J.-Pierre	G	LHJMQ	0				
123	PHILADELPHIA	Dalpé	Richard	C	LHJMQ	0	0	0	0	0
124	MONTRÉAL	Sévigny	Richard	G	LHJMQ	176				
125	DETROIT	Roy	Raymond	C	LHJMQ	0	0	0	0	0
127	WASHINGTON	Tremblay	Brent	D	LHJMQ	10	1	0	1	6

RANK	TEAM	SURNAME	FIRST NAME	P	LEAGUE	GP	G	A	PTS	PIM
138	BOSTON	Claude	Mario	D	LHJMQ	0	0	0	0	0
167	**MONTRÉAL**	**Poulin**	**Daniel**	D	LHJMQ	3	1	1	2	0
170	DETROIT	Bélanger	Alain	W	LHJMQ	0	0	0	0	0
178	**DETROIT**	**Cloutier**	**Roland**	C	LHJMQ	34	8	9	17	2
179	MONTRÉAL	Beslisle	Jean	G	LHJMQ	0				
182	MONTRÉAL	Boileau	Robert	C	US	0	0	0	0	0
1978										
8	**MONTRÉAL**	**Geoffrion**	**Daniel**	W	LHJMQ	111	20	32	52	99
42	**MONTRÉAL**	**David**	**Richard**	W	LHJMQ	31	4	4	8	10
60	**NY Rangers**	**Doré**	**André**	D	LHJMQ	257	14	81	95	261
95	DETROIT	Locas	Sylvain	C	LHJMQ	0	0	0	0	0
98	TORONTO	Lefebvre	Normand	W	LHJMQ	0	0	0	0	0
118	NY ISLANDERS	Pepin	Richard	W	LHJMQ	0	0	0	0	0
122	WASHINGTON	Sirois	Richard	G	LHI	0	0	0	0	0
139	WASHINGTON	Pomerleau	Denis	W	LHJMQ	0	0	0	0	0
181	ST. LOUIS	Boutin	J.-F.	W	LHJMQ	0	0	0	0	0
186	MONTRÉAL	Metivier	Daniel	W	LHJMQ	0	0	0	0	0
188	ST. LOUIS	Ménard	Serge	W	LHJMQ	0	0	0	0	0
192	NY RANGERS	Daigneault	Pierre	D	COL QC.	0	0	0	0	0
193	LOS ANGELES	Larochelle	Claude	W	LHJMQ	0	0	0	0	0
229	MONTRÉAL	Leblanc	Serge		US	0	0	0	0	0
233	**MONTRÉAL**	**Sleigher**	**Louis**	W	LHJMQ	194	46	53	99	146
1979										
8	**BOSTON**	**Bourque**	**Raymond**	D	LHJMQ	1612	410	1169	1579	1141
20	**QUÉBEC**	**Goulet**	**Michel**	W	AMH	1089	548	604	1152	823
27	**MONTRÉAL**	**Gingras**	**Gaston**	D	AMH	476	61	174	235	161
44	**MONTRÉAL**	**Carbonneau**	**Guy**	C	LHJMQ	1318	260	403	663	820
51	**TORONTO**	**Aubin**	**Normand**	W	LHJMQ	69	18	13	31	30
55	**BUFFALO**	**Cloutier**	**Jacques**	G	LHJMQ	255				
70	CHICAGO	Bégin	Louis	C	LHJMQ	0	0	0	0	0
72	**TORONTO**	**Tremblay**	**Vincent**	G	LHJMQ	58				
74	**BUFFALO**	**Hamel**	**Gilles**	W	LHJMQ	519	127	147	274	276
82	**WINNIPEG**	**Daley**	**Patrick**	W	LHJMQ	12	1	0	1	13
95	**BUFFALO**	**Haworth**	**Allan**	C	LHJMQ	524	189	211	400	425
99	**BOSTON**	**Baron**	**Marco**	G	LHJMQ	86				
104	**QUÉBEC**	**Lacroix**	**Pierre**	W	LHJMQ	274	24	107	131	197
107	ST. LOUIS	Leduc	Gilles	D	LHJMQ	0	0	0	0	0
1980										
2	**CHICAGO**	**Savard**	**Denis**	C	LHJMQ	1196	473	865	1338	1336
13	**CALGARY**	**Cyr**	**Denis**	W	LHJMQ	193	41	43	84	36
24	**QUÉBEC**	**Rochefort**	**Normand**	D	LHJMQ	598	39	119	158	570
29	**HARTFORD**	**Galarneau**	**Michel**	C	LHJMQ	78	7	10	17	34
65	WINNIPEG	Fournier	Guy	W	LHJMQ	0	0	0	0	0
76	CALGARY	Roy	Marc		LHJMQ	0	0	0	0	0

➤

RANK	TEAM	SURNAME	FIRST NAME	P	LEAGUE	GP	G	A	PTS	PIM
96	ST. LOUIS	Lemieux	Alain	C	LHJMQ	119	28	44	72	38
103	MONTRÉAL	Gagné	Rémi	C	LHJMQ	0	0	0	0	0
125	BUFFALO	Naud	Daniel	D	LHJMQ	0	0	0	0	0
129	QUÉBEC	Therrien	Gaston	D	LHJMQ	22	0	8	8	12
150	QUÉBEC	Bolduc	Michel	D	LHJMQ	10	0	0	0	6
160	CALGARY	Drouin	Claude		LHJMQ	0	0	0	0	0
166	MONTRÉAL	Penney	Steve	G	LHJMQ	91				
171	QUÉBEC	Tanguay	Christian	W	LHJMQ	2	0	0	0	0
1981										
14	BOSTON	Léveillé	Normand	W	LHJMQ	75	17	25	42	49
18	MONTRÉAL	Delorme	Gilbert	D	LHJMQ	541	31	92	123	520
35	BOSTON	Dufour	Luc	C	LHJMQ	167	23	21	44	199
44	DETROIT	Micalef	Corado	G	LHJMQ	113				
52	VANCOUVER	Lanthier	J.-Marc	W	LHJMQ	105	16	16	32	29
53	QUÉBEC	Gaulin	J.-Marc	W	LHJMQ	26	4	3	7	8
90	TORONTO	Lefrançois	Normand	W	LHJMQ	0	0	0	0	0
94	NY ISLANDERS	Sylvestre	Jacques	W	LHJMQ	0	0	0	0	0
121	PHILADELPHIA	Villeneuve	André	D	LHJMQ	0	0	0	0	0
151	HARTFORD	Doré	Denis	W	LHJMQ	0	0	0	0	0
152	WASHINGTON	Duchesne	Gaétan	W	LHJMQ	1028	179	254	433	629
153	TORONTO	Turmel	Richard	D	LHJMQ	0	0	0	0	0
158	QUÉBEC	Côté	André	W	LHJMQ	0	0	0	0	0
161	BOSTON	Parisée	Armei	D	LHJMQ	0	0	0	0	0
167	ST. LOUIS	Vigneault	Alain	D	LHJMQ	42	2	5	7	82
179	QUÉBEC	Brisebois	Marc	W	LHJMQ	0	0	0	0	0
198	NY RANGERS	Proulx	Mario	G	US	0				
199	VANCOUVER	Vignola	Réjean	W	LHJMQ	0	0	0	0	0
201	CHICAGO	Roy	Sylvain	D	LHJMQ	0	0	0	0	0
203	BOSTON	Bourque	Richard	W	LHJMQ	0	0	0	0	0
1982										
11	VANCOUVER	Petit	Michel	D	LHJMQ	827	90	238	328	1839
19	MONTRÉAL	Héroux	Alain	W	LHJMQ	0	0	0	0	0
23	DETROIT	Courteau	Yves	W	LHJMQ	22	2	5	7	4
28	CHICAGO	Badeau	René	D	LHJMQ	0	0	0	0	0
31	MONTRÉAL	Gauvreau	Jocelyn	D	LHJMQ	2	0	0	0	0
53	VANCOUVER	Lapointe	Yves	W	LHJMQ	0	0	0	0	0
55	QUÉBEC	Gosselin	Mario	G	LHJMQ	242				
99	TORONTO	Charland	Sylvain	W	LHJMQ	0	0	0	0	0
105	NY ISLANDERS	Breton	René	W	LHJMQ	0	0	0	0	0
107	DETROIT	Vilgrain	Claude	W	LHJMQ	89	21	32	53	78
131	QUÉBEC	Poudrier	Daniel	D	LHJMQ	25	1	5	6	10
161	PHILADELPHIA	Lavigne	Alain	W	LHJMQ	0	0	0	0	0
163	BUFFALO	Verret	Claude	C	LHJMQ	14	2	5	7	2
223	QUÉBEC	Martin	André	D	LHJMQ	0	0	0	0	0

RANK	TEAM	SURNAME	FIRST NAME	P	LEAGUE	GP	G	A	PTS	PIM
1983										
2	HARTFORD	Turgeon	Sylvain	W	LHJMQ	669	269	225	494	691
10	BUFFALO	Lacombe	Normand	W	US	319	53	62	115	196
26	MONTRÉAL	Lemieux	Claude	W	LHJMQ	1197	379	406	785	1756
27	MONTRÉAL	Momesso	Sergio	W	LHJMQ	710	152	193	345	1557
32	QUÉBEC	Heroux	Yves	W	LHJMQ	1	0	0	0	0
45	MONTRÉAL	Letendre	Daniel	W	LHJMQ	0	0	0	0	0
59	CHICAGO	Bergevin	Marc	D	LHJMQ	1191	36	145	181	1090
67	LOS ANGELES	Benoit	Guy	W	LHJMQ	0	0	0	0	0
92	QUÉBEC	Guénette	Luc	G	LHJMQ	0				
95	WASHINGTON	Bouliane	Martin	C	LHJMQ	0	0	0	0	0
101	PHILADELPHIA	Carrier	Jérôme	D	LHJMQ	0	0	0	0	0
103	PITTSBURGH	Emond	Patrick	C	LHJMQ	0	0	0	0	0
109	WINNIPEG	Baillargeon	Joël	W	LHJMQ	20	0	2	2	31
143	HARTFORD	Duperron	Christian	D	LHJMQ	0	0	0	0	0
162	BOSTON	Olivier	François		LHJMQ	0	0	0	0	0
195	WASHINGTON	Beaudoin	Yves	D	LHJMQ	11	0	0	0	5
209	WINNIPEG	Cormier	Éric		QC COLL.	0	0	0	0	0
215	WASHINGTON	Raymond	Alain	G	LHJMQ	1				
219	CHICAGO	Pepin	Steve	W	LHJMQ	0	0	0	0	0
234	BUFFALO	Hamelin	Marc	G	LHJMQ	0	.			
238	MONTRÉAL	Bergeron	J.-Guy	D	LHJMQ	0	0	0	0	0
1984										
1	PITTSBURGH	Lemieux	Mario	C	LHJMQ	915	690	1033	1723	834
10	VANCOUVER	Daigneault	J.-Jacques	D	LHJMQ	899	53	197	250	687
11	HARTFORD	Côté	Sylvain	D	LHJMQ	1171	122	313	435	545
29	MONTRÉAL	Richer	Stéphane	W	LHJMQ	1054	421	398	819	614
51	MONTRÉAL	Roy	Patrick	G	LHJMQ	1029				
123	BUFFALO	Gasseau	James	D	LHJMQ	0	0	0	0	0
167	NY ISLANDERS	Desantis	Franco	D	LHJMQ	0	0	0	0	0
171	LOS ANGELES	Robitaille	Luc	W	LHJMQ	1431	668	726	1394	1177
176	ST. LOUIS	Jomphe	Daniel	W	LHJMQ	0	0	0	0	0
179	MONTRÉAL	Demers	Éric	D	LHJMQ	0	0	0	0	0
183	QUÉBEC	Ouellette	Guy		LHJMQ	0	0	0	0	0
1985										
12	MONTRÉAL	Charbonneau	José	W	LHJMQ	71	9	13	22	67
31	BOSTON	Côté	Alain	D	LHJMQ	119	2	18	20	124
35	BUFFALO	Hogue	Benoit	W	LHJMQ	863	222	231	543	877
51	MINNESOTA	Roy	Stéphane	C	LHJMQ	12	1	0	1	0
60	WINNIPEG	Berthiaume	Daniel	G	LHJMQ	215				
74	CHICAGO	Vincelette	Daniel	W	LHJMQ	193	20	22	42	351
75	MONTRÉAL	Desjardins	Martin	C	LHJMQ	8	0	2	2	2
103	WASHINGTON	Dumas	Claude	C	LHJMQ	0	0	0	0	0
117	MONTRÉAL	Dufresne	Donald	D	LHJMQ	268	6	36	42	258

➤

RANK	TEAM	SURNAME	FIRST NAME	P	LEAGUE	GP	G	A	PTS	PIM
162	QUÉBEC	Brunetta	Mario	G	LHJMQ	40				
175	NY Rangers	Brochu	Stéphane	D	LHJMQ	1	0	0	0	0
179	CHICAGO	Laplante	Richard	W	US	0	0	0	0	0
209	EDMONTON	Barbe	Mario	D	LHJMQ	0	0	0	0	0
224	BUFFALO	Larose	Guy	C	ONT	70	10	9	19	63
246	QUÉBEC	Bois	Jean	W	LHJMQ	0	0	0	0	0
1986										
6	TORONTO	Damphousse	Vincent	C	LHJMQ	1378	432	773	1205	1190
10	ST. LOUIS	Lemieux	Jocelyn	W	LHJMQ	598	80	84	164	740
27	MONTRÉAL	Brunet	Benoit	W	LHJMQ	539	101	161	262	229
39	QUÉBEC	Routhier	J.-Marc	W	LHJMQ	8	0	0	0	9
41	QUÉBEC	Guérard	Stéphane	D	LHJMQ	34	0	0	0	40
65	LOS ANGELES	Couturier	Sylvain	W	LHJMQ	33	4	5	9	4
94	MONTRÉAL	Aubertin	Éric	W	LHJMQ	0	0	0	0	0
110	BUFFALO	Baldris	Miguel	D	LHJMQ	0	0	0	0	0
111	TORONTO	Giguère	Stéphane	W	LHJMQ	0	0	0	0	0
119	CHICAGO	Doyon	Mario	D	LHJMQ	28	3	4	7	16
144	QUÉBEC	Nault	J.-François	W	LHJMQ	0	0	0	0	0
152	BUFFALO	Guay	François	C	LHJMQ	1	0	0	0	0
168	EDMONTON	Beaulieu	Nicolas	W	LHJMQ	0	0	0	0	0
186	QUÉBEC	Millier	Pierre	W	LHJMQ	0	0	0	0	0
192	NEW JERSEY	Chabot	Frédéric	G	MID.AAA	32				
204	MONTRÉAL	Bohémier	Éric	G	LHJMQ	0				
228	QUÉBEC	Latreille	Martin	D	LHJMQ	0	0	0	0	0
1987										
1	BUFFALO	Turgeon	Pierre	C	LHJMQ	1294	515	812	1327	452
11	DETROIT	Racine	Yves	D	LHJMQ	508	37	194	231	439
14	BOSTON	Quintal	Stéphane	D	LHJMQ	1037	63	180	243	1320
25	CALGARY	Matteau	Stéphane	D	LHJMQ	848	144	172	316	742
28	TORONTO	Marois	Daniel	W	LHJMQ	350	117	93	210	419
31	NY Rangers	Lacroix	Daniel	W	LHJMQ	188	11	7	18	379
38	MONTRÉAL	Desjardins	Éric	D	LHJMQ	1143	136	439	575	757
45	VANCOUVER	Veilleux	Steve	D	LHJMQ	0	0	0	0	0
46	NY RANGERS	Gagne	Simon	W	LHJMQ	0	0	0	0	0
57	WASHINGTON	Maltais	Steve	W	ONT	120	8	18	27	53
58	MONTRÉAL	Gravel	François	G	LHJMQ	0				
185	MONTRÉAL	Tremblay	Éric	W	LHJMQ	0	0	0	0	0
212	NEW JERSEY	Charland	Alain	W	LHJMQ	0	0	0	0	0
1988										
5	QUÉBEC	Doré	Daniel	W	LHJMQ	17	2	3	5	59
7	LOS ANGELES	Gélinas	Martin	W	LHJMQ	1273	309	351	660	820
14	PHILADELPHIA	Boivin	Claude	W	LHJMQ	132	12	19	31	364
15	WASHINGTON	Savage	Réginald	W	LHJMQ	34	5	7	12	28
19	EDMONTON	Leroux	François	D	LHJMQ	249	3	20	23	577
20	MONTRÉAL	Charron	Éric	D	LHJMQ	130	2	7	9	127

RANK	TEAM	SURNAME	FIRST NAME	P	LEAGUE	GP	G	A	PTS	PIM
24	QUÉBEC	Fiset	Stéphane	G	LHJMQ	390				
34	MONTRÉAL	St-Amour	Martin	W	LHJMQ	1	0	0	0	2
38	DETROIT	Anglehart	Serge	D	LHJMQ	0	0	0	0	0
47	DETROIT	Dupuis	Guy	D	LHJMQ	0	0	0	0	0
52	WINNIPEG	Beauregard	Stéphane	G	LHJMQ	90				
62	PITTSBURGH	Gauthier	Daniel	C	LHJMQ	5	0	0	0	0
63	PHILADELPHIA	Roussel	Dominic	G	LHJMQ	205				
79	NY ISLANDERS	Brassard	André	D	LHJMQ	0	0	0	0	0
81	BOSTON	Juneau	Joé	C	US	828	156	416	572	272
87	QUÉBEC	Venne	Stéphane	D	US	0	0	0	0	0
99	NY RANGERS	Bergeron	Martin	C	LHJMQ	0	0	0	0	0
101	WINNIPEG	Lebeau	Benoit	W	US	0	0	0	0	0
104	MONTRÉAL	Bergeron	J.-Claude	G	LHJMQ	72				
142	ISLANDERS	Gaucher	Yves	W	LHJMQ	0	0	0	0	0
152	NY RANGERS	Couvrette	Yves	W	LHJMQ	0	0	0	0	0
197	CHICAGO	Maurice	Daniel	W	LHJMQ	0	0	0	0	0
210	CALGARY	Darveau	Guy	D	LHJMQ	0	0	0	0	0
234	QUÉBEC	Lapointe	Claude	C	LHJMQ	879	127	178	305	721
1989										
30	MONTRÉAL	Brisebois	Patrice	D	LHJMQ	1009	98	322	420	623
41	MONTRÉAL	Larouche	Steve	C	LHJMQ	26	9	9	18	10
43	QUÉBEC	Morin	Stéphane	C	LHJMQ	90	16	39	55	52
51	MONTRÉAL	Sévigny	Pierre	W	LHJMQ	78	4	5	9	64
75	MINNESOTA	Quintin	J.-F.	W	LHJMQ	22	5	5	10	4
76	QUÉBEC	Dubois	Éric	D	LHJMQ	0	0	0	0	0
83	MONTRÉAL	Racicot	André	G	LHJMQ	68				
93	ST. LOUIS	Laperriere	Daniel	D	US	48	2	5	7	27
102	LOS ANGELES	Ricard	Éric	D	LHJMQ	0	0	0	0	0
104	MONTRÉAL	Deschamps	Marc	D	US	0	0	0	0	0
157	HARTFORD	Saumier	Raymond	W	LHJMQ	0	0	0	0	0
167	MONTRÉAL	Lebeau	Patrick	W	LHJMQ	15	3	2	5	6
178	HARTFORD	Picard	Michel	W	LHJMQ	166	28	42	70	103
183	BUFFALO	Audette	Donald	W	LHJMQ	735	260	249	509	584
234	TORONTO	Chartrand	Steve	W	LHJMQ	0	0	0	0	0
251	MONTRÉAL	Cadieux	Steve	C	LHJMQ	0	0	0	0	0
1990										
16	CHICAGO	Dykhuis	Karl	D	LHJMQ	644	42	91	133	495
20	NEW JERSEY	Brodeur	Martin	G	LHJMQ	999				
26	CALGARY	Perreault	Nicolas	D	ONT	0	0	0	0	0
31	TORONTO	Potvin	Félix	G	LHJMQ	640				
38	EDMONTON	Legault	Alexandre	D	US	0	0	0	0	0
41	CALGARY	Belzile	Étienne	D	US	0	0	0	0	0
54	ST. LOUIS	Tardif	Patrice	C	US	65	7	11	18	78
58	MONTRÉAL	Poulin	Charles	C	LHJMQ	0	0	0	0	0

➤

RANK	TEAM	SURNAME	FIRST NAME	P	LEAGUE	GP	G	A	PTS	PIM
60	MONTRÉAL	Guillet	Robert	W	LHJMQ	0	0	0	0	0
67	EDMONTON	Blain	Joël	W	LHJMQ	0	0	0	0	0
81	MONTRÉAL	Dionne	Gilbert	W	ONT	223	61	79	140	108
86	VANCOUVER	Odjick	Gino	W	LHJMQ	605	64	73	137	2567
92	MINNESOTA	Cicone	Enrico	D	LHJMQ	374	10	18	28	1469
108	DETROIT	Barthe	Claude	D	LHJMQ	0	0	0	0	0
136	TORONTO	Lacroix	Éric	W	US	472	67	70	137	361
153	NY ISLANDERS	Fleury	Sylvain	C	LHJMQ	0	0	0	0	0
163	CHICAGO	Bélanger	Hugo	W	US	0	0	0	0	0
175	LOS ANGELES	Leblanc	Denis	W	LHJMQ	0	0	0	0	0
208	BUFFALO	Naud	Sylvain	W	LHJMQ	0	0	0	0	0
216	NY ISLANDERS	Lacroix	Martin	W	US	0	0	0	0	0
241	TORONTO	Vachon	Nicholas	W	US	1	0	0	0	0
246	HARTFORD	Chalifoux	Denis	C	LHJMQ	0	0	0	0	0
SUPP	TORONTO	Robitaille	Martin	C	US	0	0	0	0	0
1991										
9	HARTFORD	Poulin	Patrick	W	LHJMQ	634	101	134	235	299
10	DETROIT	Lapointe	Martin	W	LHJMQ	991	181	200	381	1417
13	BUFFALO	Boucher	Philippe	D	LHJMQ	748	94	206	300	702
24	QUÉBEC	Corbet	René	W	LHJMQ	362	58	74	132	420
25	WASHINGTON	Lavigne	Éric	D	LHJMQ	1	0	0	0	0
41	CALGARY	Groleau	François	D	LHJMQ	8	0	1	1	6
47	TORONTO	Perreault	Yanic	C	LHJMQ	859	247	269	516	402
50	PHILADELPHIA	Dupré	Yanick	W	LHJMQ	35	2	0	2	16
61	MONTRÉAL	Sarault	Yves	W	LHJMQ	106	10	10	20	51
62	BOSTON	Cousineau	Marcel	G	LHJMQ	26				
78	EDMONTON	Nobili	Mario	W	LHJMQ	0	0	0	0	0
83	MONTRÉAL	Lapointe	Sylvain	D	US	0	0	0	0	0
90	QUÉBEC	Labrecque	Patrick	G	LHJMQ	2				2
94	PHILADELPHIA	Degrace	Yanick	G	LHJMQ	0				
132	CHICAGO	Auger	Jacques	D	US	0	0	0	0	0
146	WASHINGTON	Morissette	Dave	W	LHJMQ	11	0	0	0	57
173	CALGARY	St-Pierre	David	C	LHJMQ	0	0	0	0	0
179	TORONTO	Lehoux	Guy	D	LHJMQ	0	0	0	0	0
212	WASHINGTON	Leblanc	Carl	D	LHJMQ	0	0	0	0	0
240	LOS ANGELES	Boulianne	André	G	LHJMQ	0				
244	QUÉBEC	Meloche	Éric	W	LHJMQ	0	0	0	0	0
1992										
28	QUÉBEC	Brousseau	Paul	W	LHJMQ	26	1	3	4	29
50	OTTAWA	Traverse	Patrick	D	LHJMQ	279	14	51	65	113
52	QUÉBEC	Fernandez	Emmanuel	G	LHJMQ	325				
61	EDMONTON	Roy	Simon	D	LHJMQ	0	0	0	0	0
70	DETROIT	Cloutier	Sylvain	C	ONT	7	0	0	0	0
71	WASHINGTON	Gendron	Martin	W	LHJMQ	30	4	2	6	10
82	MONTRÉAL	Bernard	Louis	D	LHJMQ	0	0	0	0	0

RANK	TEAM	SURNAME	FIRST NAME	P	LEAGUE	GP	G	A	PTS	PIM
98	OTTAWA	Guérard	Daniel	W	LHJMQ	2	0	0	0	0
115	PITTSBURGH	Derouville	Philippe	G	LHJMQ	3				
122	TAMPA BAY	Tanguay	Martin	C	LHJMQ	0	0	0	0	0
129	CALGARY	Bouchard	Joël	D	LHJMQ	364	22	53	75	264
147	SAN JOSE	Bellerose	Éric	W	LHJMQ	0	0	0	0	0
148	QUÉBEC	Lepage	Martin	D	LHJMQ	0	0	0	0	0
158	ST. LOUIS	Laperrière	Ian	C	LHJMQ	1101	118	198	316	1794
164	MONTRÉAL	Proulx	Christian	D	LHJMQ	7	1	2	3	20
175	PHILADELPHIA	Jutras	Claude	W	LHJMQ	0	0	0	0	0
194	OTTAWA	Savoie	Claude	W	LHJMQ	0	0	0	0	0
200	NY ISLANDERS	Paradis	Daniel	W	LHJMQ	0	0	0	0	0
218	TAMPA BAY	Tardif	Marc	W	LHJMQ	0	0	0	0	0
247	PHILADELPHIA	Paquin	Patrice	W	LHJMQ	0	0	0	0	0
1993										
1	OTTAWA	Daigle	Alexandre	W	LHJMQ	616	129	198	327	186
10	QUÉBEC	Thibault	Jocelyn	G	LHJMQ	596				
24	CHICAGO	Lecompte	Éric	W	LHJMQ	0	0	0	0	0
53	OTTAWA	Charbonneau	Patrick	G	LHJMQ	0				
69	WASHINGTON	Boileau	Patrick	D	LHJMQ	48	5	11	16	26
73	MONTRÉAL	Bordeleau	Sébastien	C	LHJMQ	251	37	61	98	118
88	BOSTON	Paquette	Charles	D	LHJMQ	0	0	0	0	0
90	CHICAGO	Dazé	Éric	W	LHJMQ	601	226	172	398	176
91	OTTAWA	Dupaul	Cosmo	W	LHJMQ	0	0	0	0	0
99	MONTRÉAL	Houle	J.-F.	W	US	0	0	0	0	0
100	DETROIT	Larose	Benoit	D	LHJMQ	0	0	0	0	0
105	LOS ANGELES	Beaubien	Frédérik	G	LHJMQ	0				
135	Florida	Nasreddine	Alain	D	LHJMQ	74	1	4	5	84
143	NEW JERSEY	Brûlé	Steve	W	LHJMQ	2	0	0	0	0
153	QUÉBEC	Matte	Christian	W	LHJMQ	25	2	3	5	12
156	PITTSBURGH	Lalime	Patrick	G	LHJMQ	421				
159	TAMPA BAY	Raby	Mathieu	D	LHJMQ	0	0	0	0	0
211	TAMPA BAY	Laporte	Alexandre	D	LHJMQ	0	0	0	0	0
229	MONTRÉAL	Duchesne	Alex	W	LHJMQ	0	0	0	0	0
231	QUÉBEC	Auger	Vincent	W	ONT	0	0	0	0	0
247	NEW JERSEY	Provencher	Jimmy	W	LHJMQ	0	0	0	0	0
248	NY ISLANDERS	Larocque	Stéphane	W	LHJMQ	0	0	0	0	0
265	FLORIDA	Montreuil	Éric	C	LHJMQ	0	0	0	0	0
274	NY ISLANDERS	Charland	Carl	W	LHJMQ	0	0	0	0	0
1994										
16	TORONTO	Fichaud	Éric	G	LHJMQ	95				
26	NY Rangers	Cloutier	Dan	G	ONT	351				147
40	CHICAGO	Leroux	J.-Yves	W	LHJMQ	220	16	22	38	146
44	MONTRÉAL	Théodore	José	G	LHJMQ	501				
47	BOSTON	Goneau	Daniel	W	LHJMQ	VOIR REP. DE 1996				

►

RANK	TEAM	SURNAME	FIRST NAME	P	LEAGUE	GP	G	A	PTS	PIM
49	DETROIT	Dandenault	Mathieu	D	LHJMQ	868	68	135	203	516
61	QUÉBEC	Bety	Sébastien	D	LHJMQ	0	0	0	0	0
68	ST. LOUIS	Roy	Stéphane	C	LHJMQ	0	0	0	0	0
74	MONTRÉAL	Bélanger	Martin	D	LHJMQ	0	0	0	0	0
101	PHILADELPHIA	Vallée	Sébastien	G	LHJMQ	0				
104	NY Rangers	Blouin	Sylvain	W	LHJMQ	115	3	4	7	336
114	DETROIT	Deschesnes	Frédérik	G	LHJMQ	0				
117	VANCOUVER	Dubé	Yanick	C	LHJMQ	0	0	0	0	0
119	WASHINGTON	Jean	Yanick	D	LHJMQ	0	0	0	0	0
122	MONTRÉAL	Drolet	Jimmy	D	LHJMQ	0	0	0	0	0
129	NEW JERSEY	Gosselin	Christian	D	LHJMQ	0	0	0	0	0
130	NY RANGERS	Éthier	Martin	D	LHJMQ	0	0	0	0	0
143	WINNIPEG	Vézina	Steve	G	LHJMQ	0				
151	BOSTON	Roy	André	W	LHJMQ	515	35	33	68	1169
156	RANGERS	Brosseau	David	W	LHJMQ	0	0	0	0	0
161	PITTSBURGH	Aubin	Serge	C	LHJMQ	374	44	64	108	361
168	BUFFALO	Plouffe	Steve	G	LHJMQ	0				
183	FLORIDA	Boudrias	Jason	W	LHJMQ	0	0	0	0	0
207	NEW JERSEY	Bertrand	Éric	W	LHJMQ	15	0	0	0	4
210	OTTAWA	Cassivi	Frédéric	G	LHJMQ	13				
211	OTTAWA	Dupont	Danny	D	LHJMQ	0	0	0	0	0
271	SAN JOSE	Beauregard	David	W	LHJMQ	0	0	0	0	0
SUPP	TAMPA BAY	Bouchard	François	D	US	0	0	0	0	0
1995										
13	HARTFORD	Giguère	J.-Sébastien	G	LHJMQ	457				
16	BUFFALO	Biron	Martin	G	LHJMQ	433				
20	CALGARY	Gauthier	Denis	D	LHJMQ	554	17	60	77	748
25	COLORADO	Denis	Marc	G	LHJMQ	349				
31	EDMONTON	Laraque	Georges	W	LHJMQ	667	52	98	150	1098
32	WINNIPEG	Chouinard	Marc	C	LHJMQ	320	37	41	78	123
37	DALLAS	Côté	Patrick	W	LHJMQ	105	1	2	3	377
39	NY Rangers	Dubé	Christian	W	LHJMQ	33	1	1	2	4
45	CHICAGO	Laflamme	Christian	D	LHJMQ	324	2	45	47	282
52	DETROIT	Audet	Philippe	W	LHJMQ	4	0	0	0	0
68	BUFFALO	Sunderland	Mathieu	W	LHJMQ	0	0	0	0	0
76	PITTSBURGH	Aubin	J.-Sébastien	G	LHJMQ	218				
78	NEW JERSEY	Gosselin	David	W	LHJMQ	13	2	1	3	11
86	MONTRÉAL	Delisle	Jonathan	W	LHJMQ	1	0	0	0	0
93	WASHINGTON	Charpentier	Sébastien	G	LHJMQ	24				
95	WASHINGTON	Thériault	Joël	D	LHJMQ	0	0	0	0	0
105	WASHINGTON	Gratton	Benoit	C	LHJMQ	58	6	10	16	58
114	FLORIDA	Cloutier	François	W	LHJMQ	0	0	0	0	0
123	BUFFALO	Bienvenue	Daniel	W	LHJMQ	0	0	0	0	0
126	DETROIT	Arsenault	Dave	G	LHJMQ	0				
136	WINNIPEG	Daigle	Sylvain	G	LHJMQ	0				

RANK	TEAM	SURNAME	FIRST NAME	P	LEAGUE	GP	G	A	PTS	PIM
141	DALLAS	Marleau	Dominic	D	LHJMQ	0	0	0	0	0
145	TORONTO	Tremblay	Yannick	D	LHJMQ	390	38	87	125	178
147	WASHINGTON	Jobin	Frédérick	D	LHJMQ	0	0	0	0	0
153	ST. LOUIS	Hamel	Denis	W	LHJMQ	192	19	12	31	77
157	LOS ANGELES	Larose	Benoit	D	LHJMQ	0	0	0	0	0
164	MONTRÉAL	Robidas	Stéphane	D	LHJMQ	561	30	105	135	418
175	CHICAGO	Tardif	Steve	C	LHJMQ	0	0	0	0	0
179	ST. LOUIS	Grand-Pierre	J.-Luc	D	LHJMQ	269	7	13	20	311
200	NEW JERSEY	Henry	Frédéric	G	LHJMQ	0				
216	MONTRÉAL	Houde	Éric	C	LHJMQ	30	2	3	5	4
1996										
3	NY ISLANDERS	Dumont	Jean-Pierre	W	LHJMQ	678	187	272	459	328
16	TAMPA BAY	Larocque	Mario	D	LHJMQ	5	0	0	0	16
19	EDMONTON	Descoteaux	Mathieu	D	LHJMQ	5	1	1	2	4
24	PHOENIX	Brière	Daniel	C	LHJMQ	591	204	269	473	459
31	CHICAGO	Royer	Rémi	D	LHJMQ	18	0	0	0	67
40	CALGARY	Bégin	Steve	W	LHJMQ	409	47	39	86	482
44	MONTRÉAL	Garon	Mathieu	G	LHJMQ	204				
47	NEW JERSEY	Dagenais	Pierre	W	LHJMQ	VOIR REP. DE 1998				
48	Rangers	Goneau	Daniel	W	LHJMQ	53	12	3	15	14
50	TORONTO	Larivée	Francis	G	LHJMQ	0				
53	BOSTON	Naud	Éric	W	LHJMQ	0	0	0	0	0
54	BUFFALO	Methot	François	C	LHJMQ	0	0	0	0	0
94	CALGARY	Lefebvre	Christian	D	LHJMQ	0	0	0	0	0
96	LOS ANGELES	Belanger	Éric	C	LHJMQ	557	106	152	258	251
99	MONTRÉAL	Drapeau	Etienne	C	LHJMQ	0	0	0	0	0
127	MONTRÉAL	Archambault	Daniel	D	LHJMQ	0	0	0	0	0
137	San Jose	Larocque	Michel	G	US	3				
151	TORONTO	Demartinis	Lucio	W	LHJMQ	0	0	0	0	0
156	FLORIDA	Poirier	Gaétan	W	US	0	0	0	0	0
157	TAMPA BAY	Delisle	Xavier	C	LHJMQ	16	3	2	5	6
162	DETROIT	Jacques	Alexandre	W	LHJMQ	0	0	0	0	0
163	OTTAWA	Hardy	François	D	LHJMQ	0	0	0	0	0
168	EDMONTON	Bernier	David	W	LHJMQ	0	0	0	0	0
169	ST. LOUIS	Corso	Daniel	C	LHJMQ	77	14	11	25	20
183	FLORIDA	Couture	Alexandre	D	LHJMQ	0	0	0	0	0
186	PITTSBURGH	Meloche	Éric	W	ONT	74	9	11	20	36
217	SAN JOSE	Thibeault	David	W	LHJMQ	0	0	0	0	0
219	LOS ANGELES	Simard	Sébastien		LHJMQ	0	0	0	0	0
226	PHOENIX	Hubert	M.-Étienne	C	LHJMQ	0	0	0	0	0
233	MONTRÉAL	Tremblay	Michel		LHJMQ	0	0	0	0	0
1997										
4	NY ISLANDERS	Luongo	Roberto	G	LHJMQ	544	.			
24	NEW JERSEY	Damphousse	J.-François	G	LHJMQ	6				

➤

RANK	TEAM	SURNAME	FIRST NAME	P	LEAGUE	GP	G	A	PTS	PIM
30	PHILADELPHIA	Pelletier	J.-Marc	G	US	7				
35	WASHINGTON	Fortin	J.-François	D	LHJMQ	71	1	4	5	42
80	CAROLINE	Lessard	Francis	W	LHJMQ	91	1	3	4	268
86	ST. LOUIS	Tremblay	Didier	D	LHJMQ	0	0	0	0	0
97	PITTSBURGH	Mathieu	Alexandre	C	LHJMQ	0	0	0	0	0
113	CALGARY	Moise	Martin	W	LHJMQ	0	0	0	0	0
125	ANAHEIM	Vaillancourt	Luc	G	LHJMQ	0				
145	MONTRÉAL	Desroches	Jonathan	D	LHJMQ	0	0	0	0	0
165	TORONTO	Marchand	Hugo	D	LHJMQ	0	0	0	0	0
172	MONTRÉAL	Guité	Ben	C	US	169	19	26	45	93
185	TAMPA BAY	St-Pierre	Samuel	W	LHJMQ	0	0	0	0	0
188	NEW JERSEY	Benoit	Mathieu	W	LHJMQ	0	0	0	0	0
200	WASHINGTON	Therrien	P.-Luc	G	LHJMQ	0				
218	BOSTON	Van Acker	Éric	D	LHJMQ	0	0	0	0	0
237	FLORIDA	Côté	Benoit	W	LHJMQ	0	0	0	0	0
1998										
1	TAMPA BAY	Lecavalier	Vincent	C	LHJMQ	787	302	367	669	561
12	COLORADO	Tanguay	Alex	W	LHJMQ	659	193	387	580	345
15	OTTAWA	Chouinard	Mathieu	G	LHJMQ	VOIR 2000 OTTAWA 2000				
16	MONTRÉAL	Chouinard	Éric	C	LHJMQ	90	11	11	22	16
21	LOS ANGELES	Biron	Mathieu	D	LHJMQ	253	12	32	44	177
22	PHILADELPHIA	Gagné	Simon	W	LHJMQ	606	242	242	484	231
28	COLORADO	Ramzi	Abid	W	LHJMQ	0	VOIR PHOENIX 2000			
38	COLORADO	Sauvé	Philippe	G	LHJMQ	32				
45	MONTRÉAL	Ribeiro	Mike	C	LHJMQ	515	117	256	373	212
48	BOSTON	Girard	Jonathan	D	LHJMQ	150	10	34	44	46
65	San Jose	Laplante	Éric	W	LHJMQ	0	0	0	0	0
75	MONTRÉAL	Beauchemin	François	D	LHJMQ	246	21	69	90	172
105	NEW JERSEY	Dagenais	Pierre	W	LHJMQ	142	35	23	58	58
108	CALGARY	Sabourin	Dany	G	LHJMQ	57				
109	PHILADELPHIA	Morin	J.-P.	D	LHJMQ	0	0	0	0	0
124	PHILADELPHIA	Bélanger	Francis	W	LHJMQ	10	0	0	0	29
138	NASHVILLE	Beauchesne	Martin	D	LHJMQ	0	0	0	0	0
166	CHICAGO	Pelletier	Jonathan	G	LHJMQ	0				
172	NEW JERSEY	Larivière	Jacques	W	LHJMQ	0	0	0	0	0
181	TORONTO	Gagnon	Jonathan	W	LHJMQ	0	0	0	0	0
188	OTTAWA	Périard	Michel	D	LHJMQ	0	0	0	0	0
205	ANAHEIM	Bernier	David	W	LHJMQ	0	0	0	0	0
209	NY ISLANDERS	Brind'Amour	Frederik	G	LHJMQ	0				
213	EDMONTON	Lefebvre	Christian		LHJMQ	0	0	0	0	0
238	CHICAGO	Couture	Alexandre		LHJMQ	0	0	0	0	0
253	PHILADELPHIA	St-Jacques	Bruno	D	LHJMQ	67	3	7	10	47
1999										
22	PHILADELPHIA	Ouellet	Maxime	G	LHJMQ	12				

RANK	TEAM	SURNAME	FIRST NAME	P	LEAGUE	GP	G	A	PTS	PIM
45	COLORADO	Grenier	Martin	D	LHJMQ	18	1	0	1	14
48	OTTAWA	Lajeunesse	Simon	G	LHJMQ	1				
80	FLORIDA	Laniel	J.-François	G	LHJMQ	0				
86	PITTSBURGH	Caron	Sébastien	G	LHJMQ	92				
133	LOS ANGELES	Nogues	J.-François	G	LHJMQ	0				
139	EDMONTON	Fauteux	Jonathan	D	LHJMQ	0	0	0	0	0
145	MONTRÉAL	Thinel	M.-André	W	LHJMQ	0	0	0	0	0
178	BUFFALO	Hyacinthe	Sénèque	W	LHJMQ	0	0	0	0	0
213	OTTAWA	Giroux	Alexandre	C	LHJMQ	22	3	3	6	12
227	FLORIDA	Charron	Jonathan	G	LHJMQ	0	0	0	0	0
229	SAN JOSE	Betournay	Éric	C	LHJMQ	0	0	0	0	0
253	MONTRÉAL	Marois	Jérôme	W	LHJMQ	0	0	0	0	0
270	ST. LOUIS	Desmarais	James	C	LHJMQ	0	0	0	0	0
2000										
45	OTTAWA	Chouinard	Mathieu	G	LHJMQ	1				
55	OTTAWA	Vermette	Antoine	C	LHJMQ	376	87	93	180	213
85	PHOENIX	Abid	Ramzi	W	LHJMQ	68	14	16	30	78
86	LOS ANGELES	Lehoux	Yanick	C	LHJMQ	10	2	2	4	6
90	TORONTO	Racine	J.-François	G	LHJMQ	0				
96	ST. LOUIS	Bergeron	Antoine	D	LHJMQ	0	0	0	0	0
107	ATLANTA	Malette	Carl	C	LHJMQ	0	0	0	0	0
111	BUFFALO	Rousseau	Ghyslain	G	LHJMQ	0				
114	MONTRÉAL	Larrivée	Christian	C	LHJMQ	0	0	0	0	0
124	PITTSBURGH	Ouellet	Michel	W	LHJMQ	190	52	64	116	58
227	PHILADELPHIA	Lefebvre	Guillaume	W	LHJMQ	38	2	4	6	13
265	TORONTO	Côté	J.-Philippe	D	LHJMQ	8	0	0	0	4
275	MONTRÉAL	Gauthier	Jonathan	D	LHJMQ	0	0	0	0	0
290	ATLANTA	Gamache	Simon	W	LHJMQ	48	6	7	13	18
292	COLUMBUS	Mandeville	Louis	D	LHJMQ	0	0	0	0	0
2001										
8	COLUMBUS	Leclaire	Pascal	G	LHJMQ	125				
55	BUFFALO	Pominville	Jason	W	LHJMQ	304	99	145	244	90
67	NEW JERSEY	Leblanc	Robin	W	LHJMQ	0	0	0	0	0
88	TORONTO	Corbeil	Nicolas	W	LHJMQ	0	0	0	0	0
93	MINNESOTA	Veilleux	Stéphane	W	LHJMQ	361	43	47	90	254
96	PITTSBURGH	Rouleau	Alexandre	D	LHJMQ	0	0	0	0	0
137	ANAHEIM	Perreault	Joel	C	LHJMQ	87	11	14	25	68
165	COLORADO	Emond	J.-Luc	C	LHJMQ	0	0	0	0	0
181	CAROLINE	Boisclair	Daniel	G	LHJMQ	0				
208	PHILADELPHIA	Douville	Thierry	D	LHJMQ	0	0	0	0	0
252	TAMPA BAY	Soucy	J.-François	W	LHJMQ	0	0	0	0	0
264	ANAHEIM	Parenteau	P.-Alexandre	W	LHJMQ	5	0	1	1	2
288	DETROIT	Senez	François	G	US	0				

►

RANK	TEAM	SURNAME	FIRST NAME	P	LEAGUE	GP	G	A	PTS	PIM
2002										
8	**MINNESOTA**	Bouchard	P.-Marc	C	LHJMQ	425	77	190	267	136
31	**EDMONTON**	Deslauriers	Jeff	G	LHJMQ	10				
59	WASHINGTON	Daigneault	Maxime	G	LHJMQ	0				
76	BUFFALO	Tessier	Micheal	W	LHJMQ	0	0	0	0	0
88	TORONTO	D'Amour	Dominic	D	LHJMQ	0	0	0	0	0
99	MONTRÉAL	Lambert	Michael	W	LHJMQ	0	0	0	0	0
201	PHILADELPHIA	Brunelle	Mathieu	W	LHJMQ	0	0	0	0	0
205	EDMONTON	Dufort	J.-François	W	LHJMQ	0	0	0	0	0
212	MONTRÉAL	Ferland	Jonathan	W	LHJMQ	7	1	0	1	2
214	VANCOUVER	Roy	M.-André	W	LHJMQ	0	0	0	0	0
234	**PITTSBURGH**	Talbot	Maxime	C	LHJMQ	261	42	38	80	228
259	**BOSTON**	Stastny	Yan	C	US	87	5	10	15	58
260	DETROIT	Beaulieu	P.-Olivier	D	LHJMQ	0	0	0	0	0
261	ANAHEIM	Caron	François	D	LHJMQ	0	0	0	0	0
2003										
1	**PITTSBURGH**	Fleury	M.-André	G	LHJMQ	235				
16	San Jose	Bernier	Steve	W	LHJMQ	258	60	62	122	155
22	**EDMONTON**	Pouliot	M.-Antoine	C	LHJMQ	141	14	25	39	53
45	**BOSTON**	Bergeron	Patrice	C	LHJMQ	303	80	148	228	88
60	VANCOUVER	Bernier	M.-André	W	LHJMQ	0	0	0	0	0
61	**MONTRÉAL**	Lapierre	Maxim	C	LHJMQ	179	28	30	58	160
68	**EDMONTON**	Jacques	J.-François	W	LHJMQ	60	1	0	1	44
85	**PHILADELPHIA**	Picard	Alexandre	D	LHJMQ	139	12	30	42	39
96	TAMPA BAY	Boutin	Jonathan	G	LHJMQ	0				
104	**COLUMBUS**	Dupuis	Philippe	C	LHJMQ	8	0	0	0	4
116	ATLANTA	Desbiens	Guillaume	W	LHJMQ	0	0	0	0	0
127	**ST. LOUIS**	Bolduc	Alexandre	C	LHJMQ	7	0	1	1	4
140	PHILADELPHIA	Tremblay	David	G	LHJMQ	0				
182	**NY ISLANDERS**	Gervais	Bruno	D	LHJMQ	207	6	39	45	103
201	SAN JOSE	Tremblay	Jonathan	W	LHJMQ	0	0	0	0	0
206	CALGARY	Bellemare	Thomas	W	LHJMQ	0	0	0	0	0
215	**EDMONTON**	Roy	Mathieu	D	LHJMQ	30	2	1	3	57
222	VANCOUVER	Guénette	F.-Pierre	C	LHJMQ	0	0	0	0	0
223	FLORIDA	Roussin	Dany	W	LHJMQ	0	0	0	0	0
233	COLUMBUS	Gravel	Mathieu	W	LHJMQ	0	0	0	0	0
241	MONTRÉAL	Bonneau	Jimmy	W	LHJMQ	0	0	0	0	0
247	BOSTON	Mondou	Benoit	W	LHJMQ	0	0	0	0	0
266	BUFFALO	Martin	L.-Philippe	W	LHJMQ	0	0	0	0	0
281	MINNESOTA	Bolduc	J.-Michel	D	LHJMQ	0	0	0	0	0
2004										
8	**COLUMBUS**	Picard	Alexandre	W	LHJMQ	58	0	2	2	48
107	NASHVILLE	Fugère	Nick	W	LHJMQ	0	0	0	0	0
114	MINNESOTA	Bordeleau	Patrick	W	LHJMQ	0	0	0	0	0
124	PHILADELPHIA	Laliberte	David	W	LHJMQ	0	0	0	0	0

RANK	TEAM	SURNAME	FIRST NAME	P	LEAGUE	GP	G	A	PTS	PIM
171	PHILADELPHIA	Cabana	Frédérik	C	LHJMQ	0	0	0	0	0
181	MONTRÉAL	Lacasse	Loic	G	LHJMQ	0				
189	VANCOUVER	Ellis	Julien	G	LHJMQ	0				
203	ANAHEIM	Bouthillette	Gabriel	G	LHJMQ	0				
208	EDMONTON	Goulet	Stéphane	W	LHJMQ	0	0	0	0	0
216	**NEW JERSEY**	**Leblond Létourneau P.-Luc**		**W**	**LHJMQ**	**8**	**0**	**1**	**1**	**2**
232	**PHILADELPHIA**	**Houle**	**Martin**	**G**	**LHJMQ**	**1**				
247	NY RANGERS	Paiement	Jonathan	D	LHJMQ	0	0	0	0	0
276	NY ISLANDERS	Michaud	Sylvain	G	LHJMQ	0				
277	ST. LOUIS	Boutin	Jonathan	W	LHJMQ	0	0	0	0	0
278	MONTRÉAL	Dulac-Lemelin	Alexandre	D	LHJMQ	0	0	0	0	0
2005										
16	ATLANTA	Bourret	Alex	W	LHJMQ	0	0	0	0	0
35	**San Jose**	**Vlasic M.-Édouard**		**D**	**LHJMQ**	**245**	**11**	**65**	**76**	**84**
44	**COLORADO**	**Stastny**	**Paul**	**C**	**US**	**193**	**63**	**122**	**185**	**88**
45	**MONTRÉAL**	**Latendresse**	**Guillaume**	**W**	**LHJMQ**	**209**	**46**	**36**	**82**	**133**
50	LOS ANGELES	Roussin	Dany	W	LHJMQ	0	0	0	0	0
56	NY RANGERS	Cliché	M.-André	C	LHJMQ	0	0	0	0	0
59	PHOENIX	Pelletier	P.-Olivier	G	LHJMQ	0				
62	**PITTSBURGH**	**Letang**	**Kristopher**	**D**	**LHJMQ**	**144**	**18**	**34**	**52**	**51**
87	**BUFFALO**	**Gragnani**	**M.-André**	**D**	**LHJMQ**	**6**	**0**	**0**	**0**	**6**
93	FLORIDA	Legault	Olivier	W	LHJMQ	0	0	0	0	0
114	VANCOUVER	Vincent	Alexandre	G	LHJMQ	0				
119	PHILADELPHIA	Duchesne	Jeremy	G	LHJMQ	0				
130	MONTRÉAL	Aubin	Mathieu	C	LHJMQ	0	0	0	0	0
192	CAROLINE	Blanchard	Nicolas	C	LHJMQ	0	0	0	0	0
194	PITTSBURGH	Paquet	J.-Philippe	D	LHJMQ	0	0	0	0	0
197	ANAHEIM	Levasseur	J.-Philippe	G	LHJMQ	0				
229	MONTRÉAL	Paquet	Philippe	D	US	0	0	0	0	0
2006										
6	**COLUMBUS**	**Brassard**	**Dérick**	**C**	**LHJMQ**	**48**	**11**	**16**	**27**	**23**
11	**LOS ANGELES**	**Bernier**	**Jonathan**	**G**	**LHJMQ**	**4**				
35	WASHINGTON	Bouchard	François	W	LHJMQ	0	0	0	0	0
53	MONTRÉAL	Carle	Mathieu	D	LHJMQ	0	0	0	0	0
61	CHICAGO	Danis-Pepin	Simon	D	US	0	0	0	0	0
118	CALGARY	Carpentier	Hugo	C	LHJMQ	0	0	0	0	0
121	OTTAWA	Lessard	P.-Luc	D	LHJMQ	0	0	0	0	0
127	WASHINGTON	Lacroix	Maxime	W	LHJMQ	0	0	0	0	0
142	COLUMBUS	Fréchette	Maxime	D	LHJMQ	0	0	0	0	0
144	LOS ANGELES	Nolet	Martin	D	JRA QC	0	0	0	0	0
148	NEW JERSEY	Magan-Grenier	Olivier	D	LHJMQ	0	0	0	0	0
153	CAROLINE	Chaput	Stéphane	C	LHJMQ	0	0	0	0	0
175	PHILADELPHIA	Dupont	Michael	G	LHJMQ	0				
177	WASHINGTON	Perreault	Mathieu	C	LHJMQ	0	0	0	0	0
207	BUFFALO	Breault	Benjamin	C	LHJMQ	0	0	0	0	0

➤

RANK	TEAM	SURNAME	FIRST NAME	P	LEAGUE	GP	G	A	PTS	PIM
2007										
20	PITTSBURGH	Esposito	Angelo	C	LHJMQ	0	0	0	0	0
26	**ST. LOUIS**	**Perron**	**David**	**C**	**LHJMQ**	**143**	**28**	**49**	**77**	**88**
48	NY RANGERS	Lafleur	Antoine	G	LHJMQ	0				
51	PITTSBURGH	Veilleux	Kevin	C	LHJMQ	0	0	0	0	0
63	ANAHEIM	Macenauer	Maxime	C	LHJMQ	0	0	0	0	0
65	MONTRÉAL	Fortier	Olivier	C	LHJMQ	0	0	0	0	0
69	CHICAGO	Tanguay	Maxime	C	LHJMQ	0	0	0	0	0
145	VANCOUVER	Messier	C.-Antoine	C	LHJMQ	0	0	0	0	0
147	BUFFALO	Allard	J.-Simon	C	LHJMQ	0	0	0	0	0
196	NY ISLANDERS	Lacroix	Simon	D	LHJMQ	0	0	0	0	0
2008										
35	ANAHEIM	Deschamps	Nicolas	C	LHJMQ	0	0	0	0	0
41	VANCOUVER	Sauvé	Yann	D	LHJMQ	0	0	0	0	0
47	BOSTON	Sauvé	Maxime	C	LHJMQ	0	0	0	0	0
55	MINNESOTA	Scandella	Marco	D	LHJMQ	0	0	0	0	0
64	ATLANTA	Paquette	Danick	W	LHJMQ	0	0	0	0	0
67	PHILADELPHIA	Bourdon	M.-André	D	LHJMQ	0	0	0	0	0
76	PHOENIX	Brodeur	Mathieu	D	LHJMQ	0	0	0	0	0
83	ANAHEIM	Cousineau	Marco	G	LHJMQ	0	0	0	0	0
92	SAN JOSE	Groulx	Samuel	D	LHJMQ	0	0	0	0	0
107	COLUMBUS	Delisle	Steven	D	LHJMQ	0	0	0	0	0
126	NY ISLANDERS	Poulin	Kevin	G	LHJMQ	0	0	0	0	0
129	TORONTO	Champagne	Joël	C	LHJMQ	0	0	0	0	0
133	EDMONTON	Cornet	Philippe	W	LHJMQ	0	0	0	0	0
134	BUFFALO	Lagacé	Jacob	W	LHJMQ	0	0	0	0	0
151	DETROIT	Cayer	Julien	C	US	0	0	0	0	0
167	COLORADO	Chouinard	Joël	D	LHJMQ	0	0	0	0	0
186	SAN JOSE	Demers	Jason	D	LHJMQ	0	0	0	0	0
195	CAROLINE	Morneau	Samuel	W	LHJMQ	0	0	0	0	0
205	NEW JERSEY	Bérubé	J.-Sébastien	W	LHJMQ	0	0	0	0	0
2009										
18	MONTRÉAL	Leblanc	Louis	C	US					
25	BOSTON	Caron	Jordan	W	LHJMQ					
27	CAROLINE	Paradis	Philippe	C	LHJMQ					
30	PITTSBURGH	Després	Simon	D	LHJMQ					
38	DALLAS	Chiasson	Alex	W	US					
42	NASHVILLE	Roussel Charles-Olivier		d	LHJMQ					
54	NEW JERSEY	Gélinas	Éric	D	LHJMQ					
84	LOS ANGELES	Deslauriers	Éric	D	LHJMQ					
90	DETROIT	Fournier	Gleason	D	LHJMQ					
94	COLUMBUS	Savard	David	D	LHJMQ					
95	LOS ANGELES	Bérubé Jean -François		G	LHJMQ					
132	NASHVILLE	Bourque	Gabriel	W	LHJMQ					
133	EDMONTON	Roy	Olivier	G	LHJMQ					

RANK	TEAM	SURNAME	FIRST NAME	P	LEAGUE	GP	G	A	PTS	PIM
139	MONTRÉAL	Dumont	Gabriel	C	LHJMQ					
142	PHILADELPHIA	Riopel	Nicolas	G	LHJMQ					
153	PHILADELPHIA	Labrecque	Dave	C	LHJMQ					
194	BUFFALO	Legault	Maxime	W	LHJMQ					
205	WASHINGTON	Casavant	Benjamin	W	LHJMQ					
209	CHICAGO	Gilbert	David	C	LHJMQ					

TABLE 2.18

Draft results for French-speaking Quebecers 1970-2009

YEAR	PLAYERS DRAFTED	ORIGIN				PLAYERS WHO PLAYED	GAMES PLAYED	
		LHJMQ	ONTARIO	US	OTHER		1 to 199	200 +
1970	17	9	8	–	–	9	3	6
1971	17	12	5	–	–	10	4	6
1972	29	26	3	–	–	11	5	6
1973	22	20	2	–	–	4	1	3
1974	31	29	–	2	–	12	2	10
1975	21	20	–	1	–	6	4	2
1976	9	9	–	–	–	4	3	1
1977	28	27	–	1	–	13	8	5
1978	15	12	–	1	2	4	3	1
1979	14	12	–	–	2	12	4	8
TOTAL	**203**	**176**	**18**	**5**	**4**	**85**	**37**	**48**
1980	14	14	–	–	–	9	7	2
1981	20	19	–	1	–	8	6	2
1982	14	14	–	–	–	7	5	2
1983	21	19	–	1	1	9	4	5
1984	11	11	–	–	–	6	–	6
1985	15	13	1	1	–	11	8	3
1986	17	16	–	–	1	9	6	3
1987	13	12	1	–	–	8	2	6
1988	24	21	–	3	–	14	8	6
1989	16	14	–	2	–	10	8	2
TOTAL	**165**	**153**	**2**	**8**	**2**	**91**	**54**	**37**
1990	23	13	2	8	–	9	2	7
1991	21	19	–	2	–	12	7	5
1992	20	19	1	–	–	10	6	4
1993	24	22	1	1	–	9	4	5
1994	28	26	1	1	–	10	4	6
1995	31	31	–	–	–	20	9	11
1996	30	27	1	2	–	13	8	5
1997	17	15	–	2	–	6	5	1
1998	26	26	–	–	–	13	7	6
1999	14	14	–	–	–	5	5	–
TOTAL	**234**	**212**	**6**	**16**	**0**	**107**	**57**	**50**
2000	15	15	–	–	–	8	7	1
2001	13	12	–	1	–	5	3	2
2002	14	13	–	1	–	5	3	2
2003	24	24	–	–	–	11	7	4
YEAR	PLAYERS DRAFTED	ORIGIN				PLAYERS WHO PLAYED	GAMES PLAYED	
		LHJMQ	ONTARIO	US	OTHER		1 to 199	200 +
2005	17	15	–	2	–	5	3	2
2006	15	13	–	1	1	2	2	–
2007	10	10	–	–	–	1	1	–
2008	19	18	–	1	–	–	–	–
2009	19	17	–	2	–	–	–	–
TOTAL	**161**	**152**	**0**	**8**	**1**	**40**	**29**	**11**
GRAND TOTAL	**763**	**693**	**26**	**37**	**7**	**323**	**177**	**146**

TABLE 2.19

Draft of English-speaking Quebecers 1970-2009*

RANK	TEAM	SURNAME	FIRST NAME	P	LEAGUE	GP	G	A	PTS	PIM
1970										
2	VANCOUVER	Tallon	Dale	D	ONT	642	98	238	336	568
49	PITTSBURGH	Forey	Connie	W	ONT	4	0	0	0	0
57	BUFFALO	Morton	Mike	W	LHJMQ	0	0	0	0	0
69	BOSTON	Roselle	Bob	C	LHJMQ	0	0	0	0	0
75	CALIFORNIA	Moyes	Doug	W	LHJMQ	0	0	0	0	0
88	CALIFORNIA	Murray	Terry	D	ONT	302	4	76	80	199
99	PHILADELPHIA	Cunningham	Gary	D	ONT	0	0	0	0	0
1971										
17	VANCOUVER	Lalonde	Bobby	C	ONT	641	124	210	334	298
43	CALIFORNIA	Monahan	Hartland	W	ONT	334	61	80	141	163
77	MINNESOTA	Globensky	Allan	D	ONT	0	0	0	0	0
83	NY Rangers	Wood	Wayne	G	ONT	0	0	0	0	0
98	TORONTO	Johnson	Steve	D	LHJMQ	0	0	0	0	0
1972										
25	BUFFALO	Carriere	Larry	D	UC	367	16	74	90	462
59	TORONTO	Bowles	Brian	D	LHJMQ	0	0	0	0	0
73	ST. LOUIS	Johnson	Dave	D	LHJMQ	0	0	0	0	0
105	ST. LOUIS	Coughlin	Brian	D	LHJMQ	0	0	0	0	0
138	DETROIT	Kuzmicz	George	D	US	0	0	0	0	0
1973										
15	TORONTO	Turnbull	Ian	D	ONT	628	123	317	440	736
131	VANCOUVER	Folco	Peter	D	LHJMQ	2	0	0	0	0
148	ATLANTA	Surbey	Glen	D	UC	0	0	0	0	0
166	MONTRÉAL	Halliday	Gordon	W	US	0	0	0	0	0
1974										
88	CHICAGO	Logan	Dave	D	LHJMQ	218	5	29	34	470
90	BOSTON	Bateman	Jamie	D	LHJMQ	0	0	0	0	0
139	NY Rangers	Holts	Greg	C	ONT	11	0	0	0	0
168	BUFFALO	Smith	Derek	W	ONT	335	78	116	194	60
200	CHICAGO	Byers	Dwayne	W	LHJMQ	0	0	0	0	0
1975										
8	ATLANTA	Mulhern	Richard	D	LHJMQ	303	27	93	120	217
13	PITTSBURGH	Laxton	Gordie	G	AMH	17				
55	WASHINGTON	Mackasey	Blair	D	LHJMQ	1	0	0	0	2
87	LOS ANGELES	Miglia	Dave	D	LHJMQ	0	0	0	0	0
1976										
25	ST. LOUIS	Smrke	John	W	ONT	103	11	17	28	33
28	ATLANTA	Simpson	Robert	W	LHJMQ	175	35	29	64	98
83	PITTSBURGH	Lowe	Brendan	D	LHJMQ	0	0	0	0	0

* Hockey players who played more than one game in the NHL are in bold.

➤

RANK	TEAM	SURNAME	FIRST NAME	P	LEAGUE	GP	G	A	PTS	PIM
1977										
4	VANCOUVER	Gillis	Jerry	W	LHJMQ	386	78	95	173	230
15	NY ISLANDERS	Bossy	Michael	W	LHJMQ	752	573	553	1126	210
64	MONTRÉAL	Holland	Robbie	G	LHJMQ	44				
78	CHICAGO	Platt	Gary	W	LHJMQ	0	0	0	0	0
95	CLEVELAND	Allan	Jeff	D	LHJMQ	4	0	0	0	2
98	NY Rangers	Bethel	John	W	US	17	0	2	2	4
114	CHICAGO	Lahache	Floyd	D	LHJMQ	0	0	0	0	0
116	NY Rangers	Sullivan	Bob	W	LHJMQ	VOIR 1978				
144	CHICAGO	Ough	Steve	D	LHJMQ	0	0	0	0	0
151	PHILADELPHIA	Baumen	Michel	D	LHJMQ	0	0	0	0	0
184	DETROIT	James	Val	W	LHJMQ	11	0	0	0	30
1978										
32	BUFFALO	Mckegney	Tony	W	ONT	912	320	319	639	517
36	MONTRÉAL	Carter	Ron	W	LHJMQ	2	0	0	0	0
38	WASHINGTON	Currie	Glen	W	LHJMQ	326	39	79	118	100
165	ATLANTA	Green	Mark	C	LHJMQ	0	0	0	0	0
171	MONTRÉAL	Swan	John		UC	0	0	0	0	0
180	ATLANTA	Sullivan	Bob	W	LHI	62	18	19	37	18
1979										
19	WINNIPEG	Mann	Jimy	W	LHJMQ	293	10	20	30	895
21	EDMONTON	Lowe	Kevin	D	LHJMQ	1254	84	348	432	1498
30	LOS ANGELES	Hardy	Mark	D	LHJMQ	926	62	306	368	1293
120	BOSTON	Krushelnysky	Mike	W	LHJMQ	897	241	328	569	699
1980										
47	WASHINGTON	Miele	Dan	W	US	0	0	0	0	0
53	MINNESOTA	Velischek	Randy	D	US	509	21	76	97	403
56	BUFFALO	Mckenna	Sean	W	LHJMQ	414	82	80	162	181
81	BOSTON	Kasper	Steve	W	LHJMQ	821	177	291	468	554
84	PHILADELPHIA	Zytynsky	Taras	D	LHJMQ	0	0	0	0	0
202	CALGARY	Fletcher	Steven	W	LHJMQ	3	0	0	0	5
1981										
13	MINNESOTA	Meighan	Ron	D	ONT	48	3	7	10	18
62	ST. LOUIS	Donnely	Gord	D	LHJMQ	554	28	41	69	2069
164	BUFFALO	Orlando	Gates	W	US	98	18	26	44	51
194	WASHINGTON	Valentine	Chris	W	LHJMQ	105	43	52	95	127
1982										
47	PHILADELPHIA	Campbell	Bill	D	LHJMQ	0	0	0	0	0
54	NEW JERSEY	Kasper	Dave	W	LHJMQ	0	0	0	0	0
56	HARTFORD	Dineen	Kevin	W	US	1188	355	405	760	2229
79	BUFFALO	Hamilton	Jeff	W	US	0	0	0	0	0
100	BUFFALO	Logan	Robert	W	US	42	10	5	15	0

RANK	TEAM	SURNAME	FIRST NAME	P	LEAGUE	GP	G	A	PTS	PIM
165	BOSTON	Fiore	Tony	C	LHJMQ	0	0	0	0	0
181	QUÉBEC	Hough	Mike	W	ONT	707	100	156	256	675
246	NY Rangers	Robinson	Dwayne	D	US					
1983										
14	WINNIPEG	Dollas	Bobby	D	LHJMQ	646	42	96	138	467
15	PITTSBURGH	Errey	Bobby	W	ONT	895	120	212	382	1005
100	LOS ANGELES	Galley	Gary	D	US	1149	125	474	599	1218
141	PHILADELPHIA	Mormina	Bobby	W	LHJMQ	0	0	0	0	0
149	WINNIPEG	Pesetti	Ronnie	D	US	0	0	0	0	0
240	EDMONTON	Woodburn	Steve	D	LHJMQ	0	0	0	0	0
1984										
27	PHILADELPHIA	Mellanby	Scott	W	US	1431	364	476	840	2479
37	PHILADELPHIA	Chychrun	Jeff	D	ONT	262	3	22	25	742
57	QUÉBEC	Finn	Steven	D	LHJMQ	725	34	78	112	1724
71	ST. LOUIS	Herring	Graham	D	LHJMQ	0	0	0	0	0
150	LOS ANGELES	Deegan	Shannon	F	US	0	0	0	0	0
174	CHICAGO	Di Fiori	Ralph	D	LHJMQ	0	0	0	0	0
1985										
113	DETROIT	Mckay	Randy	W	US	932	162	201	363	1731
114	PITTSBURGH	Marston	Stuart-Lee		LHJMQ	0	0	0	0	0
115	BOSTON	Hynes	Gord	D	OHL	52	3	9	12	22
165	WINNIPEG	Draper	Tom	G	US	53				
198	MONTRÉAL	Mansi	Maurice	W	US	0	0	0	0	0
207	WINNIPEG	Quigley	Dave	G	UC	0	0	0	0	0
1986										
3	NEW JERSEY	Brady	Neil	C	LHW	89	9	22	31	95
5	BUFFALO	Anderson	Shawn	D	US	255	11	51	62	117
55	MINNESOTA	Zettler	Rob	D	ONT	569	5	65	70	920
61	WASHINGTON	Hrivnac	Jim	G	US	85				
70	VANCOUVER	Stern	Ronnie	W	LHJMQ	638	75	86	161	2077
113	WINNIPEG	Bateman	Rob	D	CO CA	0	0	0	0	0
117	QUÉBEC	White	Scott	D	US	0	0	0	0	0
173	BUFFALO	Witham	Sean	D	US	0	0	0	0	0
220	ST. LOUIS	Maclean	Terry	C	LHJMQ	0	0	0	0	0
1987										
8	CHICAGO	Waite	Jimmy	G	LHJMQ	106				
24	VANCOUVER	Murphy	Rob	D	LHJMQ	125	9	12	21	152
124	CALGARY	Aloi	Joe	D	LHJMQ	0	0	0	0	0
1988										
30	ST. LOUIS	Plavsic	Adrien	D	US	214	16	56	72	161
SUPP	WINNIPEG	O Neill	Mike	G	US	21				

➤

RANK	TEAM	SURNAME	FIRST NAME	P	LEAGUE	GP	G	A	PTS	PIM
1989										
92	EDMONTON	White	Peter	C	E.U	220	23	37	60	36
124	ST. LOUIS	Frenette	Derek	W	E.U	0	0	0	0	0
173	NEW JERSEY	Faust	André	W	E.U	47	10	7	17	14
244	NY Rangers	Macdermid	Kenneth	W	LHJMQ	0	0	0	0	0
1990										
22	QUÉBEC	Hughes	Ryan	C	E.U	3	0	0	0	0
162	HARTFORD	D Orsonnens	Martin	D	E.U	0	0	0	0	0
226	CHICAGO	Dubinsky	Steve	C	E.U	375	25	45	70	164
1991										
100	MONTRÉAL	Layzell	Brad	D	US	0	0	0	0	0
186	DETROIT	Bermingham	Jim	C	LHJMQ	0	0	0	0	0
262	LOS ANGELES	Gaul	Michael	D	US	3	0	0	0	0
SUPP	CHICAGO	Gravelle	Dan	W	US	0	0	0	0	0
1992										
76	QUÉBEC	Mcintyre	Ian	W	LHJMQ	0	0	0	0	0
145	TAMPA BAY	Wilkinson	Derek	G	ONT	22				
193	TAMPA BAY	Kemper	Andréw	D	OHL	0	0	0	0	0
1993										
171	WINNIPEG	Woods	Martin	D	LHJMQ	0	0	0	0	0
1994										
139	QUÉBEC	Windsor	Nicholas	D	ONT	0	0	0	0	0
181	NEW JERSEY	Williams	Jeff	W	ONT	0	0	0	0	0
285	QUÉBEC	Low	Steven	D	LHJMQ	0	0	0	0	0
SUPP	HARTFORD	Martins	Steven	C	US	267	21	25	46	142
1995										
34	WINNIPEG	Doig	Jason	D	LHJMQ	158	6	18	24	285
166	Florida	Worrell	Peter	W	LHJMQ	391	19	27	46	1554
1996										
235	Florida	Smith	Russell	D	LHJMQ	0	0	0	0	0
1997										
77	DALLAS	Gainey	Steve	W	OHL	33	0	2	2	34
106	ST. LOUIS	Pollock	James	D	OHL	9	0	0	0	6
149	ST. LOUIS	Bilotto	Nicholas	D	LHJMQ	0	0	0	0	0
1998										
133	LOS ANGELES	Rullier	Joe	D	LHJMQ	0	0	0	0	0
229	TAMPA BAY	Lyness	Chris	D	LHJMQ	0	0	0	0	0
248	LOS ANGELES	Yeats	Matthew	G	US	5				
1999										
108	TORONTO	Murovic	Mirko	W	LHJMQ	0	0	0	0	0
166	CALGARY	Pecker	Cory	W	ONT	0	0	0	0	0

RANK	TEAM	SURNAME	FIRST NAME	P	LEAGUE	GP	G	A	PTS	PIM
2000										
189	COLORADO	Bahen	Chris	D	US	0	0	0	0	0
208	VANCOUVER	Reid	Brandon	C	LHJMQ	13	2	4	6	0
215	EDMONTON	Lombardi	Matthew	C	LHJMQ	See CALGARY 2002				
2001										
10	NY Rangers	Blackburn	Dan	G	OHL	63				
139	NY Rangers	Collymore	Shawn	W	LHJMQ	0	0	0	0	0
2002										
90	CALGARY	Lombardi	Matthew	C	LHJMQ	297	56	81	137	195
105	PHILADELPHIA	Ruggeri	Rosario	D	LHJMQ	0	0	0	0	0
193	PHILADELPHIA	Mormina	Joey	D	US	1	0	0	0	0
2003										
25	Florida	Stewart	Anthony	W	ONT	105	4	8	12	38
52	CHICAGO	Crawford	Corey	G	LHJMQ	7				
197	NEW JERSEY	Smith	Jason	G	QJRA	0	0	0	0	0
2004										
126	San Jose	Mitchell	Torrey	C	US	82	10	10	20	50
160	BOSTON	Walter	Ben	C	US	22	1	0	1	4
273	BUFFALO	Hunter	Dylan	W	ONT	0	0	0	0	0
2005										
14	WASHINGTON	Pokulok	Sasha	D	US	0	0	0	0	0
2006										
147	BUFFALO	Biega	Alex	D	US	0	0	0	0	0
208	NEW JERSEY	Henegan	Kyell	D	LHJMQ	0	0	0		0
2007										
41	PHILADELPHIA	Marshall	Kevin	D	LHJMQ	0	0	0	0	0
2008										
104	BUFFALO	Southorn	Jordon	D	LHJMQ	0	0	0	0	0
152	TAMPA BAY	Barberio	Mark	D	LHJMQ	0	0	0	0	0
2009										
121	PITTSBURGH	Peterson	Nick	W	LHJMQ					
123	PITTSBURGH	Velischek	Alex	D	US					

TABLE 2.20

Draft results for English-speaking Quebecers 1970-2009

YEAR	,PLAYERS DRAFTED	ORIGIN					PLAYERS WHO PLAYED	GAMES PLAYED	
		LHJMQ	ONTARIO	US	C.U.	OTHER		1 to 199	200 +
1970	7	3	4	–	–	–	3	1	2
1971	5	1	4	–	–	–	2	–	2
1972	5	3	–	1	1	–	1	–	1
1973	4	1	1	1	1	–	2	1	1
1974	5	3	2	–	–	–	3	1	2
1975	4	3	–	–	–	1	3	2	1
1976	3	2	1	–	–	–	2	2	–
1977	11	10	–	1	–	–	6	4	2
1978	6	3	1	–	1	1	4	2	2
1979	4	4	–	–	–	2	4	–	4
TOTAL	54	33	13	3	3	2	30	13	17
1980	6	4	–	2	–	–	4	1	3
1981	4	2	1	1	–	–	4	3	1
1982	8	3	1	4	–	–	3	1	2
1983	6	3	1	2	–	–	3	–	3
1984	6	3	1	2	–	–	3	–	3
1985	6	1	–	3	1	1·	3	2	1
1986	9	2	1	4	1	1	5	2	3
1987	3	3	–	–	–	–	2	2	–
1988	2	–	–	2	–	–	2	1	1
1989	4	1	–	3	–	–	2	1	1
TOTAL	54	22	5	23	2	2	31	13	18
1990	3	–	–	3	–	–	2	1	1
1991	4	1	–	3	–	–	1	1	–
1992	3	1	1	–	–	1	1	1	–
1993	1	1	–	–	–	–	–	–	–
1994	4	1	2	1	–	–	1	–	1
1995	2	2	–	–	–	–	2	1	1
1996	1	1	–	–	–	–	–	–	–
1997	3	1	–	–	–	2	2	2	–
1998	3	2	–	1	–	–	1	1	–
1999	2	1	1	–	–	–	–	–	–
TOTAL	26	11	4	8	0	3	10	7	3
2000	3	2	–	1	–	–	1	1	–
2001	2	1	–	–	–	1	1	1	–
2002	3	2	–	1	–	–	2	1	1
2003	3	1	1	–	–	1	2	2	–
2004	3	–	1	2	–	–	2	2	–
2005	1	–	–	1	–	–	–	–	–
2006	2	1	–	1	–	–	–	–	–
2007	2	2	–	–	–	–	–	–	–
2008	2	2	–	–	–	–	–	–	–
2009	2	1	–	1	–	–	–	–	–
TOTAL	23	12	2	7	0	2	8	7	1
GRAND	157	78	24	41	5	9	79	40	39

Chapter 3

NHL Teams and Their Use of Quebec Hockey Players

Which National Hockey League teams have used the most Quebec hockey players? What proportion of Quebec players drafted by these NHL teams played at least one game? Are some NHL teams allergic to Quebec players? Answers to these questions and more are provided in the following pages.

The NHL teams are presented in the same order as previously for the NHL Entry Draft (Table 2.16). NHL teams that no longer exist are presented after the thirty teams now in the league.

NOTE: Two lists of Quebec players are provided at the end of Chapter 3: players drafted by the respective hockey teams (Table 3.1) and players who played for those teams (Table 3.2). The statistics for players who were drafted indicate their NHL career results. The statistics for hockey players who played indicate the results they obtained with their NHL teams. Table 1 in the Appendix provides the number of Montreal Canadiens games played by French-speaking Quebec hockey players during seasons 1970-71 to 2008-09.

Figures for the Montreal Canadiens (1970-2009)

- The Montreal Canadiens top the league in the average number of French-speaking Quebec hockey players drafted, with 2.63 players per year (a total of 105).
- Of the 101 players drafted before 2006, fifty played in the NHL, or 49.5 percent.
- The Canadiens are also tops in the use French-speaking Quebec hockey players. Of the 374 players who played for them, 128 were French-speaking Quebecers, or 34.22 percent.
- 51.56 percent of those 128 Quebec hockey players (or 66 players) used by the Canadiens played with the team for more than one season.

Figures for the Buffalo Sabres (1970-2009)

· The Sabres are second for the average number of French-speaking Quebec hockey players drafted, with 1.20 player per year (a total of 48).

· Of the 44 players picked before 2006, seventeen played in the NHL, or 38.64 percent.

· The Sabres are third as regards use of French-speaking Quebec hockey players. Of the 372 players who played for them, fifty-one were French-speaking Quebecers, or 13.71 percent.

· 47.05 percent of those fifty-one Quebec hockey players (or 24 players) used by the Sabres played with the team for more than one season.

Figures for the Philadelphia Flyers (1970-2009)

· The Flyers are third for the average number of French-speaking Quebec hockey players drafted, with 1.13 player per year (a total of 45).

· Of the forty players picked before 2006, sixteen played in the NHL, or 40 percent.

· The Flyers are fifth as regards use of French-speaking Quebec hockey players. Of the 491 players they used, sixty-four were French-speaking Quebecers, or 13.03 percent.

· 31.25 percent of those sixty-four Quebec hockey players (or 20 players) used by the Flyers played with the team for more than one season.

Figures for the New York Rangers (1970-2009)

· The Rangers are fourth for the average number of French-speaking Quebec hockey players drafted, with 0.90 player per year (a total of 36).

· Of the thirty-five players picked before 2006, thirteen played in the NHL, or 37.14 percent.

· The Rangers are fifteenth as regards use of French-speaking Quebec hockey players. Of the 555 players who played for them, fifty-five were French-speaking Quebecers, or 9.91 percent.

· 29.09 percent of those fifty-five (or 16 players) played more than one season with the Rangers.

Figures for the Columbus Blue Jackets from 2000 to 2009

- The Blue Jackets are fifth for the average number of French-speaking Quebec hockey players drafted, with 0.9 player per year (a total of 9).
- Of the five players picked before 2006, two played in the NHL, or 40 percent;
- The Blue Jackets are twenty-third as regards use of French-speaking Quebec hockey players. Of the 149 players who played for them, thirteen were French-speaking Quebecers, or 8.72 percent;
- 38.46 percent of those Quebec hockey players (or 5 players) played more than one season with Columbus.

Figures for the Ottawa Senators from 1992 to 2009

- The Ottawa Senators are sixth for the average number of French-speaking Quebec hockey players drafted, with 0.89 player per year (a total of 16).
- Of the fifteen players picked before 2006, eight played in the NHL, or 53.33 percent.
- The Ottawa Senators are seventh as regards use of French-speaking Quebec hockey players. Of the 257 players who played for them, thirty were French-speaking Quebecers, or 11.67 percent.
- 23.33 percent of those thirty Quebec hockey players (or seven players) played more than one season with the Senators.

Figures for the Washington Capitals from 1974 to 2009

- The Washington Capitals are sixth for the average number of French-speaking Quebec hockey players drafted, with 0.89 player per year (a total of 32).
- Of the twenty-eight players picked before 2006, fifteen played in the NHL, or 53.57 percent.
- The Capitals are ninth as regards use of French-speaking Quebec hockey players. Of the 450 players who played for them, fifty-two were French-speaking Quebecers, or 11.56 percent.
- 25 percent of those fifty-two Quebec hockey players (or 13 players) played more than one season with the Capitals.

Figures for the Toronto Maple Leafs (1970-2009)

· The Maple Leafs are eighth for the average number of French-speaking Quebec hockey players drafted, with 0.875 player per year (a total of 35).

· Of the thirty-four players picked before 2006, eleven played in the NHL, or 32.35 percent;

· The Maple Leafs are twenty-first as regards use of French-speaking Quebec hockey players. Of the 498 players who played for them, forty-five were French-speaking Quebecers, or 9.04 percent;

· 40 percent of those forty-five Quebec hockey players (or 18 players) played more than one season with the Maple Leafs.

Figures for the Detroit Red Wings (1970-2009)

· The Red Wings are ninth for the average number of French-speaking Quebec hockey players drafted, with 0.85 player per year (a total of 34).

· Of the thirty-two players picked before 2006, sixteen played in the NHL, or 50 percent.

· The Red Wings are twentieth as regards use of French-speaking Quebec hockey players. Of the 476 players who played for them, forty-four were French-speaking Quebecers, or 9.24 percent.

· 45 percent of those forty-four Quebec hockey players (or 20 players) played more than one season with the Red Wings.

Figures for the Chicago Blackhawks (1970-2009)

· The Blackhawks are tenth for the average number of French-speaking Quebec hockey players drafted, with 0.80 player per year (a total of 32).

· Of the twenty-nine players picked before 2006, fifteen played in the NHL, or 51.72 percent.

· The Blackhawks are eighth as regards use of French-speaking Quebec hockey players. Of the 455 players who played for them, fifty-three were French-speaking Quebecers, or 11.65 percent.

· 35.84 percent of those fifty-three Quebec hockey players (or 19 players) played more than one season with the Blackhawks.

Figures for the New York Islanders (1972-2009)

- The Islanders are eleventh for the average number of French-speaking Quebec hockey players drafted, with 0.76 player per year (a total of 32).
- Of the twenty-seven players picked before 2006, seven played in the NHL, or 25.93 percent;
- The Islanders are twenty-fourth as regards use of French-speaking Quebec hockey players. Of the 441 players who played for them, thirty-three were French-speaking Quebecers, or 7.48 percent;
- 30.30 percent of those thirty-three Quebec hockey players (or 10 players) played more than one season with the Islanders.

Figures for the Boston Bruins (1970-2009)

- The Bruins are twelfth for the average number of French-speaking Quebec hockey players drafted, with 0.73 player per year (a total of 29).
- Of the twenty-seven players picked before 2006, fifteen played in the NHL, or 55.55 percent;
- The Bruins are twenty-second as regards use of French-speaking Quebec hockey players. Of the 506 players who played for them, forty-five were French-speaking Quebecers, or 8.89 percent;
- 35.55 percent of those forty-five Quebec hockey players (or 16 players) played more than one season with the Bruins.

Figures for the Los Angeles Kings (1970-2009)

- The Kings are thirteenth for the average number of French-speaking Quebec hockey players drafted, with 0.68 player per year (a total of 27).
- Of the twenty-three players picked before 2006, eight played in the NHL, or 34.78 percent.
- The Kings are eleventh as regards use of French-speaking Quebec hockey players. Of the 533 players who played for them, sixty-one were French-speaking Quebecers, or 11.44 percent.
- 31.14 percent of those sixty-one Quebec hockey players (or 19 players) played more than one season with the Kings.

Figures for the New Jersey Devils (1982-2009)

- The Devils are fourteenth for the average number of French-speaking Quebec hockey players drafted, with 0.68 player per year (a total of 19).
- Of the seventeen players picked before 2006, seven played in the NHL, or 41.17 percent.
- The Devils are twenty-eighth as regards use of French-speaking Quebec hockey players. Of the 282 players who played for them, eighteen were French-speaking Quebecers, or 6.38 percent.
- 27.77 percent of those eighteen Quebec hockey players (or 5 players) played more than one season with the Devils.

Figures for the Pittsburgh Penguins (1970-2009)

- The Penguins are fifteenth for the average number of French-speaking Quebec hockey players drafted, with 0.65 player per year (a total of 26).
- Of the twenty-three players picked before 2006, seventeen played in the NHL, or 73.91 percent.
- The Penguins are sixth as regards use of French-speaking Quebec hockey players. Of the 526 players who played for them, sixty-two were French-speaking Quebecers, or 11.79 percent.
- 33.87 percent of those 62 Quebec hockey players (or 21 players) played more than one season with the Penguins.

Figures for the Florida Panthers (1993-2009)

- The Panthers are sixteenth for the average number of French-speaking Quebec hockey players drafted, with 0.65 player per year (a total of 11).
- Of the ten players picked before 2006, only one played in the NHL, or ten percent.
- The Panthers are twenty-fifth as regards use of French-speaking Quebec hockey players. Of the 232 players who played for them, seventeen were French-speaking Quebecers, or 7.33 percent.
- 23.53 percent of those seventeen Quebec hockey players (or 4 players) played more than one season with the Panthers.

Figures for the Edmonton Oilers (1979-2009)

· The Oilers are seventeenth for the average number of French-speaking Quebec hockey players drafted, with 0.65 player per year (a total of 20).

· Of the eighteen players picked before 2006, six played in the NHL, or 33.33 percent.

· The Oilers are twenty-seventh as regards use of French-speaking Quebec hockey players. Of the 408 players who played for them, twenty-eight were French-speaking Quebecers, or 6.87 percent.

· 17.85 percent of those twenty-eight Quebec hockey players (or 5 players) played more than one season with the Oilers.

Figures for the Tampa Bay Lightning (1992-2009)

· The Lightning is eighteenth for the average number of French-speaking Quebec hockey players drafted, with 0.61 player per year (a total of 11).

· Of the ten players picked before 2006, three played in the NHL, or 30 percent.

· The Lightning is fourth as regards use of French-speaking Quebec hockey players. Of the 288 players who played for them, thirty-nine were French-speaking Quebecers, or 13.54 percent.

· 33.33 percent of those thirty-nine Quebec hockey players (or 13 players) played more than one season with the Lightning.

Figures for the St. Louis Blues (1970-2009)

· The Blues are nineteenth for the average number of French-speaking Quebec hockey players drafted, with 0.6 player per year (a total of 24).

· Of the twenty-four players picked before 2006, eleven played in the NHL, or 45.83 percent;

· The Blues are tenth as regards use of French-speaking Quebec hockey players. Of the 548 players who played for them, sixty-three were French-speaking Quebecers, or 11.50 percent;

· 34.92 percent of those sixty-three Quebec hockey players (or 22 players) played more than one season with the Blues.

Figures for the Anaheim Ducks (1993- 2009)

· The Ducks are twentieth for the average number of French-speaking Quebec hockey players drafted, with 0.59 player per year (a total of 10).
· Of the seven players picked before 2006, two played in the NHL, or 28.57 percent.
· The Ducks are twenty-ninth as regards use of French-speaking Quebec hockey players. Of the 236 players who played for them, fourteen were French-speaking Quebecers, or 5.93 percent;
· 50 percent of those fourteen Quebec hockey players (or 7 players) played more than one season with the Ducks.

Figures for the San Jose Sharks (1991- 2009)

· The Sharks are twenty-first for the average number of French-speaking Quebec hockey players drafted, with 0.58 player per year (a total of 11).
· Of the nine players picked before 2006, three played in the NHL, or 33.33 percent.
· The Sharks are twenty-sixth as regards use of French-speaking Quebec hockey players. Of the 236 players who played for them, seventeen were French-speaking Quebecers, or 7.20 percent.
· 29.41 percent of those seventeen Quebec hockey players (or 5 players) played more than one season with the Sharks.

Figures for the Calgary Flames (1980-2009)

· The Flames are twenty-second for the average number of French-speaking Quebec hockey players drafted, with 0.57 player per year (a total of 17).
· Of the sixteen players picked before 2006, seven played in the NHL, or 43.75 percent.
· The Flames are eighteenth as regards use of French-speaking Quebec hockey players. Of the 383 players who played for them, thirty-six were French-speaking Quebecers, or 9.35 percent.
· 27.77 percent of those thirty-six Quebec hockey players (or 10 players) played more than one season with the Flames.

Figures for the Colorado Avalanche (1995-2009)

- The Avalanche is twenty-third for the average number of French-speaking Quebec hockey players drafted, with 0.53 player per year (a total of 8).
- Of the seven players picked before 2006, six played in the NHL, or 85.71 percent.
- The Avalanche is second as regards use of French-speaking Quebec hockey players. Of the 178 players who played for them, twenty-nine were French-speaking Quebec hockey players, or 16.29 percent.
- 55.17 percent of those twenty-nine Quebec hockey players (or 16 players) played more than one season with the Avalanche.

Figures for the Minnesota Wild (2000-2009)

- The Wild is twenty-fourth for the average number of French-speaking Quebec hockey players drafted, with 0.50 player per year (a total of 5).
- Of the four players picked before 2006, two played in the NHL, or 50 percent.
- The Wild is twelfth as regards use of French-speaking Quebec hockey players. Of the 116 players who played for them, thirteen were French-speaking Quebecers, or 11.21 percent.
- 69.23 percent of those thirteen Quebec hockey players (or 9 players) played more than one season with the Wild.

Figures for the Vancouver Canucks (1970-2009)

- The Canucks are twenty-fifth for the average number of French-speaking Quebec hockey players drafted, with 0.50 player per year (a total of 20).
- Of the eighteen players picked before 2006, seven played in the NHL, or 38.89 percent.
- The Canucks are nineteenth as regards use of French-speaking Quebec hockey players. Of the 473 players who played for them, forty-four were French-speaking Quebecers, or 9.30 percent.
- 43.18 percent of those forty-four Quebec hockey players (or 19 players) played more than one season with the Canucks.

Figures for the Carolina Hurricanes (1997-2009)

· The Hurricanes are twenty-sixth for the average number of French-speaking Quebec hockey players drafted, with 0.46 player per year (a total of 6).

· Of the three players picked before 2006, only one played in the NHL, or 33.33 percent.

· The Hurricanes are thirtieth as regards use of French-speaking Quebec hockey players. Of the 146 players who played for them, six were French-speaking Quebecers, or 4.11 percent.

· 16.66 percent of those six Quebec hockey players (or one player) played more than one season with the Hurricanes.

Figures for the Atlanta Thrashers (1999-2009)

· The Thrashers are twenty-seventh for the average number of French-speaking Quebec hockey players drafted, with 0.45 player per year (a total of 5).

· Of the four players picked before 2006, only one played in the NHL, or 25 percent.

· The Thrashers are sixteenth as regards use of French-speaking Quebec hockey players. Of the 172 players who played for them, seventeen were French-speaking Quebecers, or 9.88 percent.

· 35.29 percent of those seventeen Quebec hockey players (or six players) played more than one season with the Thrashers.

Figures for the Phoenix Coyotes (1996-2009)

· The Coyotes are twenty-eighth for the average number of French-speaking Quebec hockey players drafted, with 0.36 player per year (a total of 5).

· Of the four players picked before 2006, two played in the NHL, or 50 percent.

· The Coyotes are seventeenth as regards use of French-speaking Quebec hockey players. Of the 230 players who played for them, twenty-two were French-speaking Quebecers, or 9.57 percent.

· 13.63 percent of those twenty-two Quebec hockey players (or three players) played more than one season with the Coyotes.

Figures for the Nashville Predators (1998-2009)

· The Predators are twenty-ninth for the average number of French-speaking Quebec hockey players drafted, with 0.33 player per year (a total of 4).

· Of the 2 players picked before 2006, not one played in the NHL, or 0 percent.

· The Predators are fourteenth as regards use of French-speaking Quebec hockey players. Of the 161 players who played for them, sixteen were French-speaking Quebecers, or 10 percent.

· 25 percent of those sixteen Quebec hockey players (or 4 players) played more than one season with the Predators.

Figures for the Dallas Stars (1994-2009)

· The Stars are thirtieth for the average number of French-speaking Quebec hockey players drafted, with 0.18 player per year (a total of 3).

· Of the two players picked before 2006, only one played in the NHL, or 50 percent.

· The Stars are thirteenth as regards use of French-speaking Quebec hockey players. Of the 223 players who played for them, twenty-three were French-speaking Quebecers, or 10.31 percent.

· 26.08 percent of those twenty-three Quebec hockey players (or six players) played more than one season with the Stars.

The NHL teams that were dissolved

The position of these teams is determined by the rank they would have if they still existed.

Figures for the Quebec Nordiques (1979-95)

· The Nordiques are second for the average number of French-speaking Quebec hockey players drafted, with 2.38 players per year (a total 38).

· Of the thirty-eight players picked by the Nordiques, twenty-three played in the NHL, or 60.52 percent.

- The Nordiques are second as regards use of French-speaking Quebec hockey players. Of the 245 players who played for them, seventy-five were French-speaking Quebecers, or 30.61 percent.
- 40 percent of those seventy-five Quebec hockey players (or 30 players) played more than one season with the Nordiques.

Figures for the Atlanta Flames (1972-81)

- The Flames are sixth for the average number of French-speaking Quebec hockey players drafted, with 0.89 player per year (a total of 8).
- Of the eight players picked by the Flames, three played in the NHL, or 37.50 percent.
- The Flames are third as regards use of French-speaking Quebec hockey players. Of the ninety-four players who played for them, twenty-one were French-speaking Quebecers, or 22.34 percent.
- 42.86 percent of those twenty-one Quebec hockey players (or 9 players) played more than one season with the Flames.

Figures for the Oakland Seals (1967-76)

- The Seals are fourth for the average number of French-speaking Quebec hockey players drafted, with 1.12 player per year (a total of 5).
- Of the five players picked by the Seals, two played in the NHL, or 40 percent.
- The Seals are twenty-fourth as regards use of French-speaking Quebec hockey players. Of the 102 players who played for them, eight were French-speaking Quebecers, or 7.84 percent.
- 50 percent of those eight Quebec hockey players (or 4 players) played more than one season with the Seals.

Figures for the Cleveland Barons (1976-78)

- The Barons are fourth for the average number of French-speaking Quebec hockey players drafted, with one player per year (one player in total).
- The Barons picked one player, who also played in the NHL, making it 100 percent.

- The Barons are twenty-ninth as regards use of French-speaking Quebec hockey players. Of the 49 players who played for them, three were French-speaking Quebecers, or 6.12 percent.
- 66.66 percent of those Quebec hockey players (or 2 players) played more than one season with the Barons.

Figures for the Hartford Whalers (1979-97)

- The Whalers are eighteenth for the average number of French-speaking Quebec hockey players drafted, with 0.63 player per year (a total of 10).
- Of the ten players the Whalers picked, six played in the NHL, making it 60 percent.
- The Whalers are twenty-ninth as regards use of French-speaking Quebec hockey players. Of the 275 players who played for them, seventeen were French-speaking Quebecers, or 6.20 percent.
- 35.29 percent of those seventeen Quebec hockey players (or 6 players) played more than one season with the Whalers.

Figures for the Winnipeg Jets (1979-96)

- The Jets are twentieth for the average number of French-speaking Quebec hockey players drafted, with 0.59 player per year (a total of 10).
- Of the ten players the Jets picked, four played in the NHL, making it 40 percent.
- The Jets are sixth as regards use of French-speaking Quebec hockey players. Of the 243 players who played for them, thirty were French-speaking Quebecers, or 12.35 percent.
- 40 percent of those thirty Quebec hockey players (or 12 players) played more than one season with the Jets.

Figures for the Minnesota North Stars (1967-94)

- The North Stars are twenty-ninth for the average number of French-speaking Quebec hockey players drafted, with 0.35 player per year (a total of 8).
- Of the eight players the North Stars picked, four played in the NHL, making it 50 percent.

- The North Stars twenty-fifth as regards use of French-speaking Quebec hockey players. Of the 310 players who played for them, twenty-three were French-speaking Quebecers, or 7.42 percent.
- 21.74 percent of those twenty-three Quebec hockey players (or 5 players) played more than one season with the North Stars.

Figures for the Kansas City Scouts (1974-76)

- The Scouts are twenty-ninth for the average number of French-speaking Quebec hockey players drafted, with 0.33 player per year (one player in total).
- The player that was picked never played in the NHL, making it 0 percent.
- The Scouts are fourth as regards use of French-speaking Quebec hockey players. Of the 50 players who played for them, ten were French-speaking Quebecers, or 20 percent.
- 60 percent of those ten Quebec hockey players (or 6 players) played more than one season with the Scouts.

Figures for the Colorado Rockies (1976-82)

- The Rockies are thirtieth for the average number of French-speaking Quebec hockey players drafted, with 0.0 player per year.
- The Rockies are twenty-eighth as regards use of French-speaking Quebec hockey players. Of the 125 players who played for them, eight were French-speaking Quebecers, or 6.4 percent.
- 75 percent of those eight Quebec hockey players (or 6 players) played more than one season with the Rockies.

NHL teams: analysis and facts

These figures and tables may appear fastidious but they are a pre-requisite for any serious analysis.

First, the Montreal Canadiens and the Quebec Nordiques should be put aside for the time being. There is an enormous difference between picking more than one French-speaking hockey player per year during the NHL draft, as has been the case for the Buffalo Sabres and the Philadelphia Flyers, and picking one every six years, as was the case for the Dallas Stars for many years.

Reasons such as great people and great cities explain the large statistical gap regarding the number of French-speaking Quebec hockey players picked by NHL teams.

The Buffalo Sabres and Punch Imlach

The Buffalo Sabres started out in the National Hockey League in 1970, but the organization's involvement with French-speaking Quebec hockey players began twenty-five years earlier in 1945.

In the mid-1940s a young man from Toronto moved to Quebec City to find a job. His name was Punch Imlach.[1] He played hockey for the Quebec Aces in Quebec's Senior Hockey League and then became coach and general manager. During that period the Quebec Aces went through difficult financial straits. Punch Imlach partnered with the team dentist, became co-owner of the franchise, and saved the Quebec team from disappearing. During his twelve-year stint in Quebec City, he must have come to the realization that Quebec's Capital City, perched as it is in north-eastern North America, was not some barbarian Gallic holdout but rather home to some top-notch hockey players. He was Jean Béliveau's last coach before Béliveau joined the Montreal Canadiens. Punch Imlach died on December 1, 1987 and until he died he always said that Jean Béliveau was the best player he had ever had the privilege to see playing hockey. It is not surprising therefore to note that many years earlier, in 1970, when he was coach and general manager of the Buffalo Sabres, Punch Imlach chose Gilbert Perreault, an exceptional hockey player, as his first draft pick. The following year, in the first round of the draft, he picked another Quebecer, Richard Martin, and then signed René Robert as a free agent. Perreault, Martin, and Robert went on to form the famous offensive line known as the *French Connection.*

The relationship between the Buffalo Sabres and French-speaking Quebec hockey players didn't end there. Since their first amateur draft in 1970 the Buffalo Sabres have drafted more French-speaking Quebec hockey players than any other team except the Montreal Canadiens. Punch Imlach's legacy lives on in Buffalo. Each year, the

1. Punch Imlach, *Hockey is a Battle, Punch Imlach*, Macmillan Company of Canada, 1969.

Quebec government honours people who have made exceptional contributions to Quebec's development in various areas of activity by naming them to the *Ordre national du Québec*. It is my firm belief that Punch Imlach deserves such an honour posthumously, either as *Grand Officier, Officier or Chevalier*.

The Philadelphia Flyers: Keith Allen and Bobby Clarke

The Philadelphia Flyers have drafted the most Quebecers over the past decade, even more than the Montreal Canadiens. Between 2000 and 2009 the Flyers drafted thirteen French-speaking and three English-speaking Quebec hockey players, while over the same time period the Montreal Canadiens drafted fifteen French-speaking Quebecers. As was the case with the Buffalo Sabres, the relationship between French-speaking Quebec hockey players and Philadelphia Flyers originated in Quebec City. The Quebec Aces hockey team is once again at the heart of the matter.

The Philadelphia Flyers joined the National Hockey League in 1967. Its farm team was that same famous Quebec City Aces team that played in the American Hockey League. The Flyers operated that franchise until the Nordiques entered the World Hockey Association in 1972. During that time, between 1967 and 1971, the Quebec Aces always had a minimum of thirteen French-speaking Quebec hockey players on their regular line-up.[2] More than fifteen Quebec Aces hockey players ended up wearing the Flyers' trademark orange hockey sweater.

One of those fifteen players, Simon Nolet, was employed as a scout for many years. Today, the Flyers continue to recruit French-speaking Quebec hockey players. Simon Nolet was always Bobby Clarke's point man. Even when Bobby Clarke was General Manager of the Florida Panthers, Simon Nolet was always the man he trusted. In the 1970s, before the Clarke-Nolet duo began to operate, General Manager Keith Allen and scout Marcel Pelletier, who later became head of hockey personnel, had also teamed up and were the decision-makers for the Philadelphia Flyers in 1967. Their legacy of supporting French-speaking Quebec hockey players is still alive and well in Philadelphia.

---

2. asdequebec.hockeydb.com

Quebec City

Quebec City is a beautiful city that is affectionately nicknamed *Notre grand Village*. It is largely responsible for debunking the myths, stereotypes, and legends about French-speaking Quebec culture. Great Canadians like Punch Imlach, Keith Allen, and Bobby Clarke were positively influenced by the hockey players from Quebec City. The team's draft results and use of Quebec hockey players bear witness.

The Quebec Nordiques, who played in the NHL from 1979 to 1995, also played a key role by giving seventy-four Quebec hockey players a chance to play in the NHL and gain visibility.

On the other hand, Colorado *Nordiks*, formerly a French-speaking organization, have a poor and disappointing record with respect to recruitment of Quebec hockey players. The *Nordiks* should learn from the Sabres and Flyers, two teams that have never forgotten where they came from.

Quebec hockey fans should applaud Quebec City and the people of that city for having such a positive impact on two major NHL organizations: the Sabres and the Flyers. I have a modest proposal for Quebec City Mayor Régis Labaume or his successor. One of these summers, he should invite all NHL managers to Quebec City for a huge banquet and give them a first-hand experience of what Quebec culture is all about. It might just be helpful.

The enigmatic Dallas Stars

The Dallas Stars, whose farm team is in Montreal, has only used a total of eighteen French-speaking Quebec hockey players—eight of whom had already played for the Montreal Canadiens—since the team joined the NHL in 1994. During that same time period, they drafted a total of three French-speaking Quebec hockey players: two in 1995 and the last one in 2009. Anybody capable of explain this paradox is invited to communicate with the author.

The unequivocal Carolina Hurricanes

The Carolina Hurricanes are at least consistent. They simply don't want any French-speaking Quebec hockey players. Since 1997, they have used five Quebec players and only one played more than one season with their team. From what I've heard, however, many Quebecers winter in Carolina and so the people in Raleigh should know what a Quebecer looks like by now!

The Montreal Canadiens

A big event takes place every fall in Quebec. It's not apple picking, the Fall Colours Festival, the Fall Fair or the beginning of the school year. It's the beginning of the legendary Montreal Canadiens' training camp. Hockey town wakes up, or better yet, the Canadiens' town wakes up. It's a challenge even to say anything about the Canadiens that has not already been said many times.

On December 4, 1890, John Ambrose O'Brien and Jimmy Gardner, two English-speaking Ontario businessmen, founded Le club de hockey le Canadien de Montréal with the overriding goal of uniting the best French-Canadian hockey players on one team so as to attract French-speaking Montreal fans who tended to avoid hockey arenas since they had no team to cheer on and no French-speaking players with whom they could identify.

More than one hundred years later, the Montreal Canadiens clearly missed their chance to celebrate their centennial in a way that is consistent with the team's history. The Canadiens have always boasted a very significant number of French-speaking Quebec hockey players who led the way. The players and the team were nicknamed the *Flying Frenchmen* for many years because of the large numbers of French-speaking players who wore the team's colours with pride, honour, and courage. I learned this during the six seasons that I played against them. It was always an honour to play them, not only for me but also for my teammates who were mostly English Canadians. Why an honour? Well simply because for all hockey professionals between 1970 and 1980, playing against the *Flying Frenchmen*, the *Habs* or the Montreal Canadiens, was like making history. It was like playing against the descendents of Maurice Richard, Jean Béliveau, Dickie Moore, and Doug Harvey, all great Quebecers who built the National Hockey League. It was every Canadian kid's dream to wear that uniform one day. So just to play against them was our consolation prize. But those are memories.

When I finished writing the original French version of this book, on August 10, 2009, the Montreal Canadiens were starting their season with only three French-speaking Quebecers in their line-up. When the English version was about to go to the printer, the team had only two. Was it not an insult for that team to shun its own history at a time when they were celebrating the centennial of the glorious *Flying Frenchmen*?

In fact, it is not surprising that so few French-speaking Quebec hockey players start the season with the Montreal Canadiens. In the seven years following the arrival of the Gainey-Timmins tandem in Montreal the Canadiens, who used to draft on average 2.85 Quebecers per year, only selected 1.57 Quebec hockey player a year. Since 1970 the Canadiens would draft on average thirty Quebec players per decade. Yet over the past decade, the team only drafted fifteen French-speaking Quebec hockey players. A fifty-percent drop compared to the earlier decades. There's no point in looking anywhere else to understand the problem. The Serge Savard era is over. He was known to say, "If the talent is equal, I will choose a player from Quebec." Serge Savard's philosophy is now in the dumpster. This is not normal. Something is rotten in the kingdom of the Montreal Canadiens.

The Montreal Canadiens are one of the rare NHL teams that favoured players and coaches from Quebec. It was a winning strategy to which the team's many Stanley Cup victories bear witness. These players and coaches have gone on to prove to many NHL teams that despite the myths and prejudice about the "frogs" Quebec abounds with hockey talent.

The way the Montreal Canadiens operate today is troubling. It makes one wonder what its future relationship with Quebec society will be.

The time has come for Quebec City to have an NHL hockey team.

TABLEAU 3.1
Quebecers drafted by team 1970 to 2009*

Anaheim Ducks – 1993-09

YEAR	RANK	SURNAME	FIRST NAME	P	TEAM	GP	G	A	PTS	PIM
1997	125	Vaillancourt	Luc	G	BEAUPORT	0	0	0	0	0
1998	205	Bernier	David	W	QUÉBEC	0	0	0	0	0
2001	137	**Perreault**	**Joël**	C	**BAIE-COMEAU**	87	11	14	25	68
	264	**Parenteau**	**P.-Alexandre**	W	**CHICOUTIMI**	5	0	1	1	2
2002	261	Caron	François	D	MONCTON	0	0	0	0	0
2004	203	Bouthillette	Gabriel	G	GATINEAU	0	0	0	0	0
2005	197	Levasseur	Jean-Philippe	G	ROUYN	0	0	0	0	0
2007	63	Macenauer	Maxime	C	ROUYN	0	0	0	0	0
2008	35	Deschamps	Nicolas	C	CHICOUTIMI	0	0	0	0	0
	83	Cousineau	Marco	G	BAIE-COMEAU	0	0	0	0	0

Atlanta Thrashers – 1999-09

YEAR	RANK	SURNAME	FIRST NAME	P	TEAM	GP	G	A	PTS	PIM
2000	107	Mallette	Carl	C	VICTORIAVILLE	0	0	0	0	0
	290	**Gamache**	**Simon**	W	**VAL D'OR**	48	6	7	13	18
2003	116	Desbiens	Guillaume	W	ROUYN	0	0	0	0	0
2005	16	Bourret	Alex	W	LEWISTON	0	0	0	0	0
2008	64	Paquette	Danick	W	LEWISTON	0	0	0	0	0

Atlanta Flames – 1972-79

YEAR	RANK	SURNAME	FIRST NAME	P	TEAM	GP	G	A	PTS	PIM
1972	2	**Richard**	**Jacques**	C	**QUÉBEC**	556	160	187	347	307
	34	**Lemieux**	**Jean**	D	**SHERBROOKE**	204	23	63	86	39
	130	Roy	Pierre	D	QUÉBEC	0	0	0	0	0
	132	Lamarre	Jean	C	QUÉBEC	0	0	0	0	0
1973	148	Surbey	Glen	D	LOYOLA	0	0	0	0	0
	149	Ross	Guy	D	SHERBROOKE	0	0	0	0	0
1974	28	**Chouinard**	**Guy**	C	**QUÉBEC**	578	205	370	575	120
	167	Granger	Louis	W	SHAWINIGAN	0	0	0	0	0
1975	8	**Mulhern**	**Richard**	D	**SHERBROOKE**	303	27	93	120	217
	150	Sanza	Nick	G	MONTRÉAL JR	0	0	0	0	0
1976	28	**Simpson**	**Bobby**	W	**SHERBROOKE**	175	35	29	64	98
1977	100	Harbec	Bernard	C	LAVAL	0	0	0	0	0
1978	165	Green	Mark	C	SHERBROOKE	0	0	0	0	0
	180	**Sullivan**	**Bob**	W	**TOLEDO IHL**	62	18	19	37	18

Boston Bruins – 1970-09

YEAR	RANK	SURNAME	FIRST NAME	P	TEAM	GP	G	A	PTS	PIM
1970	27	**Bouchard**	**Dan**	G	**LONDON**	655				
	69	Roselle	Bob	C	SOREL	0	0	0	0	0

• Hockey players who played more than one game in the NHL are in bold.

						GP	G	A	PTS	PIM
1972	48	Boudreault	Michel	C	LAVAL	0	0	0	0	0
1973	6	Savard	André	C	QUÉBEC	790	211	271	482	411
	95	Bourgouyne	Jean-Pierre	D	SHAWINIGAN	0	0	0	0	0
	157	Bouillon	Yvon	W	CORNWALL	0	0	0	0	0
1974	90	Bateman	Jamie	W	QUÉBEC	0	0	0	0	0
1975	68	Daigle	Denis	C	MONTRÉAL JR	0	0	0	0	0
1977	138	Claude	Mario	D	SHERBROOKE	0	0	0	0	0
1979	8	Bourque	Raymond	D	VERDUN	1612	410	1169	1579	1141
	99	Baron	Marco	G	MONTRÉAL JR	86				
	120	Krushelnyski	Mike	C	MONTRÉAL JR	897	241	328	569	699
1980	81	Kasper	Steve	W	MONTRÉAL JR	821	177	291	468	554
1981	14	Léveillé	Normand	W	CHICOUTIMI	75	17	25	42	49
	35	Dufour	Luc	C	CHICOUTIMI	167	23	21	44	199
	161	Parisée	Armel	D	CHICOUTIMI	0	0	0	0	0
	203	Bourque	Richard	W	SHERBROOKE	0	0	0	0	0
1982	165	Fiore	Tony	C	MONTRÉAL JR	0	0	0	0	0
1983	162	Olivier	François	W	ST-JEAN	0	0	0	0	0
1985	31	Côté	Alain	D	QUÉBEC	119	2	18	20	124
	115	Hynes	Gord	D	MEDICINE HAT	0	0	0	0	0
1987	14	Quintal	Stéphane	D	GRANBY	1037	63	180	243	1320
1988	81	Juneau	Joey	C	R.P.I. NCAA	828	156	416	572	272
1991	62	Cousineau	Marcel	G	BEAUPORT	26				
1993	88	Paquette	Charles	D	SHERBROOKE	0	0	0	0	0
1994	47	Goneau	Daniel	W	LAVAL	SEE RANKERS 1996				
	151	Roy	André	W	CHICOUTIMI	515	35	33	68	1169
1996	53	Naud	Éric	W	ST-HYACINTHE	0	0	0	0	0
1997	218	Van Acker	Éric	D	CHICOUTIMI	0	0	0	0	0
1998	48	Girard	Jonathan	D	LAVAL	150	10	34	44	46
2002	259	Statsny	Yan	C	NOTRE-DAME	87	5	10	15	58
2003	2	Bergeron	Patrice	C	ACADIE-BATHURST	303	80	148	228	88
	247	Mondou	Benoit	W	SHAWINIGAN	0	0	0	0	0
2004	160	Walter	Ben	C	LOWELL NCAA	22	1	0	1	4
2008	47	Sauvé	Maxime	C	VAL D'OR	0	0	0	0	0
2009	25	Caron	Jordan	W	RIMOUSKI					

Buffalo Sabres – 1970-09

YEAR	RANK	SURNAME	FIRST NAME	P	TEAM	GP	G	A	PTS	PIM
1970	1	Perreault	Gilbert	C	MONTRÉAL JR	1191	512	814	1326	500
	57	Morton	Mike	W	SHAWINIGAN	0	0	0	0	0
	107	Nadeau	Luc	W	DRUMMONDVILLE	0	0	0	0	0
1971	5	Martin	Richard	W	MONTRÉAL JR	685	384	317	701	477
	47	Richer	Bob	D	TROIS-RIVIÈRES	3	0	0	0	0

➤

	75	Duguay	Pierre	C	QUÉBEC	0	0	0	0	0
1972	25	Carrière	Larry	D	LOYOLA	367	16	74	90	462
	53	Campeau	Rychard	D	SOREL	0	0	0	0	0
	69	Gratton	Gilles	G	OSHAWA	47				
1973	28	Landry	Jean	D	QUÉBEC	0	0	0	0	0
	44	Deschamps	André	W	QUÉBEC	0	0	0	0	0
	60	Dupuis	Yvon	W	QUÉBEC	0	0	0	0	0
1974	47	Déziel	Michel	W	SOREL	0	0	0	0	0
	119	Noreau	Bernard	W	LAVAL	0	0	0	0	0
	136	Constantin	Charles	W	QUÉBEC	0	0	0	0	0
	168	Smith	Derek	W	OTTAWA 67s	335	78	116	194	60
	196	Geoffrion	Robert	W	CORNWALL	0	0	0	0	0
1975	17	Sauvé	Robert	G	LAVAL	420				
1976	105	Lemieux	Donald	D	TROIS-RIVIÈRES	0	0	0	0	0
1977	86	Sirois	Richard	G	SHERBROOKE	0	0	0	0	0
1978	32	McKegney	Tony	W	KINGSTON	912	320	319	639	517
1979	55	Cloutier	Jacques	G	TROIS-RIVIÈRES	255				
	74	Hamel	Gilles	W	LAVAL	519	127	147	274	276
	95	Haworth	Alan	C	SHERBROOKE	524	189	211	400	425
1980	56	McKenna	Sean	W	SHERBROOKE	414	82	80	162	181
	125	Naud	Daniel	D	VERDUN	0	0	0	0	0
1981	164	Orlando	Gates	W.	PROVIDENCE COL.	98	18	26	44	51
1982	79	Hamilton	Jeff	W	PROVIDENCE COL.	0	0	0	0	0
	100	Logan	Bobby	W	WEST ISLAND JR	42	10	5	15	0
	163	Verret	Claude	C	TROIS-RIVIÈRES	14	2	5	7	2
1983	10	Lacombe	Normand	W	U.N.H. NCAA	319	53	62	115	196
	234	Hamelin	Marc	G	SHAWINIGAN	0	0	0	0	0
1984	123	Gasseau	James	D	DRUMMONDVILLE	0	0	0	0	0
1985	35	Hogue	Benoit	W	ST-JEAN	863	222	231	543	877
	224	Larose	Guy	C	GUELPH	70	10	9	19	63
1986	5	Anderson	Shawn	D	Univ. MAINE	255	11	51	62	117
	110	Baldris	Miguel	D	SHAWINIGAN	0	0	0	0	0
	152	Guay	François	C	LAVAL	1	0	0	0	0
	173	Whitham	Sean	D	PROVIDENCE COL.	0	0	0	0	0
1987	1	Turgeon	Pierre	C	GRANBY	1294	515	812	1327	452
1989	183	Audette	Donald	W	LAVAL	735	260	249	509	584
1990	208	Naud	Sylvain	W	LAVAL	0	0	0	0	0
1991	13	Boucher	Philippe	D	GRANBY	748	94	206	300	702
1994	168	Plouffe	Steve	G	GRANBY	0	0	0	0	0
1995	16	Biron	Martin	G	BEAUPORT	433				
	68	Sunderland	Mathieu	W	DRUMMONDVILLE	0	0	0	0	0
	123	Bienvenue	Daniel	W	VAL D'OR	0	0	0	0	0
1996	54	Méthot	François	C	ST-HYACINTHE	0	0	0	0	0
1999	178	Hyacinthe Jr.	Sénèque	W	VAL D'OR	0	0	0	0	0

2000	111	Rousseau	Ghyslain	G	BAIE-COMEAU	0	0	0	0	0
2001	55	Pominville	Jason	W	SHAWINIGAN	304	99	145	244	90
2002	76	Messier	Michael	W	ACADIE-BATHURST	0	0	0	0	0
2003	266	Martin	L-Philippe	W	BAIE-COMEAU	0	0	0	0	0
2004	273	Hunter	Dylan	W	LONDON	0	0	0	0	0
2005	87	Gragnani	Marc-André	D	P.E.I.	6	0	0	0	6
2006	147	Biega	Alex	D	HARVARD	0	0	0	0	0
	207	Breault	Benjamin	C	BAIE-COMEAU	0	0	0	0	0
2007	147	Allard	Jean Simon	C	ST-JOHN'S	0	0	0	0	0
	179	Byron	Paul	C	GATINEAU	0	0	0	0	0
2008	104	Southorn	Jordon	D	P.E.I.	0	0	0	0	0
	134	Lagacé	Jacob	W	CHICOUTIMI	0	0	0	0	0
2009	194	Legault	Maxime	W	SHAWINIGAN					

Calgary Flames – 1980-09

YEAR	RANK	SURNAME	FIRST NAME	P	TEAM	GP	G	A	PTS	PIM
1980	13	Cyr	Denis	W	MONTRÉAL JR	193	41	43	84	36
	76	Roy	Marc	W	TROIS-RIVIÈRES	0	0	0	0	0
	160	Drouin	Claude	W	QUÉBEC	0	0	0	0	0
	202	Fletcher	Steven	W	HULL	3	0	0	0	5
1987	25	Matteau	Stéphane	D	HULL	848	144	172	316	742
	124	Aloi	Joe	D	HULL	0	0	0	0	0
1988	10	Darveau	Guy	D	VICTORIAVILLE	0	0	0	0	0
1990	26	Perreault	Nicolas	D	HAWKESBURY JR B	0	0	0	0	0
	41	Belzile	Étienne	D	CORNELL	0	0	0	0	0
1991	41	Groleau	François	D	SHAWINIGAN	8	0	1	1	6
	173	St-Pierre	David	C	LONGUEUIL	0	0	0	0	0
1992	129	Bouchard	Joël	D	VERDUN	364	22	53	75	264
1995	20	Gauthier	Denis	D	DRUMMONDVILLE	489	15	58	73	658
1996	40	Bégin	Steve	D	VAL D'OR	347	40	34	74	440
	94	Lefebvre	Christian	D	GRANBY	0	0	0	0	0
1997	113	Moise	Martin	W	BEAUPORT	0	0	0	0	0
1998	108	Sabourin	Dany	G	SHERBROOKE	38				
1999	166	Pecker	Cory	W	SAULT STE-MARIE	0	0	0	0	0
2002	90	Lombardi	Matthew	C	VICTORIAVILLE	297	56	81	137	195
2003	206	Bellemare	Thomas	W	DRUMMONDVILLE	0	0	0	0	0
2006	118	Carpentier	Hugo	C	ROUYN	0	0	0	0	0

California Seals – 1970-77

YEAR	RANK	SURNAME	FIRST NAME	P	TEAM	GP	G	A	PTS	PIM
1970	75	Moyes	Doug	W	SOREL	0	0	0	0	0
	88	Murray	Terry	D	OTTAWA 67s	302	4	76	80	199
1971	29	Leduc	Richard	W	TROIS-RIVIERES	130	28	38	66	69

➤

	43	Monahan	Hartland	W	MONTRÉAL JR	334	61	80	141	163
	57	Bélanger	Reynald	G	SHAWINIGAN	0	0	0	0	0
1972	54	St-Sauveur	Claude	C	SHERBOOKE	79	24	24	48	23
	86	Lefebvre	Jacques	G	SHAWINIGAN	0	0	0	0	0
	134	Meloche	Denis	W	DRUMMONDVILLE	0	0	0	0	0

Carolina Hurricanes – 1997-2009

YEAR	RANK	SURNAME	FIRST NAME	P	TEAM	GP	G	A	PTS	PIM
1997	80	Lessard	Francis	W	VAL D'OR	91	1	3	4	268
2001	181	Boisclair	Daniel	G	CAP BRETON	0	0	0	0	0
2005	192	Blanchard	Nicolas	C	CHICOUTIMI	0	0	0	0	0
2006	153	Chaput	Stéphane	C	LEWISTON	0	0	0	0	0
2008	195	Morneau	Samuel	W	BAIE-COMEAU	0	0	0	0	0
2009	27	Paradis	Philippe	C	SHAWINIGAN					

Cleveland Barons – 1977-78

YEAR	RANK	SURNAME	FIRST NAME	P	TEAM	GP	G	A	PTS	PIM
1977	23	Chicoine	Daniel	W	SHERBROOKE	31	1	2	3	12
	95	Allen	Jeff	D	HULL	4	0	0	0	2

Coloroado Rockies – 1976-82

YEAR	RANK	SURNAME	FIRST NAME	P	TEAM	GP	G	A	PTS	PIM
1977-	0									
1980-	0									

Chicago Blackhawks – 1970-2009

YEAR	RANK	SURNAME	FIRST NAME	P	TEAM	GP	G	A	PTS	PIM
1970	28	Archambault	Michel	W	DRUMMONDVILLE	3	0	0	0	0
	70	Meloche	Gilles	G	VERDUN	788				
1972	77	Giroux	Réjean	W	QUÉBEC	0	0	0	0	0
1974	34	Daigle	Alain	W	TROIS-RIVIÈRES	389	56	50	106	122
	88	Logan	Dave	D	LAVAL	218	5	29	34	470
	188	Bernier	Jean	D	SHAWINIGAN	0	0	0	0	0
	200	Byers	Dwayne	W	SHERBROOKE	0	0	0	0	0
1975	61	Giroux	Pierre	W	HULL	6	1	0	1	17
1976	9	Cloutier	Réal	W	QUÉBEC	317	146	198	344	119
1977	19	Savard	Jean	C	QUÉBEC	43	7	12	19	29
	78	Platt	Gary	W	SOREL	0	0	0	0	0
	114	Lahache	Floyd	D	SHERBROOKE	0	0	0	0	0
	144	Ough	Steve	D	LAVAL	0	0	0	0	0
1979	70	Bégin	Louis	C	SHERBROOKE	0	0	0	0	0
1980	2	Savard	Denis	C	MONTRÉAL JR	1196	473	865	1338	1336
1981	201	Roy	Sylvain	D	HULL	0	0	0	0	0
1982	28	Badeau	René	D	QUÉBEC	0	0	0	0	0

1983	59	Bergevin	Marc	D	CHICOUTIMI	1191	36	145	181	1090
	219	Pépin	Steve	W	ST-JEAN	0	0	0	0	0
1984	174	Difiori	Ralph	D	SHAWINIGAN	0	0	0	0	0
1985	74	Vincelette	Daniel	W	DRUMMONDVILLE	193	20	22	42	351
	179	Laplante	Richard	W	UNIV. VERMONT	0	0	0	0	0
1986	119	Doyon	Mario	D	DRUMMONDVILLE	28	3	4	7	16
1987	8	Waite	Jimmy	G	CHICOUTIMI	106				
1988	197	Maurice	Daniel	C	CHICOUTIMI	0	0	0	0	0
1990	16	Dykhuis	Karl	D	HULL	644	42	91	133	495
	163	Bélanger	Hugo	D	UNIV. CLARKSON	0	0	0	0	0
	226	Dubinsky	Steve	C	UNIV. CLARKSON	375	25	45	70	164
1991	132	Auger	Jacques	D	UNIV. WISCONSIN	0	0	0	0	0
	Supp.	Gravelle	Daniel	W	MERRIMACK	0	0	0	0	0
1993	24	Lecompte	Éric	W	HULL	0	0	0	0	0
	90	Dazé	Éric	W	BEAUPORT	601	226	172	398	176
1994	40	Leroux	Jean-Yves	W	BEAUPORT	324	2	45	47	282
1995	45	Laflamme	Christian	D	BEAUPORT	324	2	45	47	282
	175	Tardif	Steve	C	DRUMMONDVILLE	0	0	0	0	0
1996	31	Royer	Rémi	D	ST-HYACINTHE	18	0	0	0	67
1998	166	Pelletier	Jonathan	G	DRUMMONDVILLE	0	0	0	0	0
	238	Couture	Alexandre	D	SHERBROOKE	0	0	0	0	0
2003	52	Crawford	Corey	G	MONCTON	7				
2006	61	Danis-Pépin	Simon	D	UNIV. MAINE	0	0	0	0	0
2007	69	Tanguay	Maxime	C	RIMOUSKI	0	0	0	0	0
2009	209	Gilbert	David	C	QUÉBEC					

Colorado Avalanche – 1995-2009

YEAR	RANK	SURNAME	FIRST NAME	P	TEAM	GP	G	A	PTS	PIM
1995	25	Denis	Marc	G	CHICOUTIMI	349				
1998	12	Tanguay	Alex	W	HALIFAX	659	193	387	580	345
	28	Abid	Ramzi	W	CHICOUTIMI	68	14	16	30	78
	38	Sauvé	Philippe	G	RIMOUSKI	32				
1999	45	Grenier	Martin	D	QUÉBEC	18	1	0	1	14
2000	189	Bahen	Chris	D	UNIV. CLARKSON	0	0	0	0	0
2001	165	Émond	Pierre-Luc	C	DRUMMONDVILLE	0	0	0	0	0
2005	44	Stastny	Paul	C	UNIV. DENVER	193	63	122	185	88
2008	167	Chouinard	Joël	D	VICTORIAVILLE	0	0	0	0	0

Columbus Blue Jackets – 2000-09

YEAR	RANK	SURNAME	FIRST NAME	P	TEAM	GP	G	A	PTS	PIM
2000	292	Mandeville	Louis	D	ROUYN	0	0	0	0	0
2001	8	Leclaire	Pascal	G	HALIFAX	125				
2003	104	Dupuis	Philippe	C	HULL	0	0	0	0	0

➤

	223	Gravel	Mathieu	W	SHAWINIGAN	0	0	0	0	0
2004	8	Picard	Alexandre	W	LEWISTON	58	0	2	2	48
2006	6	Brassard	Dérick	C	DRUMMONDVILLE	48	11	16	27	23
	142	Fréchette	Maxime	D	DRUMMONDVILLE	0	0	0	0	0
2008	107	Delisle	Steven	D	GATINEAU	0	0	0	0	0

Dallas Stars– 1993-2009

YEAR	RANK	SURNAME	FIRST NAME	P	TEAM	GP	G	A	PTS	PIM
1995	37	Côté	Patrick	W	BEAUPORT	105	1	2	3	377
	141	Marleau	Dominic	D	VICTORIAVILLE	0	0	0	0	0
1997	77	Gainey	Steve	W	KAMLOOPS	33	0	2	2	34
2009	38	Chiasson	Alex	W	DES MOINES U.S.A.					

Detroit Red Wings– 1970-2009

YEAR	RANK	SURNAME	FIRST NAME	P	TEAM	GP	G	A	PTS	PIM
1970	12	Lajeunesse	Serge	D	MONTRÉAL JR	103	1	4	5	103
	26	Guindon	Bob	W	MONTRÉAL JR	6	0	1	1	0
	40	Lambert	Yvon	W	DRUMMONDVILLE	683	206	273	479	340
1971	1	Dionne	Marcel	C	ST. CATHERINES	1348	731	1040	1771	600
1972	26	Guité	Pierre	W	ST. CATHERINES	0	0	0	0	0
	138	Kuzmicz	George	D	CORNELL	0	0	0	0	0
1973	139	Bibeau	Raymond	D	MONTRÉAL JR	0	0	0	0	0
1974	63	Bergeron	Michel	W	SOREL	229	80	58	138	165
1975	113	Phaneuf	Jean-Luc	C	MONTRÉAL JR	0	0	0	0	0
	164	Thibodeau	Jean-Luc	C	SHAWINIGAN	0	0	0	0	0
1976	111	Leblanc	Fernand	W	SHERBROOKE	34	5	6	11	0
	120	Legris	Claude	G	SOREL	4				
1977	125	Roy	Raymond	C	SHERBROOKE	0	0	0	0	0
	170	Bélanger	Alain	W	TROIS-RIVIÈRES	0	0	0	0	0
	178	Cloutier	Roland	C	TROIS-RIVIÈRES	34	8	9	17	2
	184	James	Val	W	QUÉBEC	11	0	0	0	20
1978	95	Locas	Sylvain	C	SHERBROOKE	0	0	0	0	0
1981	44	Micalef	Corrado	G	SHERBROOKE	113				
1982	23	Courteau	Yves	W	LAVAL	22	2	5	7	4
	107	Vilgrain	Claude	W	LAVAL	89	21	32	53	78
1985	113	McKay	Randy	W	MICHIGAN TECH	932	162	201	363	1731
1987	11	Racine	Yves	D	LONGUEUIL	508	37	194	231	439
1988	38	Anglehart	Serge	D	DRUMMONDVILLE	0	0	0	0	0
1988	47	Dupuis	Guy	D	HULL	0	0	0	0	0
1990	108	Barthe	Claude	D	VICTORIAVILLE	0	0	0	0	0
1991	10	Lapointe	Martin	W	LAVAL	991	181	200	381	1417
	186	Bermingham	Jim	C	LAVAL	0	0	0	0	0
1992	70	Cloutier	Sylvain	C	GUELPH	7				

1993	100	Larose	Benoit	D	LAVAL	0	0	0	0	0
1994	49	**Dandenault**	**Mathieu**	D	**SHERBROOKE**	827	64	127	191	499
	114	Deschenes	Frédérick	G	GRANBY	0	0	0	0	0
1995	52	**Audet**	**Philippe**	W	**GRANBY**	4	0	0	0	0
	126	Arsenault	Dave	G	DRUMMONDVILLE	0	0	0	0	0
1996	162	Jacques	Alexandre	W	SHAWINIGAN	0	0	0	0	0
2001	288	Senez	François	G	R.P.I. NCAA	0	0	0	0	0
2002	260	Beaulieu	Pierre-Olivier	D	QUÉBEC	0	0	0	0	0
2008	151	Cayer	Julien	G	NORTHWOOD N.Y.	0	0	0	0	0
2009	90	Fournier	Gleason	D	RIMOUSKI					

Edmonton Oilers – 1979-2009

YEAR	RANK	SURNAME	FIRST NAME	P	TEAM	GP	G	A	PTS	PIM
1979	21	**Lowe**	**Kevin**	D	**SHERBROOKE**	1254	84	348	432	1498
1983	240	Woodburn	Steve	D	VERDUN	0	0	0	0	0
1985	209	Barbe	Mario	D	CHICOUTIMI	0	0	0	0	0
1986	168	Beaulieu	Nick	W	DRUMMONDVILLE	0	0	0	0	0
1988	19	**Leroux**	**François**	D	**ST-JEAN**	249	3	20	23	577
1989	92	White	Peter	C	MICHIGAN ST.	220	23	37	60	36
1990	38	Legault	Alexandre	D	UNIV. BOSTON	0	0	0	0	0
	67	Blain	Joel	W	HULL	0	0	0	0	0
1991	78	Nobili	Mario	W	LONGUEUIL	0	0	0	0	0
1992	61	Roy	Simon	D	SHAWINIGAN	0	0	0	0	0
1995	31	**Laraque**	**Georges**	W	**ST-JEAN**	634	52	96	148	1037
1996	19	**Descoteaux**	**Mathieu**	D	**SHAWINIGAN**	5	1	1	2	4
	168	Bernier	David	W	ST-HYACINTHE	0	0	0	0	0
1998	213	Lefebvre	Christian		BAIE-COMEAU	0	0	0	0	0
1999	139	Fauteux	Jonathan		VAL D'OR	0	0	0	0	0
2000	215	Lombardi	Matthew	C	VICTORIAVILLE	VOIR CALGARY 2002				
2002	31	**Deslauriers**	**Jeff**	G	**CHICOUTIMI**	10	0	0	0	0
	205	Dufort	J.-François	W	CAP BRETON	0	0	0	0	0
2003	22	**Pouliot**	**Marc-Antoine**	C	**RIMOUSKI**	78	6	13	19	30
	68	**Jacques**	**J.-François**	D	**BAIE-COMEAU**	53	0	0	0	35
	215	**Roy**	**Mathieu**		**VAL D OR**	30	2	1	3	57
2004	208	Goulet	Stéphane		QUÉBEC	0	0	0	0	0
2008	133	Cornet	Philippe	W	RIMOUSKI	0	0	0	0	0
2009	133	Roy	Olivier	G	CAP BRETON					

Florida Panthers – 1993-2009

YEAR	RANK	SURNAME	FIRST NAME	P	TEAM	GP	G	A	PTS	PIM
1993	135	Nasreddine	Alain	D	DRUMMONDVILLE	74	1	4	5	84
	265	Montreuil	Éric	C	CHICOUTIMI	0	0	0	0	0
1994	183	Boudrias	Jason	W	LAVAL	0	0	0	0	0

➤

1995	114	Cloutier	François	W	HULL	0	0	0	0	0
	165	Worrell	Peter	W	HULL	391	19	27	46	1554
1996	156	Poirier	Gaétan	W	MERRIMACK NCAA	0	0	0	0	0
	183	Couture	Alexandre	D	VICTORIAVILLE	0	0	0	0	0
	235	Smith	Russell	D	HULL	0	0	0	0	0
1997	237	Côté	Benoit	W	SHAWINIGAN	0	0	0	0	0
1999	80	Laniel	Jean-François	G	SHAWINIGAN	0	0	0	0	0
	227	Charron	Jonathan	G	VAL D'OR	0	0	0	0	0
2003	25	Stewart	Anthony	W	KINGSTON	105	4	8	12	38
	223	Roussin	Dany		RIMOUSKI	0	0	0	0	0
2005	93	Legault	Olivier	W	LEWISTON	0	0	0	0	0

Hartford Whaliers – 1979-97

YEAR	RANK	SURNAME	FIRST NAME	P	TEAM	GP	G	A	PTS	PIM
1980	29	Galarneau	Michel	C	HULL	78	7	10	17	
1981	151	Doré	Denis	W	CHICOUTIMI	0	0	0	0	
1982	56	Dineen	Kevin	W	UNIV. DENVER	1188	355	405	760	
1983	2	Turgeon	Sylvain	W	HULL	669	269	226	495	
	143	Duperron	Chris	D	CHICOUTIMI	0	0	0	0	
1984	11	Côté	Sylvain	D	QUÉBEC	1171	122	313	435	
1989	157	Saumier	Raymond	W	TROIS-RIVIÈRES	0	0	0	0	
	178	Picard	Michel	W	TROIS-RIVIÈRES	166	28	42	70	
1990	162	D'Orsonnens	Martin	D	UNIV. CLARKSON	0	0	0	0	
	246	Chalifoux	Denis	C	LAVAL	0	0	0	0	
1991	9	Poulin	Patrick	W	ST-HYACINTHE	634	101	134	235	
1994	Supp.	Martins	Steve	C	HARVARD	267	21	25	46	
1995	13	Giguère	J.-Sébastien	G	HALIFAX	457				

Kansas City Scouts – 1974-76

YEAR	RANK	SURNAME	FIRST NAME	P	TEAM	GP	G	A	PTS	PIM
1974	162	Carufel	Denis	W	SOREL	0	0	0 .	0	0
1975	0									

Los Angeles Kings – 1970-2009

YEAR	RANK	SURNAME	FIRST NAME	P	TEAM	GP	G	A	PTS	PIM
1971	76	Lapierre	Camille	W	MONTRÉAL JR	0	0	0	0	0
	90	Dubé	Normand	W	SHERBROOKE	57	8	10	18	54
1974	154	Lessard	Mario	G	SHERBROOKE	240				
	184	Locas	Jacques	C	QUÉBEC	0	0	0	0	0
1975	69	Leduc	André	D	SHERBROOKE	0	0	0	0	0
	87	Miglia	Dave	D	TROIS-RIVIÈRES	0	0	0	0	0
	197	Viens	Mario	G	CORNWALL	0	0 .	0	0	0
1978	193	Larochelle	Claude	W	HULL	0	0	0	0	0
1979	30	Hardy	Mark	D	MONTRÉAL JR	926	62	306	368	1293

YEAR	RANK	SURNAME	FIRST NAME	P	TEAM	GP	G	A	PTS	PIM
1983	67	Benoit	Guy	W	SHAWINIGAN	0	0	0	0	0
	100	Galley	Gary	D	BOWLING GREEN	1149	125	474	599	1218
1984	150	Deegan	Shannon	W	VERMONT	0	0	0	0	0
	171	Robitaille	Luc	W	HULL	1431	668	726	1394	1177
1986	65	Couturier	Sylvain	W	LAVAL	33	4	5	9	4
1988	7	Gélinas	Martin	W	HULL	1273	309	351	660	820
1989	102	Ricard	Éric	D	GRANBY	0	0	0	0	0
1990	175	Leblanc	Dennis	W	ST-HYACINTHE	0	0	0	0	0
1991	240	Boulianne	André	G	LONGUEUIL	0	0	0	0	0
	262	Gaul	Michael	D	ST-LAWRENCE	3	0	0	0	0
1993	105	Beaubien	Fréderik	G	ST-HYACINTHE	0	0	0	0	0
1995	157	Larose	Benoit	D	SHERBROOKE	0	0	0	0	0
1996	96	Bélanger	Éric	C	BEAUPORT	557	106	152	258	251
	219	Simard	Sébastien		DRUMMONDVILLE	0	0	0	0	0
1998	21	Biron	Mathieu	D	SHAWINIGAN	253	12	32	44	177
	133	Rullier	Joe	D	RIMOUSKI	0	0	0	0	0
	248	Yeats	Matthew	G	OLDS GRIZZLYS	5				
1999	133	Nogues	J.-François	G	VICTORIAVILLE	0	0	0	0	0
2000	86	Lehoux	Yanick	C	BAIE-COMEAU	10	2	2	4	6
2005	50	Roussin	Dany	W	RIMOUSKI	0	0	0	0	0
2006	11	Bernier	Jonathan	G	LEWISTON	4				
	144	Nolet	Martin	D	CHAMPLAIN U.S.A.	0	0	0	0	0
2009	84	Deslauriers	Éric	D	ROUYN-NORANDA					
	95	Bérubé	J.-François	G	MONTRÉAL JR					

Montreal Canadiens – 1970-2009

YEAR	RANK	SURNAME	FIRST NAME	P	TEAM	GP	G	A	PTS	PIM
1971	1	Lafleur	Guy	W	QUÉBEC	1127	560	793	1353	399
	24	Deguise	Michel	G	SOREL	0	0	0	0	0
1972	6	Larocque	Michel	G	OTTAWA	307				
	110	Archambault	Yves	G	SOREL	0	0	0	0	0
1973	64	Latulipe	Richard	W	QUÉBEC	0	0	0	0	0
	96	Patry	Denis	W	DRUMMONDVILLE	0	0	0	0	0
	112	Belisle	Michel	W	MONTRÉAL JR	0	0	0	0	0
	128	Desjardins	Mario	W	SHERBROOKE	0	0	0	0	0
	158	Labrecque	Alain	W	TROIS-RIVIÈRES	0	0	0	0	0
	166	Halliday	Gordon	W	UNIV. PENN.	0	0	0	0	0
	168	Chiasson	Louis	W	TROIS-RIVIÈRES	0	0	0	0	0
1974	12	Tremblay	Mario	W	MONTRÉAL JR	852	258	226	584	1043
	33	Lupien	Gilles	D	MONTRÉAL JR	226	5	25	30	416
1975	15	Mondou	Pierre	W	MONTRÉAL JR	548	194	262	456	179
	106	Lachance	Michel	D	MONTRÉAL JR	21	0	4	4	22
	204	Brisebois	Michel	C	SHERBROOKE	0	0	0	0	0

➤

1976	90	Barette	Maurice	G	QUÉBEC	0	0	0	0	0
	108	Brassard	Pierre	W	CORNWALL	0	0	0	0	0
1977	18	Dupont	Normand	W	MONTRÉAL JR	256	55	85	140	52
	43	Côté	Alain	W	CHICOUTIMI	696	103	190	293	383
	46	Lagacé	Pierre	C	QUÉBEC	0	0	0	0	0
	64	Holland	Robbie	G	MONTRÉAL JR	44				
	90	Rochette	Gaétan	D	SHAWINIGAN	0	0	0	0	0
	124	Sévigny	Richard	G	SHERBROOKE	176				
	167	Poulin	Daniel	D	CHICOUTIMI	3	1	1	2	2
	179	Belisle	Jean	G	CHICOUTIMI	0	0	0	0	0
	182	Boileau	Robert	C	UNIV. BOSTON	0	0	0	0	0
1978	8	Geoffrion	Daniel	W	CORNWALL	111	20	32	52	99
	36	Carter	Ron	W	SHERBROOKE	2	0	0	0	0
	42	David	Richard	W	TROIS-RIVIÈRES	31	4	4	8	10
	171	Swan	John	C	MCGILL	0	0	0	0	0
	186	Métivier	Daniel	W	HULL	0	0	0	0	0
	229	Leblanc	Serge	W	UNIV. VERMONT	0	0	0	0	0
	233	Sleigher	Louis	W	CHICOUTIMI	194	46	53	99	146
1979	27	Gingras	Gaston	D	WHA	476	61	174	235	161
	44	Carbonneau	Guy	C	CHICOUTIMI	1318	260	403	663	820
1980	103	Gagné	Rémi	C	CHICOUTIMI	0	0	0	0	0
	166	Penney	Steve	G	SHAWINIGAN	91				
1981	18	Delorme	Gilbert	D	CHICOUTIMI	541	31	92	123	520
1982	19	Héroux	Alain	W	CHICOUTIMI	0	0	0	0	0
	31	Gauvreau	Jocelyn	D	GRANBY	2	0	0	0	0
1983	26	Lemieux	Claude	W	TROIS-RIVIÈRES	1197	379	406	785	1756
	27	Momesso	Sergio	W	SHAWINIGAN	710	152	193	345	1557
	45	Letendre	Daniel	W	QUÉBEC	0	0	0	0	0
	238	Bergeron	Jean-Guy	D	SHAWINIGAN	0	0	0	0	0
1984	29	Richer	Stéphane	W	GRANBY	1054	421	398	819	614
	51	Roy	Patrick	G	GRANBY	1029				
	179	Demers	Éric	D	SHAWINIGAN	0	0	0	0	0
1985	12	Charbonneau	José	W	DRUMMONDVILLE	71	9	13	22	67
	75	Desjardins	Martin	C	TROIS-RIVIÈRES	8	0	2	2	2
	117	Dufresne	Donald	D	TROIS-RIVIÈRES	268	6	36	42	258
	198	Mansi	Maurice	W	R.P.I. U.S.A.	0	0	0	0	0
1986	27	Brunet	Benoit	W	HULL	539	101	161	262	229
	94	Aubertin	Éric	W	GRANBY	0	0	0	0	0
	204	Bohémier	Éric	G	HULL	0	0	0	0	0
1987	38	Desjardins	Éric	D	GRANBY	1143	136	439	575	757
	58	Gravel	Francis	G	SHAWINIGAN	0	0	0	0	0
	185	Tremblay	Éric	W	DRUMMONDVILLE	0	0	0	0	0
1988	20	Charron	Éric	D	TROIS-RIVIÈRES	130	2	7	9	127
	34	St-Amour	Martin	W	VERDUN	1	0	0	0	2

	104	Bergeron	Jean-Claude	G	VERDUN	72				
1989	30	Brisebois	Patrice	D	LAVAL	947	93	309	402	604
	41	Larouche	Steve	C	TROIS-RIVIÈRES	26	9	9	18	10
	51	Sévigny	Pierre	W	VERDUN	78	4	5	9	64
	83	Racicot	André	G	GRANBY	68				
	104	Deschamps	Marc	D	CORNELL	0	0	0	0	0
	167	Lebeau	Patrick	W	ST-JEAN	15	3	2	5	6
	251	Cadieux	Steve	C	SHAWINIGAN	4	0	0	0	0
1990	58	Poulin	Charles	C	ST-HYACINTHE	0	0	0	0	0
	60	Guillet	Robert	W	LONGUEUIL	0	0	0	0	0
	81	Dionne	Gilbert	W	KITCHENER	223	61	79	140	108
1991	61	Sarault	Yves	W	ST-JEAN	106	10	10	20	51
	83	Lapointe	Sylvain	D	UNIV. CLARKSON	0	0	0	0	0
	100	Layzell	Brad	D	R.P.I. U.S.A.	0	0	0	0	0
1992	82	Bernard	Louis	D	DRUMMONDVILLE	0	0	0	0	0
	164	Proulx	Christian	D	ST-JEAN	7	1	2	3	20
1993	73	Bordeleau	Sébastien	C	HULL	251	37	61	98	118
	99	Houle	J.-François	W	NORTHWOOD U.S.A.	0	0	0	0	0
	229	Duchesne	Alex	W	DRUMMONDVILLE	0	0	0	0	0
1994	44	Théodore	José	G	ST-JEAN	501				
	74	Bélanger	Martin	D	GRANBY	0	0	0	0	0
	122	Drolet	Jimmy	D	ST-HYACINTHE	0	0	0	0	0
1995	86	Delisle	Jonathan	W	HULL	1	0	0	0	0
	164	Robidas	Stéphane	D	SHAWINIGAN	561	30	105	135	418
	216	Houde	Éric	C	HALIFAX	30	2	3	5	4
1996	44	Garon	Mathieu	G	VICTORIAVILLE	204				
	99	Drapeau	Étienne	C	BEAUPORT	0	0	0	0	0
	127	Archambault	Daniel	D	VAL D OR	0	0	0	0	0
	233	Tremblay	Michel		SHAWINIGAN	0	0	0	0	0
1997	145	Desroches	Jonathan	D	GRANBY	0	0	0	0	0
	172	Guité	Ben	C	UNIV. MAINE	169	19	26	45	93
1998	16	Chouinard	Éric	C	QUÉBEC	90	11	11	22	16
	45	Ribeiro	Mike	C	ROUYN	515	117	256	373	212
	75	Beauchemin	François	D	LAVAL	246	21	69	90	172
1999	145	Thinel	Marc-André	W	VICTORIAVILLE	0	0	0	0	0
	253	Marois	Jérome	W	QUÉBEC	0	0	0	0	0
2000	114	Larivée	Christian	C	CHICOUTIMI	0	0	0	0	0
	275	Gauthier	Jonathan	D	ROUYN	0	0	0	0	0
2002	99	Lambert	Michael	W	MONTRÉAL JR	0	0	0	0	0
	212	Ferland	Jonathan	W	ACADIE-BATHURST	7	1	0	1	2
2003	61	Lapierre	Maxim	C	MONTRÉAL JR	100	13	17	30	84
	241	Bonneau	Jimmy		MONTRÉAL JR	0	0	0	0	0
2004	181	Lacasse	Loic		BAIE-COMEAU	0	0	0	0	0

➤

	278	Dulac-Lemelin	Alexandre		BAIE-COMEAU	0	0	0	0	0
2005	45	**Latendresse**	**Guillaume**	W	**DRUMMONDVILLE**	153	32	24	56	88
	130	Aubin	Mathieu	C	LEWISTON	0	0	0	0	0
	229	Paquet	Philippe	D	SALISBURY U.S.A.	0	0	0	0	0
2006	53	Carle	Mathieu	D	ACADIE-BATHURST	0	0	0	0	0
2007	65	Fortier	Olivier	C	RIMOUSKI	0	0	0	0	0
2009	18	Leblanc	Louis	C	OMAHA U.S.A.					
	133	Dumont	Gabriel	C	DRUMMONDVILLE					

Minnesota North Stars – 1970-93

YEAR	RANK	SURNAME	FIRST NAME	P	TEAM	GP	G	A	PTS	PIM
1971	77	Globensky	Allan	D	MONTRÉAL JR	0	0	0	0	0
	117	Coutu	Richard	G	ROSEMONT	0	0	0	0	0
1974	24	**Nantais**	**Richard**	W	**QUÉBEC**	63	5	4	9	79
1975	112	Robert	François	D	SHERBROOKE	0	0	0	0	0
	190	Cloutier	Gilles	G	SHAWINIGAN	0	0	0	0	0
1977	115	Sanvido	Jean-Pierre	G	TROIS-RIVIÈRES	0	0	0	0	0
1980	53	**Velischek**	**Randy**	D	**PROVIDENCE**	509	21	76	97	403
1981	13	**Meighan**	**Ron**	D	**NIAGARA FALLS**	48	3	7	10	18
1985	51	**Roy**	**Stéphane**	C	**GRANBY**	12	1	0	1	0
1986	55	**Zettler**	**Rob**	D	**SAULT STE-MARIE**	569	5	65	70	920
1989	75	**Quintin**	**J.-François**	W	**SHAWINIGAN**	22	5	5	10	4
1990	92	**Ciccone**	**Enrico**	D	**TROIS-RIVIÈRES**	374	10	18	28	1469

Minnesota Wild – 2000-09

YEAR	RANK	SURNAME	FIRST NAME	P	TEAM	GP	G	A	PTS	PIM
2001	93	**Veilleux**	**Stéphane**	W	**VAL D'OR**	361	43	47	90	254
2002	8	**Bouchard**	**Pierre-Marc**	C	**CHICOUTIMI**	425	77	190	267	136
2003	281	Bolduc	Jean-Michel		QUÉBEC	0	0	0	0	0
2004	114	Bordeleau	Patrick		VAL D'OR	0	0	0	0	0
2008	55	Scandela	Marco	D	VAL D'OR	0	0	0	0	0

Nashville Predators – 1998-2009

YEAR	RANK	SURNAME	FIRST NAME	P	TEAM	GP	G	A	PTS	PIM
1998	138	Beauchesne	Martin	D	SHERBROOKE	0	0	0	0	0
2004	107	Fugère	Nick		GATINEAU	0	0	0	0	0
2009	42	Roussel	Ch.-Olivier	D	SHAWINIGAN					
	132	Bourque	Gabriel	W	BAIE-COMEAU					

New Jersey Devils – 1982-2009

YEAR	RANK	SURNAME	FIRST NAME	P	TEAM	GP	G	A	PTS	PIM
1982	54	Kasper	Dave	W	SHERBROOKE	0	0	0	0	0
1986	3	**Brady**	**Neil**	C	**MEDICINE HAT**	89	9	22	31	95
1986	192	**Chabot**	**Frédéric**	G	**STE-FOY AAA**	32				
1987	212	Charland	Alain	W	DRUMMONDVILLE	0	0	0	0	0

1989	173	Faust	André	W	PRINCETON	47	10	7	17	14
1990	20	Brodeur	Martin	G	ST-HYACINTHE	999				
1993	143	Brulé	Steve	W	ST-JEAN	2	0	0	0	0
	247	Provencher	Jimmy	W	ST-JEAN	0	0	0	0	0
1994	129	Gosselin	Christian	D	ST-HYACINTHE	0	0	0	0	0
	181	Williams	Jeff	W	GUELPH	0	0	0	0	0
	207	Bertrand	Éric	W	GRANBY	15	0	0	0	4
1995	78	Gosselin	David	W	SHEBROOKE	13	2	1	3	11
	200	Henry	Frédéric	G	GRANBY	0	0	0	0	0
1996	47	Dagenais	Pierre	W	MONCTON	VOIR 1998				
1997	24	Damphousse	J.-François	G	MONCTON	6				
	188	Benoit	Mathieu	W	CHICOUTIMI	0	0	0	0	0
1998	172	Larivière	Jacques	W	MONCTON	0	0	0	0	0
	105	Dagenais	Pierre	W	ROUYN	142	35	23	58	58
2001	67	Leblanc	Robin	W	BAIE-COMEAU	0	0	0	0	0
2003	197	Smith	Jason	G	LENNOXVILLE	0				
2004	216	Leblond	Pierre-Luc		BAIE-COMEAU	0	0	0	0	0
2006	148	Magnan	Olivier	D	ROUYN	0	0	0	0	0
	208	Henegan	Kyell	D	SHAWINIGAN	0	0	0	0	0
2008	205	Bérubé	J.-Sébastien	W	ROUYN	0	0	0	0	0
2009	54	Gélinas	Éric	D	LEWISTON					

New York Islanders – 1972-2009

YEAR	RANK	SURNAME	FIRST NAME	P	TEAM	GP	G	A	PTS	PIM
1972	65	Grenier	Richard	C	VERDUN	10	1	1	2	2
	97	Brodeur	Richard	G	CORNWALL	385				
	117	Levasseur	René	D	SHAWINIGAN	0	0	0	0	0
	129	Rolando	Yvan	W	DRUMMONDVILLE	0	0	0	0	0
	146	Lambert	René	W	ST-JÉRÔME	0	0	0	0	0
1973	1	Potvin	Denis	D	OTTAWA	1060	310	742	1052	1356
	49	St-Laurent	André	C	MONTRÉAL JR	644	129	187	316	749
	126	Desgagnés	Denis	W	SOREL	0	0	0	0	0
1974	76	Toresan	Carlo	D	SOREL	0	0	0	0	0
1975	65	Lepage	André	G	MONTRÉAL JR	0	0	0	0	0
1977	15	Bossy	Michael	W	LAVAL	752	573	553	1126	210
1978	118	Pépin	Richard	W	LAVAL	0	0	0	0	0
1981	94	Sylvestre	Jacques	W	SOREL	0	0	0	0	0
1982	105	Breton	René	W	GRANBY	0	0	0	0	0
1984	167	De Santis	Franco	D	VERDUN	0	0	0	0	0
1988	79	Brassard	André	D	TROIS-RIVIÈRES	0	0	0	0	0
	142	Gaucher	Yves	W	CHICOUTIMI	0	0	0	0	0
1990	153	Fleury	Sylvain	C	LONGUEUIL	0	0	0	0	0
	216	Lacroix	Martin	W	ST-LAWRENCE U.S.	0	0	0	0	0

➤

1992	200	Paradis	Daniel	W	CHICOUTIMI	0	0	0	0	0
1993	248	Larocque	Stéphane	W	SHERBROOKE	0	0	0	0	0
	274	Charland	Carl	W	HULL	0	0	0	0	0
1996	3	**Dumont**	**Jean-Pierre**	W	**VAL D'OR**	596	171	223	394	308
1997	4	**Luongo**	**Roberto**	G	**VAL D'OR**	490				
1998	209	Brind'amour	Fréderik	G	SHERBROOKE	0	0	0	0	0
2003	182	**Gervais**	**Bruno**	D	**ACADIE-BATHURST**	138	3	23	26	70
2004	276	Michaud	Sylvain		DRUMMONDVILLE	0	0	0	0	0
2007	196	Lacroix	Simon	D	SHAWINIGAN	0	0	0	0	0
2008	126	Poulin	Kevin	G	VICTORIAVILLE	0	0	0	0	0

New York Rangers – 1970-2009

YEAR	RANK	SURNAME	FIRST NAME	P	TEAM	GP	G	A	PTS	PIM
1970	11	**Gratton**	**Norm**	W	**MONTRÉAL JR**	201	39	45	84	64
	53	St-Pierre	André	D	DRUMMONDVILLE	0	0	0	0	0
	106	Brind'amour	Pierre	W	MONTRÉAL JR	0	0	0	0	0
1971	83	Wood	Wayne	G	MONTRÉAL JR	0	0	0	0	0
1971	97	Royal	Jean-Denis	D	ST-JÉRÔME	0	0	0	0	0
	111	**Péloffy**	**André**	C	**ROSEMONT**	9	0	0	0	0
	114	Lecomte	Gérald	D	SHERBROOKE	0	0	0	0	0
1972	31	Villemure	René	W	SHAWINIGAN	0	0	0	0	0
	127	Blais	Yvon	D	CORNWALL	0	0	0	0	0
	137	Archambault	Pierre	D	ST-JÉRÔME	0	0	0	0	0
1973	78	Laganière	Pierre	W	SHERBROOKE	0	0	0	0	0
1974	139	**Holts**	**Greg**	C	**KINGSTON**	11	0	0	0	0
1974	156	Arvisais	Claude	C	SHAWINIGAN	0	0	0	0	0
1975	120	**Larose**	**Claude**	W	**SHERBROOKE**	25	4	7	11	2
	169	Beaulieu	Daniel	W	QUÉBEC	0	0	0	0	0
	201	Dionne	Paul	W	PRINCETON NCAA	0	0	0	0	0
1976	60	Périard	Claude	W	TROIS-RIVIÈRES	0	0	0	0	0
	112	Lévesque	Rémi	C	QUÉBEC	0	0	0	0	0
1977	8	**Deblois**	**Lucien**	W	**SOREL**	993	249	276	525	814
	62	**Marois**	**Mario**	D	**QUÉBEC**	955	76	357	433	1746
	80	**Gosselin**	**Benoit**	W	**TROIS-RIVIÈRES**	7	0	0	0	33
	98	**Bethel**	**John**	W	**UNIV. BOSTON**	17	0	2	2	4
	116	Sullivan	Bob	W	CHICOUTIMI	SEE ATLANTA 1978				
1978	60	**Doré**	**André**	D	**QUÉBEC**	257	14	81	95	261
	192	Daigneault	Pierre	D	COLL. ST-LAURENT	0	0	0	0	0
1981	198	Proulx	Mario	G	PROVIDENCE NCA	0	0	0	0	0
1982	246	Robinson	Dwayne	D	NEW HAMPSHIRE	0	0	0	0	0
1985	175	**Brochu**	**Stéphane**	D	**QUÉBEC**	1	0	0	0	0
1987	31	**Lacroix**	**Daniel**	W	**GRANBY**	188	11	7	18	379
	46	Gagné	Simon	W	LAVAL	0	0	0	0	0
1988	99	Bergeron	Martin	C	DRUMMONDVILLE	0	0	0	0	0

	152	Couvrette	Éric	W	ST-JEAN	0	0	0	0	0
1989	244	MacDermid	Kenneth	W	HULL	0	0	0	0	0
1994	26	Cloutier	Daniel	G	SAULT ST-MARIE	351				
	104	Blouin	Sylvain	W	LAVAL	115	3	4	7	336
	130	Éthier	Martin	D	BEAUPORT	0	0	0	0	0
	156	Brosseau	David	W	SHAWINIGAN	0	0	0	0	0
1995	39	Dubé	Christian	W	SHERBROOKE	33	1	1	2	4
1996	48	Goneau	Daniel	W	GRANBY	53	12	3	15	14
2001	10	Blackburn	Dan	G	KOOTENAY	63				
	139	Collymore	Shawn	W	QUÉBEC	0	0	0	0	0
2004	247	Paiement	Jonathan		LEWISTON	0	0	0	0	0
2005	56	Cliché	Marc-André	C	LEWISTON	0	0	0	0	0
2007	48	Lafleur	Antoine	G	P.E.I.	0	0	0	0	0

Ottawa Senators – 1992-2009

YEAR	RANK	SURNAME	FIRST NAME	P	TEAM	GP	G	A	PTS	PIM
1992	50	Traverse	Patrick	D	SHAWINIGAN	279	14	51	65	113
	98	Guérard	Daniel	W	VICTORIAVILLE	2	0	0	0	0
	194	Savoie	Claude	W	VICTORIAVILLE	0	0	0	0	0
1993	1	Daigle	Alexandre	W	VICTORIAVILLE	616	129	198	327	186
	53	Charbonneau	Patrick	G	VICTORIAVILLE	0	0	0	0	0
	91	Dupaul	Cosmo	W	VICTORIAVILLE	0	0	0	0	0
1994	210	Cassivi	FredÉric	G	ST-HYACINTHE	13				
	211	Dupont	Danny	D	LAVAL	0	0	0	0	0
1996	163	Hardy	François	D	VAL D'OR	0	0	0	0	0
1998	15	Chouinard	Mathieu	G	SHAWINIGAN	VOIR 2000				
	188	Périard	Michel	D	SHAWINIGAN	0	0	0	0	0
1999	48	Lajeunesse	Simon	G	MONCTON	1				
	213	Giroux	Alexandre	C	HULL	22	3	3	6	12
2000	45	Chouinard	Mathieu	G	SHAWINIGAN	1				
2000	55	Vermette	Antoine	C	VICTORIAVILLE	376	87	93	180	213
2006	121	Lessard	Pierre-Luc	D	GATINEAU	0	0	0	0	0

Philadelphia Flyers – 1970-2009

YEAR	RANK	SURNAME	FIRST NAME	P	TEAM	GP	G	A	PTS	PIM
1970	18	Clément	Bill	C	OTTAWA	719	148	208	356	383
	46	Lapierre	Jacques	W	SHAWINIGAN	0	0	0	0	0
	99	Cunningham	Gary	D	STE-CATHERINES	0	0	0	0	0
	109	Daigle	Jean	C	SOREL	0	0	0	0	0
1971	9	Plante	Pierre	W	DRUMMONDVILLE	599	125	172	297	599
1972	103	Beaudoin	Serge	D	TROIS-RIVIÈRES	3	0	0	0	0
	135	Boutin	Raymond	G	SOREL	0	0	0	0	0
1973	74	Latreille	Michel	D	MONTRÉAL JR	0	0	0	0	0

►

1974	53	Sirois	Robert	W	MONTRÉAL JR	286	92	120	212	42
	125	Lemelin	Réjean	G	SHERBROOKE	507				
	174	Labrosse	Marcel	C	SHAWINIGAN	0	0	0	0	0
	201	Guay	Richard	G	CHICOUTIMI	0	0	0	0	0
1975	54	Ritchie	Bob	W	SOREL	29	8	4	12	10
1977	67	Guillemette	Yves	G	SHAWINIGAN	0	0	0	0	0
	71	Hamelin	René	W	SHAWINIGAN	0	0	0	0·	0
	107	Chaput	Alain	C	SHAWINIGAN	0	0	0	0	0
	123	Dalpé	Richard	C	TROIS-RIVIÈRES	0	0	0	0	0
	151	Baumen	Michel	D	HULL	0	0	0	0	0
1980	84	Zytynsky	Tars	D	MONTRÉAL JR	0	0	0	0	0
1981	121	Villeneuve	André	D	CHICOUTIMI	0	0	0	0	0
1982	47	Campbell	Bill	D	MONTRÉAL JR	0	0	0	0	0
	161	Lavigne	Alain	W	SHAWINIGAN	0	0	0	0	0
1983	101	Carrier	Jérome	D	VERDUN	0	0	0	0	0
	141	Mormina	Bobby	W	LONGUEUIL	·0	0	0	0	0
1984	27	Mellanby	Scott	W	HENRI CARR TOR.	1431	364	476	840	2479
	37	Chychrun	Jeff	D	KINGSTON	262	3	22	25	742
1988	14	Boivin	Claude	W	DRUMMONDVILLE	132	12	19	31	364
	63	Roussel	Dominic	G	TROIS-RIVIÈRES	205				
1991	50	Dupré	Yannick	W	DRUMMONDVILLE	35	2	0	2	16
	94	Degrace	Yannick	G	DRUMMONDVILLE	0	0	0	0	0
1992	175	Jutras	Claude	W	HULL	0	0	0	0	0
	247	Paquin	Patrice	W	BEAUPORT	0	0	0	0	0
1994	101	Vallée	Sébastien	W	VICTORIAVILLE	0	0	0	0	0
1997	30	Pelletier	Jean-Marc	G	CORNELL	7	0	0	0	0
1998	22	Gagné	Simon	W	QUÉBEC	606	242	242	484	231
	109	Morin	J.-P.	D	DRUMMONDVILLE	0	0	0	0	0
	124	Bélanger	Francis	W	RIMOUSKI	10	0	0	0	29
	253	St-Jacques	Bruno	D	BAIE-COMEAU	67	3	7	10	47
1999	22	Ouellet	Maxime	G	QUÉBEC	12				
2000	227	Lefebvre	Guillaume	W	ROUYN-NORANDA	38	2	4	6	13
2001	208	Douville	Thierry	D	BAIE-COMEAU	0	0	0	0	0
2002	105	Ruggeri	Rosario	D	CHICOUTIMI	0	0	0	0	0
	193	Mormina	Joey	D	COLGATE	1	0	0	0	0
	201	Brunelle	Mathieu	W	VICTORIAVILLE	0	0	0	0	0
2003	85	Picard	Alexandre	D	HALIFAX	139	12	30	42	39
	140	Tremblay	David	G	HULL	0	0	0	0	0
2004	124	Laliberté	David	W	P.E.I.	0	0	0	0	0
	171	Cabana	Frédérik	C	HALIFAX	0	0	0	0	0
	232	Houle	Martin	G	CAP BRETON	1				
2005	119	Duchesne	Jérémy	G	HALIFAX	0	0	0	0	0
2006	175	Dupont	Michael	G	BAIE-COMEAU	0	0	0	0	0
2007	41	Marshall	Kevin	D	LEWISTON	0	0	0	0	0

2008	67	Bourdon	Marc-André	D	ROUYN-NORANDA	0	0	0	0	0
2009	142	Riopel	Nicolas	G	MONCTON					
	153	Labrecque	Dave	C	SHAWINIGAN					

Phoenix Coyotes – 1992-2009

YEAR	RANK	SURNAME	FIRST NAME	P	TEAM	GP	G	A	PTS	PIM
1996	24	Brière	Daniel	C	DRUMMONDVILLE	562	193	255	448	433
	226	Hubert	M.-Étienne	C	LAVAL	0	0	0	0	0
2000	85	Abid	Ramzi	W	HALIFAX	68	14	16	30	78
2005	59	Pelletier	Pier-Olivier	G	DRUMMONDVILLE	0	0	0	0	0
2008	76	Brodeur	Mathieu	D	CAPE BRETON	0	0	0	0	0

Pittsburgh Penguins– 1970-2009

YEAR	RANK	SURNAME	FIRST NAME	P	TEAM	GP	G	A	PTS	PIM
1970	49	Forey	Connie	W	OTTAWA 67S	4	0	0	0	0
1972	40	Herron	Denis	G	TROIS-RIVIÈRES	462				
	120	Bergeron	Yves	W	SHAWINIGAN	3	0	0	0	0
1974	8	Larouche	Pierre	C	SOREL	812	395	427	822	237
	27	Cossette	Jacques	W	SOREL	64	8	6	14	29
	62	Faubert	Mario	D	ST. LOUIS NCAA	231	21	90	111	222
	181	Gamelin	Serge	W	SOREL	0	0	0	0	0
	195	Perron	Richard	D	QUÉBEC	0	0	0	0	0
1975	13	Laxton	Gordie	G	NEW WESTMINSTER	17				
1976	83	Lowe	Brendan	D	SHERBROOKE	0	0	0	0	0
1983	15	Errey	Bob	W	PETERBOROUGH	895	120	212	382	1005
	103	Émond	Patrick	C	HULL	0	0	0	0	0
1984	1	Lemieux	Mario	C	LAVAL	915	690	1033	1723	834
1985	114	Marston	Stuart-Lee	D	LONGUEUIL	0	0	0	0	0
1988	62	Gauthier	Daniel	C	VICTORIAVILLE	5	0	0	0	0
1992	115	Derouville	Philippe	G	VERDUN	3				
1993	156	Lalime	Patrick	G	SHAWINIGAN	421				
1994	161	Aubin	Serge	C	GRANBY	374	44	64	108	361
1995	76	Aubin	J.-Sébastien	G	SHERBROOKE	218				
1996	186	Meloche	Éric	W	CORNWALL	74	9	11	20	36
1997	97	Mathieu	Alexandre	C	HALIFAX	0	0	0	0	0
1999	86	Caron	Sébastien	G	RIMOUSKI	92				
2000	124	Ouellet	Michel	W	RIMOUSKI	190	52	64	116	58
2001	96	Rouleau	Alexandre	D	VAL D'OR	0	0	0	0	0
2002	234	Talbot	Maxime	C	HULL	261	42	38	80	228
2003	1	Fleury	Marc-André	G	CAPE BRETON	235				
2005	62	Letang	Kristopher	D	VAL D'OR	144	18	34	52	51
	194	Paquet	Jean-Philippe	D	SHAWINIGAN	0	0	0	0	0
2007	20	Esposito	Angelo	C	QUÉBEC	0	0	0	0	0

➤

	51	Veilleux	Kevin	C	VICTORIAVILLE	0	0	0	0	0
2009	30	Després	Simon	D	ST. JOHN					
	121	Peterson	Nick	W	SHAWINIGAN					
	123	Velischek	Alexandre	D	DELBARTON N. J.					

Québec Nordiques – 1979-1995

YEAR	RANK	SURNAME	FIRST NAME	P	TEAM	GP	G	A	PTS	PIM
1979	20	Goulet	Michel	W	BIRMINGHAM	1089	548	604	1152	825
	104	Lacroix	Pierre	W	TROIS-RIVIÈRES	274	24	107	131	197
1980	24	Rochefort	Normand	D	QUÉBEC	598	39	119	158	570
	129	Therien	Gaston	D	QUÉBEC	22	0	8	8	12
	150	Bolduc	Michel	D	CHICOUTIMI	10	0	0	0	6
	171	Tanguay	Christian	W	TROIS-RIVIÈRES	2	0	0	0	0
1981	53	Gaulin	Jean-Marc	W	SOREL	26	4	3	7	8
	158	Côté	André	W	QUÉBEC	0	0	0	0	0
	179	Brisebois	Marc	W	SOREL	0	0	0	0	0
1982	55	Gosselin	Mario	G	SHAWINIGAN	242				
	131	Poudrier	Daniel	D	SHAWINIGAN	25	1	5	6	10
	181	Hough	Mike	W	KITCHENER	707	100	156	256	675
	223	Martin	André	D	MONTRÉAL JR	0	0	0	0	0
1983	32	Héroux	Yves	W	CHICOUTIMI	1	0	0	0	0
	92	Guénette	Luc	G	QUÉBEC	0	0	0	0	0
1984	57	Finn	Steven	D	LAVAL	725	34	78	112	1724
1984	183	Ouellette	Guy		QUÉBEC	0	0	0	0	0
1985	162	Brunetta	Mario	G	QUÉBEC	40				
	246	Bois	Jean	W	TROIS-RIVIÈRES	0	0	0	0	0
1986	39	Routhier	Jean-Marc	W	HULL	8	0	0	0	9
	41	Guérard	Stéphane	D	SHAWINIGAN	34	0	0	0	40
	117	White	Scott	D	MICHIGAN TECH	0	0	0	0	0
	144	Nault	J.-François	W	GRANBY	0	0	0	0	0
	186	Millier	Pierre	W	CHICOUTIMI	0	0	0	0	0
	228	Latreille	Martin	D	LAVAL	0	0	0	0	0
1988	5	Doré	Daniel	W	DRUMMONDVILLE	17	2	3	5	59
	24	Fiset	Stéphane	G	VICTORIAVILLE	390				
	87	Venne	Stéphane	D	UNIV. VERMONT	0	0	0	0	0
	234	Lapointe	Claude	C	LAVAL	879	127	178	305	721
1989	43	Morin	Stéphane	C	CHICOUTIMI	90	16	39	55	52
	76	Dubois	Éric	D	LAVAL	0	0	0	0	0
1990	22	Hugues	Ryan	C	CORNELL	3	0	0	0	0
1991	24	Corbet	René	W	DRUMMONDVILLE	362	58	74	132	420
	90	Labrecque	Patrick	G	ST-JEAN	2				
	244	Meloche	Éric	W	DRUMMONDVILLE	0	0	0	0	0
1992	28	Brousseau	Paul	W	HULL	25	1	3	4	29
	52	Fernandez	Emmanuel	G	LAVAL	325				

	76	McIntyre	Ian	W	BEAUPORT	0	0	0	0	0
	148	Lepage	Martin	D	HULL	0	0	0	0	0
1993	10	**Thibault**	**Jocelyn**	G	**SHERBROOKE**	596				
	153	**Matte**	**Christian**	W	**GRANBY**	25	2	3	5	12
	231	Auger	Vincent	W	HAWKESBURY	0	0	0	0	0
1994	61	Bety	Sebastien	D	DRUMMONDVILLE	0	0	0	0	0
	139	Windsor	Nicholas	D	CORNWALL JR B	0	0	0	0	0
	285	Low	Steven	D	SHERBROOKE	0	0	0	0	0

St. Louis Blues – 1970-2009

YEAR	RANK	SURNAME	FIRST NAME	P	TEAM	GP	G	A	PTS	PIM
1970	79	Moreau	Claude	D	MONTRÉAL JR	0	0	0	0	0
1972	41	Hamel	Jean	D	DRUMMONDVILLE	699	26	95	121	766
	73	Johnson	Dave	D	CORNWALL	0	0	0	0	0
	105	Coughlin	Brian	D	VERDUN	0	0	0	0	0
1973	120	Tétrault	Jean	W	DRUMMONDVILLE	0	0	0	0	0
1974	149	Touzin	Paul	G	SHAWINIGAN	0	0	0	0	0
1976	25	**Smrke**	**John**	W	**TORONTO**	103	11	17	28	33
1978	181	Boutin	J.-François	W	VERDUN	0	0	0	0	0
	188	Ménard	Serge	W	MONTRÉAL JR	0	0	0	0	0
1979	107	Leduc	Gilles	W	VERDUN	0	0	0	0	0
1980	96	**Lemieux**	**Alain**	C	**CHICOUTIMI**	119	28	44	72	38
1981	62	**Donnelly**	**Gord**	D	**SHERBROOKE**	554	28	41	69	2069
	167	**Vigneault**	**Alain**	D	**TROIS-RIVIÈRES**	42	2	5	7	82
1984	71	Herring	Graham	D	LONGUEUIL	0	0	0	0	0
	176	Jomphe	Daniel	W	GRANBY	0	0	0	0	0
1986	10	**Lemieux**	**Jocelyn**	W	**LAVAL**	598	80	84	164	740
	220	Maclean	Terry	C	LONGUEUIL	0	0	0	0	0
1988	30	**Plavsic**	**Adrien**	D	**NEW HAMSHIRE**	214	16	56	72	161
1989	93	**Laperriere**	**Daniel**	D	**ST-LAWRENCE U.S.A.**	48	2	5	7	27
	124	Frenette	Derek	C	FERRIS STATE	0	0	0	0	0
1990	54	**Tardif**	**Patrice**	C	**CHAMPLAIN U.S.A.**	65	7	11	18	78
1992	158	**Laperrière**	**Ian**	C	**DRUMMONDVILLE**	927	111	186	297	1631
1994	68	Roy	Stéphane	C	VAL D'OR	0	0	0	0	0
1995	153	**Hamel**	**Denis**	W	**CHICOUTIMI**	192	19	12	31	77
	179	**Grand-Pierre**	**Jean-Luc**	D	**VAL D'OR**	269	7	13	20	311
1996	169	**Corso**	**Daniel**	C	**VICTORIAVILLE**	77	14	11	25	20
1997	86	Tremblay	Didier	D	HALIFAX	0	0	0	0	0
	106	**Pollock**	**James**	D	**SEATTLE**	9	0	0	0	6
	149	Bilotto	Nicholas	D	BEAUPORT	0	0	0	0	0
1999	270	Desmarais	James	C	ROUYN	0	0	0	0	0
2000	96	Bergeron	Antoine	D	VAL D'OR	0	0	0	0	0
2003	127	Bolduc	Alexandre	C	ROUYN	0	0	0	0	0

➤

2004	277	Boutin	Jonathan	W	SHAWINIGAN	0	0	0	0	0
2007	26	Perron	David	C	LEWISTON	143	28	49	77	88

San Jose Sharks – 1991-2009

YEAR	RANK	SURNAME	FIRST NAME	P	TEAM	GP	G	A	PTS	PIM
1992	147	Bellerose	Éric	W	TROIS-RIVIÉRES	0	0	0	0	0
1994	271	Beauregard	David	W	ST-HYACINTHE	0	0	0	0	0
1996	137	Larocque	Michel	G	UNIV. BOSTON	3				
	217	Thibeault	David	W	DRUMMONDVILLE	0	0	0	0	0
1998	65	Laplante	Éric	W	HALIFAX	0	0	0	0	0
1999	229	Betournay	Éric	C	ACADIE BATHURST	0	0	0	0	0
2003	16	Bernier	Steve	W	MONCTON	177	45	45	90	128
	201	Tremblay	Jonathan		ACADIE BATHURST	0	0	0	0	0
2004	126	Mitchell	Torrey	C	CONNECTICUT	82	10	10	20	50
2005	35	Vlasic	Marc-Édouard	D	QUÉBEC	163	5	35	40	42
2008	92	Groulx	Samuel	D	QUÉBEC	0	0	0	0	0
	186	Demers	Jason	D	VICTORIAVILLE	0	0	0	0	0

Tampa Bay Lightning – 1992-2009

YEAR	RANK	SURNAME	FIRST NAME	P	TEAM	GP	G	A	PTS	PIM
1992	122	Tanguay	Martin	C	VERDUN	0	0	0	0	0
	145	Wilkinson	Derek	G	COMPUWARE	22				
	193	Kemper	Andréw	D	SEATTLE	0	0	0	0	0
	218	Tardif	Marc	W	SHAWINIGAN	0	0	0	0	0
1993	159	Raby	Mathieu	D	VICTORIAVILLE	0	0	0	0	0
	211	Laporte	Alexandre	D	VICTORIAVILLE	0	0	0	0	0
1994	Supp.	Bouchard	François	D	NORTH EASTERN	0	0	0	0	0
1996	16	Larocque	Mario	D	HULL	5	0	0	0	16
	157	Delisle	Xavier	C	GRANBY	16	3	2	5	6
1997	185	St-Pierre	Samuel	W	VICTORIAVILLE	0	0	0	0	0
1998	1	Lecavalier	Vincent	C	RIMOUSKI	787	302	367	669	561
	229	Lyness	Chris	D	ROUYN	0	0	0	0	0
2001	252	Soucy	J.-François	W	MONTRÉAL	0	0	0	0	0
2003	96	Boutin	Jonathan	G	HALIFAX	0				
2008	152	Barberio	Mark	D	MONCTON	0	0	0	0	0

Toronto Maple Leafs – 1970-2009

YEAR	RANK	SURNAME	FIRST NAME	P	TEAM	GP	G	A	PTS	PIM
1970	64	Simard	Luc	W	TROIS-RIVIÈRES	0	0	0	0	0
	91	Larose	Paul	W	QUÉBEC	0	0	0	0	0
1971	98	Johnson	Steve	D	VERDUN	0	0	0	0	0
1972	43	Deslaurier	Denis	D	SHAWINIGAN	0	0	0	0	0
	59	Bowles	Brian	D	CORNWALL	0	0	0	0	0
	75	Plante	Michel	W	DRUMMONDVILLE	0	0	0	0	0

1973	15	Turnbull	Ian	D	MONTRÉAL JR	628	123	317	440	736
	52	Rochon	François	W	SHERBROOKE	0	0	0	0	0
1975	114	Rouillard	Mario	W	TROIS-RIVIÈRES	0	0	0	0	0
	165	Latendresse	Jean	D	SHAWINIGAN	0	0	0	0	0
1976	48	Bélanger	Alain	W	SHERBROOKE	9	0	1	1	6
1978	98	Lefebvre	Normand	W	TROIS-RIVIÈRES	0	0	0	0	0
1979	51	Aubin	Normand	W	VERDUN	69	18	13	31	30
	72	Tremblay	Vincent	G	QUÉBEC	58				
1981	90	Lefrançois	Normand	W	TROIS-RIVIÈRES	0	0	0	0	0
	153	Turmel	Richard	D	SHAWINIGAN	0	0	0	0	0
1982	99	Charland	Sylvain	W	SHAWINIGAN	0	0	0	0	0
1986	6	Damphousse	Vincent	C	LAVAL	1378	432	773	1205	1190
	111	Giguère	Stéphane	W	ST-JEAN	0	0	0	0	0
1987	28	Marois	Daniel	W	VERDUN	350	117	93	210	419
1989	234	Chartrand	Steve	W	DRUMMONDVILLE	0	0	0	0	0
1990	31	Potvin	Félix	G	CHICOUTIMI	640				
	136	Lacroix	Éric	W	GOVERNOR U.S.A.	472	67	70	137	361
	241	Vachon	Nicholas	W	GOVERNOR U.S.A.	1	0	0	0	0
	Supp.	Robitaille	Martin	C	UNIV. MAINE	0	0	0	0	0
1991	47	Perreault	Yannick	C	TROIS-RIVIÈRES	859	247	269	516	402
	179	Lehoux	Guy	D	DRUMMONDVILLE	0	0	0	0	0
1994	16	Fichaud	Éric	G	CHICOUTIMI	95				
1995	145	Tremblay	Yannick	D	BEAUPORT	390	38	87	125	178
1996	50	Larivée	Francis	G	LAVAL	0	0	0	0	0
	151	Demartinis	Lucio	W	SHAWINIGAN	0	0	0	0	0
1997	165	Marchand	Hugo	D	VICTORIAVILLE	0	0	0	0	0
1998	181	Gagnon	Jonathan	W	CAP BRETON	0	0	0	0	0
1999	108	Murovic	Mirko	W	MONCTON	0	0	0	0	0
2000	90	Racine	J.-François	G	DRUMMONDVILLE	0	0	0	0	0
	265	Côté	J.-Philippe	D	CAP BRETON	0	0	0	0	0
2001	88	Corbeil	Nicolas	C	SHERBROOKE	0	0	0	0	0
2002	88	D'Amour	Dominic	D	HULL	0	0	0	0	0
2008	129	Champagne	Joël	C	CHICOUTIMI	0	0	0	0	0

Vancouver Canucks – 1979-1997

YEAR	RANK	SURNAME	FIRST NAME	P	TEAM	GP	G	A	PTS	PIM
1970	2	Tallon	Dale	D	TORONTO JR	642	98	238	336	568
1971	3	Guèvremont	Jocelyn	D	MONTRÉAL JR	571	84	223	307	319
	17	Lalonde	Bobby	C	MONTRÉAL JR	641	124	210	334	298
	39	Lemieux	Richard	W	MONTRÉAL JR	274	39	82	121	132
1973	19	Bordeleau	Paulin	C	TORONTO JR	183	33	56	89	47
	131	Folco	Peter	D	QUÉBEC	2	0	0	0	0
1974	147	Gaudreault	Marc	D	LAKE SUPERIOR	0	0	0	0	0

➤

1975	46	Lapointe	Normand	G	TROIS-RIVIÈRES	0	0	0	0	0
1977	4	Gillis	Jere	W	SHERBROOKE	386	78	95	173	230
1981	52	Lanthier	Jean-Marc	W	SOREL	105	16	16	32	29
	199	Vignola	Réjean	W	SHAWINIGAN	0	0	0	0	0
1982	11	Petit	Michel	D	SHERBROOKE	827	90	238	328	1839
	53	Lapointe	Yves	W	SHAWINIGAN	0	0	0	0	0
1984	10	Daigneault	Jean-Jacques	D	LONGUEUIL	899	53	197	250	687
1987	24	Murphy	Rob	D	LAVAL	125	9	12	21	152
	45	Veilleux	Steve	D	TROIS-RIVIÉRES	0	0	0	0	0
1990	86	Odjick	Gino	W	LAVAL	605	64	73	137	2567
1994	117	Dubé	Yannick	C	LAVAL	0	0	0	0	0
2000	208	Reid	Brandon	C	HALIFAX	13	2	4	6	0
2002	214	Roy	Marc-André	W	BAIE-COMEAU	0	0	0	0	0
2003	60	Bernier	Marc-André	W	HALIFAX	0	0	0	0	0
	222	Guénette	F.-Pierre	C	HALIFAX	0	0	0	0	0
2004	189	Ellis	Julien	G	SHAWINIGAN	0	0	0	0	0
2005	114	Vincent	Alexandre	G	CHICOUTIMI	0	0	0	0	0
2007	145	Messier	C.-Antoine	C	BAIE-COMEAU	0	0	0	0	
2008	41	Sauvé	Yann	D	ST. JOHN	0	0	0	0	

Washington Capitals – 1974-2009

YEAR	RANK	SURNAME	FIRST NAME	P	TEAM	GP	G	A	PTS	PIM
1974	212	Plante	Bernard	W	TROIS-RIVIÈRES	0	0	0	0	0
	220	Chiasson	Jacques	W	DRUMMONDVILLE	0	0	0	0	0
	234	Plouffe	Yves	D	SOREL	0	0	0	0	0
1975	55	Mackasey	Blair	D	MONTRÉAL JR	1	0	0	0	2
1977	3	Picard	Robert	D	MONTRÉAL JR	899	104	319	423	1025
	39	Godin	Eddy	W	QUÉBEC	27	3	6	9	12
	75	Turcotte	Denis	C	QUÉBEC	0	0	0	0	0
	127	Tremblay	Brent	D	TROIS-RIVIÈRES	10	1	0	1	6
1978	38	Currie	Glen	W	LAVAL	326	39	79	118	100
	122	Sirois	Richard	G	MILWAUKEE	0	0	0	0	0
	139	Pomerleau	Denis	W	TROIS-RIVIÈRES	0	0	0	0	0
1980	47	Miele	Dan	W	PROVIDENCE	0	0	0	0	0
1981	152	Duchesne	Gaétan	W	QUÉBEC	1028	179	254	433	617
	194	Valentine	Chris	W	SOREL	105	43	52	95	127
1983	95	Boulianne	Martin	C	GRANBY	0	0	0	0	0
	195	Beaudoin	Yves	D	SHAWINIGAN	11	0	0	0	5
	215	Raymond	Alain	G	TROIS-RIVIÈRES	1				
1985	103	Dumas	Claude	C	GRANBY	0	0	0	0	0
1986	61	Hrivnac	Jim	G	MERRIMACK COL.	85				
1987	57	Maltais	Steve	W	CORNWALL	120	9	18	27	53
1988	15	Savage	Réginald	C	VICTORIAVILLE	34	5	7	12	28

1991	25	Lavigne	Éric	D	HULL	1	0	0	0	0
	146	Morissette	Dave	W	SHAWINIGAN	11	0	0	0	57
	212	Leblanc	Carl	D	GRANBY	0	0	0	0	0
1992	71	Gendron	Martin	C	ST-HYACINTHE	30	4	2	6	10
1993	69	Boileau	Patrick	D	LAVAL	48	5	11	16	26
1994	119	Jean	Yannick	D	CHICOUTIMI	0	0	0	0	0
1995	93	Charpentier	Sébastien	G	LAVAL	24				
	95	Thériault	Joël	D	BEAUPORT	0	0	0	0	0
	105	Gratton	Benoit	C	LAVAL	58	6	10	16	58
	147	Jobin	Frédérick	D	LAVAL	0	0	0	0	0
1997	35	Fortin	J.-François	D	SHERBROOKE	71	1	4	5	42
	200	Therrien	Pierre-Luc	G	DRUMMONDVILLE	0	0	0	0	0
2002	59	Daigneault	Maxime	G	VAL D'OR	0	0	0	0	0
2005	14	Pokulok	Sasha	D	CORNELL	0	0	0	0	0
2006	35	Bouchard	François	W	BAIE-COMEAU	0	0	0	0	0
	127	Lacroix	Maxime	W	QUÉBEC	0	0	0	0	0
	177	Perreault	Mathieu	C	ACADIE-BATHURST	0	0	0	0	0
2009	205	Casavant	Benjamin	W	P.E.I.					

Winnipeg Jets – 1979-1997

YEAR	RANK	SURNAME	FIRST NAME	P	TEAM	GP	G	A	PTS	PIM
1979	19	Mann	Jimmy	W	SHERBROOKE	293	10	20	30	895
	82	Daley	Patrick	W	MONTRÉAL JR.	12	1	0	1	13
1980	65	Fournier	Guy	W	SHAWINIGAN	0	0	0	0	0
1983	14	Dollas	Bobby	D	LAVAL	646	42	96	138	467
	109	Baillargeon	Joel	W	HULL	0	0	0	0	0
	149	Pesetti	Ronnie	D	UNIV. W. MICHIGAN	0	0	0	0	0
	209	Cormier	Éric	W	ST-GEORGES QC.	0	0	0	0	0
1985	60	Berthiaume	Daniel	G	CHICOUTIMI	215				
	165	Draper	Tom	G	VERMONT	53				
	207	Quigley	Dave	G	UNIV. MONCTON	0	0	0	0	0
1986	113	Bateman	Rob	D	COLL. ST-LAURENT	0	0	0	0	0
1988	52	Beauregard	Stéphane	G	ST-JEAN	90				
	101	Lebeau	Benoit	W	MERRIMACK	0	0	0	0	0
	Supp.	O'Neill	Mike	G	YALE	21				
1993	171	Woods	Martin	D	VICTORIAVILLE	0	0	0	0	0
1994	143	Vézina	Steve	G	BEAUPORT	0	0	0	0	0
1995	32	Chouinard	Marc	C	BEAUPORT	320	37	41	78	123
	34	Doig	Jason	D	LAVAL	158	6	18	24	285
	136	Daigle	Sylvain	G	SHAWINIGAN	0	0	0	0	0

TABLEAU 3.2

Quebecers who played in the NHL by team 1970 to 2009*

DUCKS D'ANAHEIM 1993 to 2009				236 Players			14 QC		5.93 %
Forwards									
Season	Surname	First name	P	GP	G	A	PTS	PIM	
1995-98	Jomphe	Jean-François	C	104	10	29	39	100	
1993-95	Lebeau	Stéphane	C	60	14	20	34	26	
2000-03	Chouinard	Marc	C	159	10	13	23	62	
Defencemen									
Season	Surname	First name	P	GP	G	A	PTS	PIM	
1993-98	Dollas	Bobby	D	305	28	61	89	213	
2005-09	Beauchemin	François	D	234	21	67	88	161	
1996-98	Daigneault	J.-Jacques	D	66	4	24	28	50	
1998-2001	Trépanier	Pascal	D	139	8	12	20	175	
2007-08	Bergeron	Marc-André	D	9	0	1	1	4	
1996-97	Plavsic	Adrien	D	6	0	0	0	2	
2005-06	St-Jacques	Bruno	D	1	1	0	1	0	
2000-01	Traverse	Patrick	D	15	1	0	1	6	
Goalies									
Season	Surname	First name	P	GP	W	L	T	AV.	%
2000-09	Giguère	J.-Sébastien	G	427	202	155	68	2.44	.915
1998-2001	Roussel	Dominic	G	51	12	15	11	2.85	.902
2006-07	Caron	Sébastien	G	1	0	0	0	2.12	.833

ATLANTA FLAMES 1972 to 1980				94 Players			21 QC		22.34 %
Forwards									
Season	Surname	First name	P	GP	G	A	PTS	PIM	
1974-80	Chouinard	Guy	C	318	126	168	294	56	
1972-78	Comeau	Reynald	C	468	88	126	214	153	
1975-80	Clément	Bill	C	297	69	107	176	136	
1978-80	Pronovost	Jean	W	155	52	58	110	42	
1972-75	Richard	Jacques	W	215	57	46	103	108	
1977-80	Lalonde	Bobby	C	154	38	56	94	54	
1972-74	Rochefort	Léon	W	110	19	30	49	23	
1975-76	St-Sauveur	Claude	C	79	24	24	48	23	
1976-78	Simpson	Bobby	W	127	23	18	41	94	
1972-73	Gratton	Normand	C	29	3	6	9	12	
1975-76	Lemieux	Richard	W	1	0	1	1	0	

* Players are classed by the number of points accumulated with the team. Goalie classification takes into account the number of games played for the team.

Defencemen

Season	Surname	First name	P	GP	G	A	PTS	PIM	
1975-79	Mulhern	Richard	D	207	25	67	92	153	
1973-76	Lemieux	Jean	D	140	10	38	48	35	
1975-77	Carriere	Larry	D	100	6	18	24	112	
1972-73	Picard	Noël	D	41	0	10	10	43	
1972-73	Harris	Ron	D	24	2	4	6	8	
1979-80	Beaudoin	Serge	D	3	0	0	0	0	

Goalies

Season	Surname	First name	P	GP	W	L	T	AV.	%
1972-80	Bouchard	Daniel	G	384	164	134	72	3.00	
1972-78	Myre	Philippe	G	211	76	95	32	3.21	
1977-79	Bélanger	Yves	G	22	8	10	0	4.08	
1978-80	Lemelin	Réjean	G	21	8	10	1	3.67	

ATLANTA THRASHERS
1999 to 2009

172 Players — **17 QC** — **9.88 %**

Forwards

Season	Surname	First name	P	GP	G	A	PTS	PIM	
1999-2001	Audette	Donald	W	78	39	43	82	76	
2005-07	Mellanby	Scott	W	140	24	46	70	118	
2007-09	Perrin	Éric	W	159	19	49	68	62	
2003-06	Aubin	Serge	W	140	17	32	49	152	
2001-03	Rhéaume	Pascal	C	98	15	18	33	49	
2006-08	Dupuis	Pascal	W	79	13	7	20	28	
2006-07	Bélanger	Éric	C	24	9	6	15	12	
2000-01	Sarault	Yves	W	20	5	4	9	26	
2001-06	Lessard	Francis	W	91	1	3	4	268	
2003-06	Abid	Ramzi	W	6	0	2	2	6	
2006-07	Hamel	Denis	W	3	1	0	1	0	
2003-04	Corso	Daniel	C	7	0	1	1	0	
2002-04	Gamache	Simon	C	4	0	1	1	2	
1999-2000	Bertrand	Éric	W	8	0	0	0	4	

Defencemen

Season	Surname	First name	P	GP	G	A	PTS	PIM	
1999-2004	Trembay	Yannick	D	300	33	74	107	144	
2003-04	Grand-Pierre	Jean-Luc	D	27	2	2	4	26	

Goalies

Season	Surname	First name	P	GP	W	L	T	AV.	%
2001-03	Cassivi	Frédéric	G	8	3	4	0	3.91	.894

➤

BOSTON BRUINS 1970 to 2009				506 Players			45 QC		8.89%
Forwards									
Season	Surname	First name	P	GP	G	A	PTS	PIM	
1970-82	Marcotte	Donald	W	826	220	251	471	331	
1975-81	Ratelle	Jean	C	419	155	295	450	84	
1980-89	Kasper	Steve	W	564	135	220	355	450	
2003-09	Bergeron	Patrice	C	303	80	148	228	88	
1991-94	Juneau	Joé	C	161	51	142	193	72	
1981-84	Krushelnyski	Mike	W	162	51	65	116	100	
1973-76	Savard	André	C	228	52	62	114	144	
1973-77	Forbes	Dave	W	284	53	52	105	220	
2001-04	Lapointe	Martin	W	205	40	43	83	255	
1979-81	Lalonde	Bobby	C	133	14	37	51	59	
1981-83	Léveillé	Normand	W	75	17	25	42	49	
1984-86	Sleigher	Louis	W	83	16	21	37	65	
1982-84	Dufour	Luc	W	114	20	15	35	154	
1996-98	Roy	Jean-Yves	W	54	10	15	25	22	
2001-04	Stock	P.-J.	W	130	1	12	13	282	
2001-02	Hogue	Benoit	C	17	4	4	8	9	
1972-74	Leduc	Richard	C	33	4	4	8	14	
2005-07	Stastny	Yan	C	38	1	5	6	29	
1995-97	Roy	André	W	13	0	2	2	12	
1994-95	Lacroix	Daniel	W	23	1	0	1	38	
1996-97	Drouin	P.-C.	W	3	0	0	0	0	
2005-06	Guité	Ben	W	1	0	0	0	0	
Defencemen									
Season	Surname	First name	P	GP	G	A	PTS	PIM	
1979-2000	Bourque	Raymond	D	1518	395	1111	1506	1087	
1971-76	Vadnais	Carol	D	263	47	134	181	433	
1988-92	Galley	Garry	D	257	24	81	105	322	
1998-2003	Girard	Jonathan	D	150	10	34	44	46	
1988-92	Quintal	Stéphane	D	158	8	19	27	217	
1983-84	Lapointe	Guy	D	45	2	16	18	34	
1985-89	Côté	Alain	D	68	2	9	11	65	
2000-01	Traverse	Patrick	D	37	2	6	8	14	
1991-92	Hynes	Gord	D	15	0	5	5	6	
1992-93	Richer	Stéphane	D	21	1	4	5	18	
1992-93	Lavoie	Dominic	D	2	0	0	0	2	
Goalies									
Season	Surname	First name	P	GP	W	L	T	AV.	%
1973-80	Gilbert	Gilles	G	277	155	73	39	2.95	
1987-93	Lemelin	Réjean	G	183	92	62	20	3.09	.884

1980-82	Vachon	Rogatien	G	91	40	30	12	3.47	
1979-83	Baron	Marco	G	64	31	23	5	3.40	
2007-09	Fernandez	Manny	G	32	18	10	3	2.76	.902
1993-95	Riendeau	Vincent	G	29	10	12	3	3.00	.879
2003-04	Potvin	Félix	G	28	12	8	10	2.50	.903
1979-80	Bélanger	Yves	G	8	2	0	3	3.48	
1991-92	Berthiaume	Daniel	G	8	1	4	2	3.16	.865
1972-73	Plante	Jacques	G	8	7	1	0	2.00	
2006-07	Sauvé	Philippe	G	2	0	0	0	5.80	.826
1986-87	Romano	Roberto	G	1	0	1	0	6.00	

BUFFALO SABRES 1970 to 2009					372 Players		50 QC		13.44%
Forwards									
Season	Surname	First name	P	GP	G	A	PTS	PIM	
1970-87	Perreault	Gilbert	C	1191	512	814	1326	500	
1971-81	Martin	Richard	W	681	382	313	695	475	
1971-79	Robert	René	W	524	222	330	552	401	
1987-92	Turgeon	Pierre	C	322	122	201	323	119	
1976-83	Savard	André	C	467	130	175	305	221	
1989-2001	Audette	Donald	W	421	166	131	297	335	
1978-83	Mckegney	Tony	W	363	127	141	268	117	
2003-09	Pominville	Jason	W	304	99	145	244	90	
2002-05	Brière	Daniel	C	225	92	138	230	219	
2000-06	Dumont	Jean-Pierre	W	362	102	121	223	218	
1980-86	Hamel	Gilles	W	365	92	114	208	60	
1975-82	Smith	Derek	W	244	65	98	163	38	
1987-92	Hogue	Benoit	C	196	45	67	112	275	
1981-86	Mckenna	Sean	W	237	56	53	109	120	
1970-72	Goyette	Philippe	C	97	18	67	85	20	
1980-82	Haworth	Alan	C	106	37	38	75	64	
1980-83	Sauvé	Jean-François	C	98	24	49	73	67	
1983-85	Cloutier	Réal	W	81	24	36	66	25	
1981-82	Lambert	Yvon	W	77	25	39	64	38	
1975-79	Richard	Jacques	W	155	24	38	62	73	
1984-87	Orlando	Gates	W	98	18	26	44	51	
1972-75	Gratton	Normand	W	103	15	22	37	30	
1984-87	Lacombe	Normand	W	94	12	18	30	46	
1999-2003	Hamel	Denis	W	130	13	9	22	67	
1979-85	Mongrain	Robert	C	70	11	11	22	12	
1986-88	Logan	Bob	W	38	10	5	15	0	
2007-08	Bernier	Steve	W	17	3	6	9	2	
1983-85	Verret	Claude	C	14	2	5	7	2	

➤

1973-74	Lemieux	Réal	W	38	1	1	2	4	
1998-99	Juneau	Joé	C	9	1	1	2	2	
1982-83	Gillis	Jerry	W	3	0	0	0	0	
1981-82	James	Val	W	7	0	0	0	16	
1989-90	Guay	François	C	1	0	0	0	0	
1971-79	Richer	Bob	C	3	0	0	0	0	

Defencemen

Season	Surname	First name	P	GP	G	A	PTS	PIM	
1974-79	Guèvremont	Jocelyn	D	324	38	130	168	189	
1994-97	Galley	Gary	D	163	15	87	102	193	
1972-78	Carriere	Larry	D	207	9	43	52	284	
1986-90	Anderson	Shawn	D	113	6	26	32	66	
1992-95	Boucher	Philippe	D	65	7	16	23	43	
1991-94	Donnelly	Gord	D	134	5	11	16	557	
1970-71	Talbot	Jean-Guy	D	57	0	7	7	36	
1998-2000	Grand-Pierre	Jean-Luc	D	27	0	1	1	32	
1970-71	Lacombe	François	D	1	0	1	1	2	
2007-09	Gragnani	Marc-André	D	6	0	0	0	0	
1970-71	Lagacé	Jean-Guy	D	3	0	0	0	2	

Goalies

Season	Surname	First name	P	GP	W	L	T	AV.	%
2007-08	Biron	Martin	G	300	134	115	37	2.53	.909
1976-85	Sauvé	Robert	G	246	119	76	39	3.21	
1981-89	Cloutier	Jacques	G	144	50	58	16	3.70	
2008-09	Lalime	Patrick	G	24	5	13	3	3.10	.900
2007-08	Thibault	Jocelyn	G	12	3	4	2	3.31	.869
1982-83	Myre	Philippe	G	5	3	2	0	4.20	

CALGARY FLAMES					385 Players		36 QC		9.35%
1980 to 2009									

Forwards

Season	Surname	First name	P	GP	G	A	PTS	PIM	
1980-83	Chouinard	Guy	W	196	67	168	235	54	
2003-09	Lombardi	Matthew	C	347	65	102	167	225	
2006-08	Tanguay	Alex	W	159	40	99	139	92	
1990-97	Stern	Ronnie	W	396	59	66	125	1288	
2002-04	Gélinas	Martin	W	157	38	49	87	121	
1980-82	Clément	Bill	C	147	16	32	48	61	
1980-83	Cyr	Denis	C	66	14	15	29	13	
1998-2000	Corbet	René	W	69	9	14	23	70	
1998-2000	St-Louis	Martin	W	69	4	16	20	32	
1997-2003	Bégin	Steve	W	123	11	7	18	192	
1998-2000	Dubinsky	Steve	C	84	4	11	15	18	

1995-96	Lapointe	Claude	C	32	4	5	9	20	
1995-96	Lemieux	Jocelyn	W	20	4	4	8	10	
1984-86	Courteau	Yves	W	18	2	5	7	4	
1990-92	Simard	Martin	W	37	1	5	6	172	
1999-2001	Gratton	Benoit	C	24	1	5	6	24	
1989-2000	Bureau	Marc	W	19	1	3	4	8	
1982-83	Rioux	Pierre	W	14	1	2	3	4	
2008-09	Roy	André	W	44	3	0	3	83	
1995-96	Sarault	Yves	W	11	2	1	3	4	
1997-99	Landry	Éric	C	15	1	1	2	4	
1993-94	Larose	Guy	C	7	0	1	1	4	
1992-93	Lebeau	Patrick	W	1	0	0	0	0	
1981-82	Lalonde	Bobby	C	1	0	0	0	0	

Defencemen									
Season	Surname	First name	P	GP	G	A	PTS	PIM	
1997-2004	Gauthier	Denis	D	384	13	45	58	515	
1991-94	Petit	Michel	D	134	8	40	48	243	
1990-92	Matteau	Stéphane	D	82	16	19	35	112	
1994-98	Bouchard	Joël	D	126	9	12	21	110	
1996-97	Racine	Yves	D	46	1	15	16	24	
1999-2000	Dollas	Bobby	D	49	3	7	10	28	
1997-2000	Charron	Éric	D	35	0	1	1	55	

Goalies									
Season	Surname	First name	P	GP	W	L	T	AV.	%
1980-87	Lemelin	Réjean	G	303	136	90	45	3.67	
1998-2000	Giguère	J.-Sébastien	G	22	7	10	2	3.07	.902
1980-81	Bouchard	Daniel	G	14	4	5	3	4.03	
2005-06	Sauvé	Philippe	G	8	3	3	0	3.28	.891
2003-04	Sabourin	Dany	G	4	0	3	1	3.56	.848

CAROLINA HURRICANES				146 Players		6 QC		4.11%	
1997 to 2009									
Forwards									
Season	Surname	First name	P	GP	G	A	PTS	PIM	
1997-2002	Gélinas	Martin	W	348	75	90	165	226	
2006-07	Bélanger	Éric	C	56	8	12	20	14	
Defencemen									
Season	Surname	First name	P	GP	G	A	PTS	PIM	
2002-04	St-Jacques	Bruno	D	53	2	7	9	43	
1997-98	Ciccone	Enrico	D	14	0	3	3	83	
2007-08	Mormina	Joey	D	1	0	0	0	0	

▶

Goalies									
Season	Surname	First name	P	GP	W	L	T	AV.	%
1999-2000	Fichaud	Éric	G	9	3	5	1	2.94	.884

CHICAGO BLACKHAWKS 1970 to 2009			455 Players			53 QC		11.65%	
Forwards									
Season	Surname	First name	P	GP	G	A	PTS	PIM	
1980-97	Savard	Denis	C	881	377	719	1096	1005	
1970-78	Martin	Hubert Pit	C	528	174	294	468	269	
1994-06	Dazé	Éric	W	601	226	172	398	176	
1970-80	Bordeleau	Jean-Pierre	W	519	97	126	223	143	
1989-94	Goulet	Michel	W	276	92	115	207	212	
1974-80	Daigle	Alain	W	389	56	50	106	122	
1989-94	Lemieux	Jocelyn	W	331	44	57	101	420	
1993-96	Poulin	Patrick	W	141	34	36	70	109	
1973-76	Gagnon	Germain	W	99	19	49	68	27	
2005-08	Lapointe	Martin	W	216	30	32	62	251	
1993-02	Dubinsky	Steve	C	237	16	26	42	132	
1982-84	Cyr	Denis	W	87	19	21	40	21	
1986-92	Vincelette	Daniel	W	166	20	20	40	288	
1998-2000	Dumont	Jean-Pierre	W	72	19	14	33	28	
1977-78	Plante	Pierre	W	77	10	18	28	59	
1977-79	Savard	Jean	C	42	7	12	19	29	
1971-72	Bordeleau	Christian	C	25	6	8	14	6	
Forwards									
Season	Surname	First name	P	GP	G	A	PTS	PIM	
2007-08	Perreault	Yanic	C	53	9	5	14	24	
1971-72	Lacroix	André	C	51	4	7	11	6	
2001-03	White	Peter	C	54	3	4	7	10	
2001-02	Rhéaume	Pascal	C	19	0	2	2	4	
2006-07	Parenteau	P.-Alexandre	W	5	0	1	1	2	
1972-73	L'abbé	Moe	W	5	0	1	1	0	
1990-91	Mckegney	Tony	W	9	0	1	1	4	
1976-77	Archambault	Michel	W	3	0	0	0	0	
1994-95	Gauthier	Daniel	W	5	0	0	0	0	
1997-98	Gendron	Martin	W	2	0	0	0	0	
1998-99	Cloutier	Sylvain	C	7	0	0	0	0	
Defencemen									
Season	Surname	First name	P	GP	G	A	PTS	PIM	
1973-78	Tallon	Dale	D	325	44	112	156	296	
1991-94	Matteau	Stéphane	D	164	35	42	77	198	
1984-89	Bergevin	Marc	D	266	12	29	41	283	
1996-2001	Leroux	Jean-Yves	D	220	16	22	38	146	

1975-80	Logan	Dave	D	178	4	24	28	348	
1996-99	Laflamme	Christian	D	138	2	23	25	131	
1999-2000	Côté	Sylvain	D	45	6	18	24	14	
2000-01	Quintal	Stéphane	D	72	1	18	19	60	
2003-04	Robidas	Stéphane	D	45	2	10	12	33	
1991-93	Dykhus	Karl	D	18	1	8	9	4	
1995-97	Ciccone	Enrico	D	78	2	3	5	281	
1988-89	Doyon	Mario	D	7	1	1	2	6	
1998-99	Nasreddine	Alain	D	7	0	0	0	19	
1998-99	Royer	Rémi	D	18	0	0	0	67	

Goalies

Season	Surname	First name	P	GP	W	L	T	AV.	%
1998-2004	Thibault	Jocelyn	G	331	137	142	49	2.63	.905
1985-87	Sauvé	Robert	G	84	38	32	7	3.74	
1988-97	Waite	Jimmy	G	58	14	23	9	3.64	.860
1989-91	Cloutier	Jacques	G	53	20	18	3	3.16	.877
2006-08	Lalime	Patrick	G	44	20	18	3	2.89	.897
1975-77	Villemure	Gilles	G	21	2	11	6	4.60	
1974-77	Dumas	Michel	G	8	2	1	2	3.98	
2000-01	Larocque	Michel	G	3	0	2	0	3.55	
1970-71	Meloche	Gilles	G	2	2	0	0	3.00	.848
2006-07	Caron	Sébastien	G	1	1	0	0	1.00	.960
1993-94	Soucy	Christian	G	1	0	0	0	0	

CLEVELAND BARONS 1976 to 1978					49 Players			3 QC	6.12%

Forwards

Season	Surname	First name	P	GP	G	A	PTS	PIM	
1976-78	Girard	Bob	W	93	11	14	25	44	
1977-78	Chicoine	Daniel	W	6	0	0	0	0	

Goalies

Season	Surname	First name	P	GP	W	L	T	AV.	%
1976-78	Meloche	Gilles	G	105	35	51	14	3.62	

COLORADO AVALANCHE 1995 to 2009					178 Players			29 QC	16.29%

Forwards

Season	Surname	First name	P	GP	G	A	PTS	PIM	
1999-2006	Tanguay	Alex	W	450	137	263	400	219	
1995-2000	Lemieux	Claude	W	297	106	106	212	381	
2006-09	Stastny	Paul	C	193	63	122	185	88	
2005-09	Laperrière	Ian	W	307	40	72	112	552	

➤

1995-99	Corbet	René	W	230	39	47	86	291	
1996-99	Lacroix	Éric	W	170	34	33	67	112	
2005-07	Turgeon	Pierre	C	79	20	33	53	42	
2006-09	Guité	Ben	W	168	19	26	45	93	
1998-2003	Aubin	Serge	W	82	6	7	13	70	
1996-2000	Matte	Christian	W	22	2	3	5	10	
1996-98	Sarault	Yves	W	30	3	1	4	6	
2003-04	Worrell	Peter	W	49	3	1	4	179	
1995-98	Brousseau	Paul	W	8	1	1	2	2	
2002-03	Brulé	Steve	W	2	0	0	0	0	
2008-09	Dupuis	Philippe	C	8	0	0	0	4	
1995-96	Lapointe	Claude	C	3	0	0	0	0	

Defencemen

Season	Surname	First name	P	GP	G	A	PTS	PIM	
1999-2001	Bourque	Raymond	D	94	11	58	73	54	
1996-2003	Messier	Éric	D	385	25	47	72	130	
1995-99	Lefebvre	Sylvain	D	303	9	50	59	175	
2005-07	Brisebois	Patrice	D	113	11	38	49	77	
1997-2002	Trépanier	Pascal	D	89	4	10	14	77	
1997-98	Leroux	François	D	50	1	2	3	140	
1998-99	Gaul	Michael	D	1	0	0	0	0	

Goalies

Season	Surname	First name	P	GP	W	L	T	AV.	%
1995-2003	Roy	Patrick	G	478	262	140	78	2.27	.918
2005-08	Théodore	José	G	91	42	39	5	2.76	.902
1995-96	Fiset	Stéphane	G	37	22	6	7	2.93	.898
1996-2000	Denis	Marc	G	28	10	10	5	2.55	.916
2003-04	Sauvé	Philippe	G	17	7	7	5	3.04	.896
1995-96	Thibault	Jocelyn	G	10	3	4	3	3.01	.874

COLORADO ROCKIES **1976 to 1981**				**125 Players**			**8 QC**		**6.4%**
Forwards									
Season	Surname	First name	P	GP	G	A	PTS	PIM	
1979-81	Deblois	Lucien	W	144	50	35	85	114	
1979-81	Robert	René	W	97	36	46	82	109	
1976-78	Dupéré	Denis	W	111	22	26	48	8	
1976-77	Nolet	Simon	W	52	12	19	31	10	
1978-80	Comeau	Reynald	C	92	10	15	25	22	
Defencemen									
Season	Surname	First name	P	GP	G	A	PTS	PIM	
1978-79	Lachance	Michel	D	21	0	4	4	22	

Goalies

Season	Surname	First name	P	GP	W	L	T	AV.	%
1976-80	Plasse	Michel	G	126	24	73	22	3.93	
1980-82	Myre	Philippe	G	34	5	23	3	4.74	

COLUMBUS BLUE JACKETS
2000 to 2009

| | | 149 Players | | 13 QC | | | | 8.72 % | |

Forwards

Season	Surname	First name	P	GP	G	A	PTS	PIM	
2000-02	Aubin	Serge	W	152	21	25	46	139	
2000-03	Dineen	Kevin	W	129	13	15	28	200	
2007-09	Brassard	Dérick	C	48	11	16	27	23	
2008-09	Vermette	Antoine	C	17	7	6	13	8	
2000-01	Maltais	Steve	W	26	0	3	3	12	
2000-03	Darche	Mathieu	W	24	1	1	2	6	

Defencemen

Season	Surname	First name	P	GP	G	A	PTS	PIM	
2005-06	Beauchemin	François	D	11	0	2	14	11	
2000-01	Gaul	Michael	D	2	0	0	2	4	
2000-04	Grand-Pierre	Jean-Luc	D	202	4	10	2	239	
2005-09	Picard	Alexandre	D	58	0	2	0	48	

Goalies

Season	Surname	First name	P	GP	W	L	T	AV.	%
2000-06	Denis	Marc	G	266	84	146	35	3.01	.905
2003-09	Leclaire	Pascal	G	125	45	55	12	2.82	.907
2001-03	Labbé	Jean-François	G	14	3	5	0	3.48	.890

STARS DE DALLAS
1993 to 2009

| | | 223 Players | | 23 QC | | | | 10.31 % | |

Forwards

Season	Surname	First name	P	GP	G	A	PTS	PIM	
2006-09	Ribeiro	Mike	C	239	67	153	220	120	
2001-04	Turgeon	Pierre	C	207	42	87	129	54	
1995-2002	Hogue	Benoit	C	238	39	73	112	179	
1995-2000	Carbonneau	Guy	C	364	34	66	100	181	
2001-02	Brunet	Benoit	W	32	4	9	13	8	
2001-02	Audette	Donald	W	20	4	8	12	12	
1997-98	Errey	Bob	W	59	2	9	11	46	
2002-03	Lemieux	Claude	W	32	2	4	6	14	
2001-02	Mckay	Randy	W	14	1	4	5	7	
2005-08	Lessard	Junior	W	8	2	0	2	14	
2008-09	Bégin	Steve	W	20	1	1	2	15	
2001-03	Montgomery	Jim	C	9	0	2	2	0	

➤

2000-04	Gainey	Steve	W	13	0	1	1	14	
1995-98	Côté	Patrick	W	8	0	0	0	47	
1996-97	Labelle	Marc	W	9	0	0	0	46	
1995-96	Marois	Daniel	W	3	0	0	0	2	

Defencemen

Season	Surname	First name	P	GP	G	A	PTS	PIM	
2002-08	Boucher	Philippe	D	330	52	107	159	365	
2002-09	Robidas	Stéphane	D	394	21	79	100	357	
1999-2000	Côté	Sylvain	D	28	2	8	10	14	
1993-95	Donnelly	Gord	D	34	1	1	2	118	
1999-2000	Bouchard	Joël	D	2	0	0	0	2	
2005-06	Traverse	Patrick	D	1	0	0	0	0	

Goalies

Season	Surname	First name	P	GP	W	L	T	AV.	%
1994-2000	Fernandez	Manny	G	33	12	11	6	2.48	.909

DETROIT RED WINGS 1970 to 2009					476 Players		44 QC		9.24%

Forwards

Season	Surname	First name	P	GP	G	A	PTS	PIM	
1971-75	Dionne	Marcel	C	309	139	227	366	59	
1991-2001	Lapointe	Martin	W	552	108	122	230	888	
1970-75	Charron	Guy	C	265	61	78	139	57	
1977-84	St-Laurent	André	C	172	50	73	123	249	
1974-78	Bergeron	Michel	W	174	64	46	110	156	
2001-03	Robitaille	Luc	W	162	41	40	81	88	
1973-75	Jarry	Pierre	W	91	23	36	59	21	
1994-97	Erry	Bob	W	137	18	34	52	124	
1975-79	Leblanc	Jean-Paul	C	147	13	28	41	87	
1971-73	Rochefort	Léon	W	84	19	16	35	12	
1981-83	Smith	Derek	W	91	13	18	31	22	
1989-91	Shank	Daniel	W	64	11	14	25	157	
1970-71	Connelly	Wayne	C	51	8	13	21	12	
1988-91	Mckay	Randy	W	83	4	13	17	234	
1970-71	Leclerc	René	C	44	8	8	16	43	
1976-78	Ritchie	Robert	W	28	8	4	12	10	
1977-79	Cloutier	Roland	C	20	6	6	12	2	
1976-79	Leblanc	Fernand	C	34	5	6	11	0	
1983-85	Aubry	Pierre	W	39	6	3	9	41	
1994-95	Krushelnyski	Mike	C	20	2	3	5	6	
1989-90	Mckegney	Tony	W	14	2	1	3	8	
1993-94	Maltais	Steve	W	4	0	1	1	0	
1974-75	Drolet	René	W	1	0	0	0	0	
1983-84	Johnson	Brian	W	3	0	0	0	5	

Defencemen									
Season	Surname	First name	P	GP	G	A	PTS	PIM	
1995-2004	Dandenault	Mathieu	D	616	48	101	149	342	
1989-93	Racine	Yves	D	231	22	102	124	230	
1999-2002	Duchesne	Steve	D	197	19	65	84	118	
1973-81	Hamel	Jean	D	451	19	62	81	574	
1986-89	Delorme	Gilbert	D	121	5	14	19	165	
1990-93	Dollas	Bobby	D	89	6	6	12	42	
1995-96	Bergevin	Marc	D	70	1	9	10	33	
2002-03	Boileau	Patrick	D	25	2	6	8	14	
1976-79	Murray	Terry	D	23	0	7	7	10	
1970-73	Lajeunesse	Serge	D	97	1	4	5	101	
1989-90	Picard	Robert	D	20	0	3	3	20	
1979-82	Cloutier	Réjean	D	5	0	2	2	2	

Goalies									
Season	Surname	First name	P	GP	W	L	T	AV.	%
1981-86	Micalef	Corrado	G	113	26	59	15	4.24	
1978-80	Vachon	Rogatien	G	109	30	57	19	3.74	
1980-83	Gilbert	Gilles	G	95	21	48	16	4.18	
1981-82	Sauvé	Robert	G	41	11	24	4	4.19	
1991-94	Riendeau	Vincent	G	32	17	8	2	3.28	.870
1986-90	St-Laurent	Sam	G	30	5	11	5	3.43	
1972-74	Dejordy	Denis	G	25	8	12	3	3.86	
1980-82	Legris	Claude	G	4	0	1	1	2.64	

EDMONTON OILERS 1979 to 2009			408 Players		28 QC		6.87%		

Forwards									
Season	Surname	First name	P	GP	G	A	PTS	PIM	
1984-88	Krushelnyski	Mike	C	290	95	131	226	213	
1988-93	Gélinas	Martin	W	258	60	60	120	156	
1997-2006	Laraque	Georges	W	490	43	68	111	826	
1991-92	Damphousse	Vincent	C	80	38	51	89	53	
1991-93	Mellanby	Scott	W	149	38	44	82	344	
1986-90	Lacombe	Normand	W	133	30	22	52	116	
2005-09	Pouliot	M.-Antoine	C	141	14	25	39	53	
1993-96	White	Peter	C	61	10	12	22	2	
2005-08	Jacques	Jean-François	W	53	1	0	1	44	
1979-80	Carter	Ron	W	2	0	0	0	0	
2000-01	Côté	Patrick	W	6	0	0	0	18	
1998-99	Lacroix	Daniel	W	4	0	0	0	13	
1999-2000	Picard	Michel	W	2	0	0	0	2	
1996-97	Bélanger	Jesse	C	6	0	0	0	0	
2005-06	Stastny	Yan	C	3	0	0	0	0	

➤

Defencemen

Season	Surname	First name	P	GP	G	A	PTS	PIM	
1979-98	Lowe	Kevin	D	1037	74	310	384	1236	
2002-07	Bergeron	Marc-André	D	189	33	55	88	101	
1995-97	Dufresne	Donald	D	64	1	7	8	31	
1997-98	Dollas	Bobby	D	30	2	5	7	22	
1998-2000	Laflamme	Christian	D	61	0	6	6	32	
1996-97	Petit	Michel	D	18	2	4	6	20	
1988-93	Leroux	François	D	11	0	3	3	11	
2005-08	Roy	Mathieu	D	30	2	1	3	57	
2006-07	Bisaillon	Sébastien	D	2	0	0	0	0	

Goalies

Season	Surname	First name	P	GP	W	L	T	AV.	%
2007-09	Garon	Mathieu	G	62	32	26	1	2.78	.909
2008-09	Deslauriers	Jeff	G	10	4	3	0	3.34	.901
2000-01	Roussel	Dominic	G	8	1	4	0	3.62	.861
1979-80	Corsi	James	G	26	8	14	3	3.65	
1984-85	Baron	Marco	G	1	0	1	0	3.64	

FLORIDA PANTHERS 1993 to 2009				232 Players		17 QC		7.33%	

Forwards

Season	Surname	First name	P	GP	G	A	PTS	PIM	
1993-2001	Mellanby	Scott	W	552	157	197	354	953	
1993-96	Bélanger	Jesse	C	180	49	68	117	44	
2005-07	Gélinas	Martin	W	164	31	54	85	116	
1993-97	Hough	Mike	W	259	27	52	79	185	
1997-2003	Worrell	Peter	W	342	16	26	42	1375	
2003-04	Audette	Donald	W	28	6	7	13	22	
2005-09	Stewart	Anthony	W	105	4	8	12	38	
2001-03	Dagenais	Pierre	W	35	7	1	8	8	
2002-03	Matteau	Stéphane	W	52	4	4	8	27	
1995-96	Dionne	Gilbert	W	5	1	2	3	0	
1994-95	Duchesne	Gaétan	W	13	1	2	3	0	
1993-94	Lebeau	Patrick	W	4	1	1	2	4	
2000-01	Brousseau	Paul	W	1	0	0	0	0	

Defencemen

Season	Surname	First name	P	GP	G	A	PTS	PIM	%
2002-04	Biron	Mathieu	D	91	4	18	22	65	
2003-04	Messier	Éric	D	21	0	3	3	16	
1993-95	Richer	Stéphane	D	3	0	1	1	2	

Goalies

Season	Surname	First name	P	GP	W	L	T	AV.	%
2000-06	Luongo	Roberto	G	317	108	154	59	2.68	.920

HARTFORD WHALERS 1979 À 1997				275 Players			23 QC		8.36%
Forwards									
Season	Surname	First name	P	GP	G	A	PTS	PIM	
1984-97	Dineen	Kevin	W	587	235	268	503	1237	
1983-89	Turgeon	Sylvain	W	370	178	150	328	366	
1979-82	Keon	Dave	C	234	31	97	128	42	
1981-83	Larouche	Pierre	C	83	43	47	90	20	
1991-94	Poulin	Patrick	W	91	22	32	54	50	
1983-84	Dupont	Normand	W	40	7	15	22	12	
1993-96	Lemieux	Jocelyn	W	86	13	8	21	82	
1980-83	Galarneau	Michel	C	78	7	10	17	34	
1979-80	Lacroix	André	C	29	3	14	17	2	
1990-92	Picard	Michel	W	30	4	5	9	8	
1995-97	Martins	Steve	C	25	1	4	5	8	
1991-92	Shank	Daniel	W	13	2	0	2	18	
1983-84	Yates	Ross	C	7	1	1	2	4	
1986-87	Courteau	Yves	W	4	0	0	0	0	
1979-80	Savard	Jean	C	1	0	0	0	0	
Defencemen									
Season	Surname	First name	P	GP	G	A	PTS	PIM	
1984-91	Côté	Sylvain	D	382	31	61	92	147	
1982-83	Lacroix	Pierre	D	56	6	25	31	18	
1990-92	Bergevin	Marc	D	79	7	17	24	68	
1980-82	Lupien	Gilles	D	21	2	5	7	41	
1984-85	Weir	Wally	D	34	2	3	5	56	
Goalies									
Season	Surname	First name	P	GP	W	L	T	AV.	%
1992-94	Gosselin	Mario	G	23	5	13	1	4.23	.871
1996-97	Giguère	J.-Sébastien	G	8	1	4	0	3.65	.881
1987-88	Brodeur	Richard	G	6	4	2	0	2.65	.894

KANSAS CITY SCOUTS 1974 to 1976				50 Players			11 QC		22%
Forwards									
Season	Surname	First name	P	GP	G	A	PTS	PIM	
1974-76	Charron	Guy	C	129	40	73	113	33	
1974-76	Nolet	Simon	W	113	36	47	83	46	
1974-76	Burns	Robin	W	149	31	33	64	107	
1974-76	Lemieux	Richard	C	81	10	20	30	64	
1974-76	Dubé	Normand	W	57	8	10	18	54	
1975-76	Dupéré	Denis	W	43	6	8	14	16	
1975-76	Gagnon	Germain	W	31	1	9	10	6	

➤

Defencemen

Season	Surname	First name	P	GP	G	A	PTS	PIM	
1974-76	Lagacé	Jean-Guy	D	88	5	19	24	130	
1974-76	Houde	Claude	D	59	3	6	9	40	

Goalies

Season	Surname	First name	P	GP	W	L	T	AV.	%
1974-76	Herron	Denis	G	86	15	52	15	3.96	
1974-75	Plasse	Michel	G	24	4	16	3	4.06	

LOS ANGELES KINGS 1970 to 2009				533 Players			61 QC		11.44%

Forwards

Season	Surname	First name	P	GP	G	A	PTS	PIM	
1975-87	Dionne	Marcel	C	921	550	757	1307	461	
1986-2006	Robitaille	Luc	W	1077	557	597	1154	924	
1970-77	Berry	Bob	W	539	159	191	350	344	
1995-2004	Laperriere	Ian	W	595	61	104	165	1017	
1994-99	Perreault	Yanic	C	288	76	80	156	118	
2000-06	Bélanger	Éric	C	323	63	87	150	169	
1988-91	Krushelnyski	Mike	C	156	43	66	109	170	
1988-91	Kasper	Steve	W	173	35	62	97	74	
1971-73	Bernier	Serge	W	101	33	57	90	55	
1998-2000	Audette	Donald	W	98	30	38	68	96	
1970-74	Lemieux	Réal	W	215	21	41	62	62	
1979-82	St-Laurent	André	C	115	18	34	52	179	
1994-99	Lacroix	Éric	W	144	25	24	49	176	
1985-88	Mckenna	Sean	W	129	21	21	42	29	
1970-72	Grenier	Lucien	W	128	12	11	23	16	
1977-78	Monahan	Hartland	W	64	10	9	19	45	
1988-92	Couturier	Sylvain	W	33	4	5	9	4	
1990-93	Breault	Francis	W	27	2	4	6	42	
1980-82	Martin	Richard	W	4	2	4	6	2	
1985-86	Mongrain	Robert	C	11	2	3	5	2	
1985-88	Currie	Glen	W	19	1	2	3	9	
1995-96	Larouche	Steve	C	7	1	2	3	4	
1995-96	Tardif	Patrice	C	15	1	1	2	37	
1978-79	Garland	Scott	W	6	0	1	1	24	
1982-83	Giroux	Pierre	C	6	1	0	1	17	
1988-89	Hamel	Gilles	W	11	0	1	1	2	
1992-93	Fortier	Marc	C	6	0	0	0	5	
1988-89	Logan	Bob	W	4	0	0	0	0	

Defencemen

Season	Surname	First name	P	GP	G	A	PTS	PIM	
1986-99	Duchesne	Steve	D	442	99	216	315	399	

Season	Surname	First name	P	GP	G	A	PTS	PIM	
1979-94	Hardy	Mark	D	616	53	250	303	858	
1984-2000	Galley	Garry	D	361	44	115	159	330	
1970-74	Marotte	Gilles	D	250	23	101	124	272	
1994-2002	Boucher	Philippe	D	312	32	77	109	255	
1981-82	Turnbull	Ian	D	42	11	15	26	81	
1994-96	Petit	Michel	D	49	5	13	18	111	
1978-80	Mulhern	Rich	D	51	2	12	14	39	
1995-97	Finn	Steven	D	104	5	5	10	186	
1993-94	Lavoie	Dominic	D	8	3	3	6	2	
1991-93	Chychrun	Jeff	D	43	0	4	4	99	
2008-09	Gauthier	Denis	D	65	2	2	4	90	
1987-88	Germain	Éric	D	4	0	1	1	13	
1977-78	Carriere	Larry	D	2	0	0	0	0	
1993-94	Dufresne	Donald	D	9	0	0	0	10	
1994-95	Lavigne	Éric	D	1	0	0	0	0	

Goalies

Season	Surname	First name	P	GP	W	L	T	AV.	%
1971-78	Vachon	Rogatien	G	389	171	148	66	2.86	
1978-84	Lessard	Mario	G	240	92	97	39	3.74	
1996-2001	Fiset	Stéphane	G	200	80	85	27	2.83	.906
2000-03	Potvin	Félix	G	136	61	52	25	2.35	.905
2005-07	Garon	Mathieu	G	95	44	36	9	3.03	.898
1970-72	Dejordy	Denis	G	65	18	34	11	4.20	
1990-92	Berthiaume	Daniel	G	56	27	21	7	3.54	.888
2006-08	Cloutier	Daniel	G	33	8	18	3	3.83	.868
1989-90	Gosselin	Mario	G	26	7	11	2	3.87	.864
1983-84	Baron	Marco	G	21	3	14	4	4.31	
2007-08	Aubin	J.-Sébastien	G	19	5	6	1	3.19	.886
1997-98	Chabot	Frédéric	G	12	3	3	2	3.14	.891
1999-2000	Cousineau	Marcel	G	5	1	1	1	2.11	.906
2007-08	Bernier	Jonathan	G	4	1	3	0	4.03	.864
1996-97	Bergeron	Jean-Claude	G	1	0	1	0	1.30	.886
2003-04	Chouinard	Mathieu	G	1	0	0	0	0.00	1.000
1980-81	Pageau	Paul	G	1	0	1	0	8.00	

North Stars Du Minnesota 1970 À 1993			310 Players			23 QC		7.42%	

Forwards

Season	Surname	First name	P	GP	G	A	PTS	PIM	
1970-75	Drouin	Jude	W	319	79	183	262	187	
1989-93	Duchesne	Gaétan	W	297	45	45	90	183	
1975-78	Jarry	Pierre	W	115	38	48	86	36	

➤

1984-87	Mckegney	Tony	W	108	28	41	69	68	
1974-76	Gratton	Normand	W	66	21	15	36	22	
1970-71	Rousseau	Robert	W	63	4	20	24	12	
1990-92	Bureau	Marc	W	55	6	10	16	54	
1974-77	Nantais	Richard	W	63	5	4	9	79	
1973-75	Langlais	Alain	W	25	4	4	8	10	
1978-80	Chicoine	Daniel	W	25	1	2	3	12	
1991-92	Maltais	Steve	W	12	2	1	3	2	
1987-88	Roy	Stéphane	C	12	1	0	1	0	
1989-90	Thyer	Mario	C	5	0	0	0	0	
1988-91	Zettler	Rob	D	80	1	12	13	164	
1988-89	Hardy	Mark	D	15	2	4	6	26	
1981-82	Poulin	Daniel	D	3	1	1	2	2	
1981-82	Meighan	Ron	D	7	1	1	2	2	
1991-93	Ciccone	Enrico	D	42	0	1	1	163	

Goalies

Season	Surname	First name	P	GP	W	L	T	AV.	%
1978-85	Meloche	Gilles	G	327	141	117	52	3.51	
1970-73	Gilbert	Gilles	G	42	14	22	5	3.39	
1970-75	Rivard	Fernand	G	28	6	15	2	4.26	
1989-90	Berthiaume	Daniel	G	5	1	3	0	3.49	.865
1979-80	Levasseur	Louis	G	1	0	1	0	7.00	

| MINNESOTA WILD 2000 to 2009 | | 116 Players | | 13 QC | | 11.21% |

Forwards

Season	Surname	First name	P	GP	G	A	PTS	PIM	
2002-09	Bouchard	Pierre-Marc	C	425	77	190	267	136	
2000-07	Dupuis	Pascal	W	334	67	74	141	162	
2002-09	Veilleux	Stéphane	W	361	43	47	90	254	
2003-06	Daigle	Alexandre	C	124	25	54	79	26	
2007-09	Bélanger	Éric	C	154	26	47	73	56	
2003-06	Chouinard	Marc	C	119	25	26	51	51	
2000-03	Blouin	Sylvain	W	86	3	4	7	251	
2003-04	Chouinard	Éric	C	31	3	4	7	6	
2001-02	Bordeleau	Sébastien	C	14	1	4	5	8	
2000-01	Matte	Christian	W	3	0	0	0	2	

Defencemen

Season	Surname	First name	P	GP	G	A	PTS	PIM	
2008-09	Bergeron	Marc-André	D	72	14	18	32	30	
2000-01	Daigneault	J.-Jacques	D	1	0	0	0	0	

Goalies

Season	Surname	First name	P	GP	W	L	T	AV.	%
2000-07	Fernandez	Manny	G	260	113	102	28	2.46	.913

MONTREAL CANADIENS 1970 to 2009				374 Players			128 QC		34.22%
Forwards									
Season	Surname	First name	P	GP	G	A	PTS	PIM	
1971-85	Lafleur	Guy	W	962	518	728	1246	381	
1970-79	Lemaire	Jacques	C	640	283	387	670	156	
1974-86	Tremblay	Mario	W	852	258	326	584	1043	
1970-79	Cournoyer	Yvan	W	562	276	287	563	146	
1980-94	Carbonneau	Guy	C	912	221	326	547	623	
1992-99	Damphousse	Vincent	C	519	184	314	498	559	
1976-85	Mondou	Pierre	C	548	194	262	456	179	
1984-98	Richer	Stéphane	W	490	225	196	421	399	
1972-81	Lambert	Yvon	W	606	181	234	415	302	
1970-83	Houle	Réjean	W	626	161	246	407	395	
1988-94	Lebeau	Stéphane	C	313	104	139	243	79	
1988-2002	Brunet	Benoit	W	494	92	149	241	221	
1977-82	Larouche	Pierre	C	236	110	126	236	59	
1970-75	Richard	Henri	C	315	54	150	204	147	
1983-90	Lemieux	Claude	W	281	97	92	189	576	
1990-93	Savard	Denis	C	210	72	107	179	215	
1999-2006	Ribeiro	Mike	C	276	50	103	153	92	
1970-73	Tardif	Marc	W	227	75	77	152	262	
2001-04	Perreault	Yanic	C	224	67	66	133	110	
1990-95	Dionne	Gilbert	W	196	60	70	130	106	
1994-97	Turgeon	Pierre	C	104	50	77	127	50	
2006-09	Latendresse	Guillaume	W	209	46	36	82	133	
1970-71	Beliveau	Jean	C	70	25	51	76	40	
1997-2002	Poulin	Patrick	C	277	31	44	75	65	
2001-04	Juneau	Joé	C	212	19	54	73	50	
1983-88	Momesso	Sergio	W	137	29	38	67	243	
2003-09	Bégin	Steve	W	266	35	31	66	275	
2005-09	Lapierre	Maxim	C	179	28	30	58	160	
1984-86	Deblois	Lucien	W	112	26	28	54	68	
1995-98	Bureau	Marc	W	182	22	22	44	74	
2008-09	Tanguay	Alex	W	50	16	25	41	34	
2003-06	Dagenais	Pierre	W	82	22	17	39	40	
2001-04	Audette	Donald	W	90	15	22	37	43	
1990-92	Turgeon	Sylvain	W	75	14	18	32	59	
1986-89	Thibaudeau	Gilles	C	58	12	15	27	6	
1995-98	Bordeleau	Sébastien	C	85	8	17	25	38	
2002-03	Mckay	Randy	W	75	6	13	19	72	
1991-2000	Bélanger	Jesse	C	39	7	8	15	6	
1970-71	Rochefort	Léon	W	57	5	10	15	4	

►

1990-95	Roberge	Mario	W	112	7	7	14	314	
2000-02	Landry	Éric	C	53	4	8	12	43	
1984-88	Boisvert	Serge	W	29	5	5	10	4	
1993-97	Brashear	Donald	W	111	3	7	10	358	
2000-02	Odjick	Gino	W	49	5	4	9	148	
1993-97	Sévigny	Pierre	W	75	4	5	9	62	
1988-90	Lemieux	Jocelyn	W	35	4	3	7	61	
1987-89	Charbonneau	José	W	25	1	5	6	12	
1979-80	Geoffrion	Daniel	W	32	0	6	6	12	
2000-01	Delisle	Xavier	C	14	3	2	5	6	
1996-99	Houde	Éric	C	30	2	3	5	4	
1970-71	Charron	Guy	C	15	2	2	4	2	
2000-01	Chouinard	Éric	C	13	1	3	4	0	
1979-80	Dupont	Normand	W	35	1	3	4	4	
2000-01	Stock	P.-J.	W	20	1	2	3	32	
1989-90	Desjardins	Martin	C	8	0	2	2	2	
2001-04	Gratton	Benoit	C	12	1	1	2	12	
2008-09	Laraque	Georges	W	33	0	2	2	61	
1990-91	Lebeau	Patrick	W	2	1	1	2	0	
1982-83	Daoust	Dan	C	4	0	1	1	4	
2005-06	Ferland	Jonathan	W	7	1	0	1	2	
1994-96	Sarault	Yves	W	22	0	1	1	4	
1983-84	Baron	Normand	W	4	0	0	0	12	
2000-01	Bélanger	Francis	W	10	0	0	0	29	
2000-01	Bertrand	Éric	W	3	0	0	0	0	
1998-2003	Blouin	Sylvain	W	22	0	0	0	62	
1971-72	Comeau	Reynald	C	4	0	0	0	0	
1998-99	Delisle	Jonathan	W	1	0	0	0	0	
1993-95	Fleming	Gerry	W	11	0	0	0	42	
1971-72	Gagnon	Germain	W	4	0	0	0	0	
1998-99	Jomphe	Jean-François	C	6	0	0	0	0	
1994-95	Montgomery	Jim	C	5	0	0	0	2	
1998-2000	Morissette	Dave	W	11	0	0	0	57	

Defencemen									
Season	Surname	First name	P	GP	G	A	PTS	PIM	
1970-82	Lapointe	Guy	D	771	121	406	527	806	
1990-2009	Brisebois	Patrice	D	896	87	284	371	546	
1970-81	Savard	Serge	D	710	78	257	335	392	
1988-95	Desjardins	Éric	D	405	43	136	179	351	
1979-88	Gingras	Gaston	D	247	34	102	136	111	
1970-72	Tremblay	Jean-Claude	D	152	17	103	120	47	
1995-2004	Quintal	Stéphane	D	507	37	78	115	637	
1999-2009	Bouillon	Francis	D	481	21	81	102	369	
1989-96	Daigneault	Jean-Jacques	D	352	22	68	90	257	

1970-78	Bouchard	Pierre	D	489	16	66	82	379	
1970-74	Laperrière	Jacques	D	221	12	66	78	79	
1980-84	Picard	Robert	D	141	11	61	72	172	
2005-09	Dandenault	Mathieu	D	252	20	34	54	174	
1981-84	Delorme	Gilbert	D	165	17	36	53	152	
1999-2004	Dykhuis	Karl	D	288	21	32	53	152	
1989-92	Lefebvre	Sylvain	D	200	11	42	53	182	
1988-93	Dufresne	Donald	D	119	3	20	23	155	
1999-2002	Robidas	Stéphane	D	122	7	16	23	28	
2000-03	Traverse	Patrick	D	109	4	19	23	48	
1977-80	Lupien	Gilles	D	174	3	19	22	341	
1994-96	Racine	Yves	D	72	4	10	14	68	
1983-84	Hamel	Jean	D	79	1	12	13	92	
1990-92	Côté	Alain	D	41	0	9	9	48	
1999-2001	Laflamme	Christian	D	54	0	5	5	50	
1993-94	Proulx	Christian	D	7	1	2	3	20	
2000-01	Descoteaux	Mathieu	D	5	1	1	2	4	
1995-98	Groleau	François	D	8	0	1	1	6	
2002-03	Beauchemin	François	D	1	0	0	0	0	
1992-93	Charron	Éric	D	3	0	0	0	2	
2000-01	Ciccone	Enrico	D	3	0	0	0	14	
2005-06	Côté	Jean-Philippe	D	8	0	0	0	4	
1990-91	Gauthier	Luc	D	3	0	0	0	2	
1983-84	Gauvreau	Jocelyn	D	0	0	0	0	0	
1998-99	Nasreddine	Alain	D	8	0	0	0	33	

Goalies									
Season	Surname	First name	P	GP	W	L	T	AV.	%
1984-96	Roy	Patrick	G	551	289	175	82	2.78	
1995-2006	Théodore	José	G	353	141	158	54	2.62	.911
1973-81	Larocque	Michel	G	231	144	48	31	2.83	
1995-99	Thibault	Jocelyn	G	158	67	56	28	2.73	.908
1979-84	Sévigny	Richard	G	141	67	41	17	3.10	
1979-82	Herron	Denis	G	86	43	18	17	2.80	
1983-86	Penney	Steve	G	76	32	30	10	3.45	
1989-94	Racicot	André	G	68	26	23	9	3.50	.880
1970-72	Vachon	Rogatien	G	48	23	13	9	2.66	
2000-04	Garon	Mathieu	G	43	16	20	5	2.49	.914
1970-72	Myre	Philippe	G	39	17	16	4	3.21	
1972-74	Plasse	Michel	·G	32	18	6	5	3.29	
1990-91	Bergeron	Jean-Claude	G	18	7	6	2	3.76	.862
1990-99	Chabot	Frédéric	G	16	1	4	3	2.63	.899
1971-72	Dejordy	Denis	G	7	3	2	1	4.52	
2005-06	Danis	Yann	G	6	3	2	0	2.69	.908

➤

2000-01	Fichaud	Éric	G	2	0	2	0	3.89	.875
2001-02	Fiset	Stéphane	G	2	0	1	0	3.85	.883
1995-96	Labrecque	Patrick	G	2	0	1	0	4.29	.851
2008-09	Denis	Marc	G	1	0	0	0	3.00	.857
2001-02	Michaud	Olivier	G	1	0	0	0	0.00	1.00
1987-88	Riendeau	Vincent	G	1	0	0	0	8.24	.773

NASHVILLE PREDATORS 1998 to 2009				161 Players			16 QC		10%
Forwards									
Season	Surname	First name	P	GP	G	A	PTS	PIM	
2006-09	Dumont	J.-P.	W	244	66	137	203	82	
1998-2001	Bordeleau	Sébastien	C	146	28	40	68	70	
2005-06	Perreault	Yanic	C	69	22	35	57	30	
2007-08	Gélinas	Martin	W	57	9	11	20	20	
2006-07	Abid	Ramzi	W	13	1	4	5	13	
1998-2000	Côté	Patrick	W	91	1	2	3	312	
1999-2002	Gosselin	David	W	13	2	1	3	11	
2003-06	Gamache	Simon	C	18	1	0	1	0	
2003-04	Darche	Mathieu	W	2	0	0	0	0	
2001-02	Sarault	Yves	W	1	0	0	0	0	
Defencemen									
Season	Surname	First name	P	GP	G	A	PTS	PIM	
1998-2000	Bouchard	Joël	D	116	5	15	20	83	
1998-99	Daigneault	J.-Jacques	D	35	2	2	4	38	
2002-03	Bouillon	Francis	D	4	0	0	0	2	
2002-03	Trépanier	Pascal	D	1	0	0	0	0	
1998-99	Zettler	Rob	D	2	0	0	0	2	
Goalies									
Season	Surname	First name	P	GP	W	L	T	AV.	%
1998-99	Fichaud	Éric	G	9	0	6	0	3.22	.895

NEW JERSEY DEVILS 1982 to 2009				282 Players			18 QC		6.38%
Forwards									
Season	Surname	First name	P	GP	G	A	PTS	PIM	
1991-2002	Mckay	Randy	W	760	151	171	322	1418	
1990-2000	Lemieux	Claude	W	423	142	155	297	627	
1991-2002	Richer	Stéphane	W	360	147	136	283	125	
1989-93	Vilgrain	Claude	W	81	20	31	51	78	
1989-90	Turgeon	Sylvain	W	72	30	17	47	81	
1989-92	Brady	Neil	C	29	2	4	6	17	
2000-02	Dagenais	Pierre	W	25	6	5	11	10	

1996-2006	Rhéaume	Pascal	C	35	5	1	6	12	
1995-96	Lemieux	Jocelyn	W	18	0	1	1	4	
2008-09	Létourneau Leblond	Pierre-Luc	W	8	0	1	1	22	
1999-2000	Bertrand	Éric	W	4	0	0	0	0	

Defencemen

Season	Surname	First name	P	GP	G	A	PTS	PIM	
1985-90	Velishek	Randy	D	304	11	52	63	299	
1982-83	Vadnais	Carol	D	51	2	7	9	64	
2001-02	Bouchard	Joël	D	1	0	1	1	0	

Goalies

Season	Surname	First name	P	GP	W	L	T	AV.	%
1991-2009	Brodeur	Martin	G	999	557	299	150	2.21	.914
1987-89	Sauvé	Robert	G	49	14	21	5	3.88	.858
2001-02	Damphousse	Jean-François	G	6	1	3	0	2.45	0.896
1985-86	St-Laurent	Sam	G	4	2	1	0	4.15	

NEW YORK ISLANDERS 1972 to 2009				441 Players			33 QC		7.48%

Forwards

Season	Surname	First name	P	GP	G	A	PTS	PIM	
1977-87	Bossy	Michael	W	752	573	553	1126	210	
1991-95	Turgeon	Pierre	C	255	147	193	340	70	
1991-95	Hogue	Benoit	C	258	105	124	229	282	
1996-2003	Lapointe	Claude	C	535	76	95	171	354	
1974-78	Drouin	Jude	W	250	64	105	169	103	
1973-78	St-Laurent	André	C	261	38	66	104	191	
1972-74	Gagnon	Germain	W	125	20	43	63	39	
1997-2000	Odjick	Gino	W	82	9	13	22	254	
1977-78	Bergeron	Michel	W	25	9	6	15	2	
1997-99	Hough	Mike	W	85	5	7	12	29	
1989-90	Thibaudeau	Gilles	C	20	4	4	8	17	
2000-01	Martins	Steve	C	39	1	3	4	20	
1972-73	Grenier	Richard	C	10	1	1	2	2	
2007-09	Walter	Ben	C	12	1	0	1	0	
2000-01	Bélanger	Jesse	W	12	0	0	0	2	
1999-2000	Lacroix	Daniel	W	1	0	0	0	0	
1996-97	Vachon	Nicholas	W	1	0	0	0	0	

Defencemen

Season	Surname	First name	P	GP	G	A	PTS	PIM	
1973-88	Potvin	Denis	D	1060	310	742	1052	1356	
2005-09	Gervais	Bruno	D	207	6	39	45	103	
2006-08	Bergeron	Marc-André	D	69	15	24	39	26	
2000-01	Galley	Garry	D	56	6	14	20	59	

➤

1988-90	Bergevin	Marc	D	76	2	17	19	92	
1991-93	Marois	Mario	D	40	4	10	14	53	
1999-2001	Biron	Mathieu	D	74	4	5	9	50	
2005-06	Bouchard	Joël	D	25	1	8	9	23	
1997-98	Daigneault	J.-Jacques	D	18	0	6	6	21	
2002-03	Nasreddine	Alain	D	3	0	0	0	2	

Goalies

Season	Surname	First name	P	GP	W	L	T	AV.	%
1995-98	Fichaud	Éric	G	75	19	34	12	3.14	.899
1998-2000	Potvin	Félix	G	33	7	21	6	3.35	.892
2008-09	Danis	Yann	G	31	10	17	3	2.86	.910
1999-2000	Luongo	Roberto	G	24	7	14	1	3.25	.904
1998-99	Cousineau	Marcel	G	6	0	4	1	2.87	.882
1979-80	Brodeur	Richard	G	2	1	0	0	4.50	

NEW YORK RANGERS 1970 to 2009					555 Players		55 QC		9.91 %

Forwards

Season	Surname	First name	P	GP	G	A	PTS	PIM	
1970-78	Gilbert	Rodrigue	W	544	235	351	586	284	
1970-76	Ratelle	Jean	C	379	182	266	448	74	
1983-88	Larouche	Pierre	C	253	123	120	243	59	
1971-75	Rousseau	Bobby	W	236	41	116	157	30	
1977-89	Deblois	Lucien	W	326	57	79	136	297	
1995-97	Robitaille	Lucien	W	146	47	70	117	128	
1986-89	Dionne	Marcel	C	118	42	56	98	50	
1986-87	Mckegney	Tony	W	64	29	17	46	56	
1988-89	Lafleur	Guy	W	67	18	27	45	12	
1980-82	Gillis	Jere	W	61	13	19	32	20	
1993-96	Matteau	Stéphane	W	11	10	21	31	49	
1978-79	Plante	Pierre	W	70	6	25	31	37	
1999-2000	Daigle	Alexandre	C	58	8	18	26	23	
1998-2001	Lacroix	Éric	W	146	8	12	20	67	
1996-2000	Goneau	Daniel	W	53	12	3	15	14	
1979-82	Larose	Claude	W	25	4	7	11	2	
1995-97	Momesso	Sergio	W	28	4	4	8	41	
1971-72	Jarry	Pierre	W	34	3	3	6	20	
1997-2000	Stock	P.-J.	W	54	2	4	6	131	
1971-72	Goyette	Philippe	C	8	1	4	5	0	
1993-96	Lacroix	Daniel	W	30	2	2	4	30	
1995-96	Laperrière	Ian	W	28	1	2	3	53	
1996-99	Dubé	Christian	C	33	1	1	2	4	
2006-07	Dupuis	Pascal	W	6	1	0	1	0	
1971-72	Gratton	Normand	W	3	0	1	1	0	

1994-95	Roy	Jean-Yves	W	3	1	0	1	2	
1974-75	Monahan	Hartland	W	6	0	1	1	4	
1996-98	Blouin	Sylvain	W	7	0	0	0	23	
1977-78	Gosselin	Benoit	W	7	0	0	0	33	
1973-74	Lemieux	Réal	W	7	0	0	0	0	
1997-98	Sévigny	Pierre	W	3	0	0	0	2	
2003-04	Dusablon	Benoit	C	3	0	0	0	2	
2005-06	Giroux	Alexandre	C	1	0	0	0	0	
1995-96	Larouche	Steve	C	1	0	0	0	0	
2003-04	Rhéaume	Pascal	C	17	0	0	0	5	
1975-78	Holst	Greg	C	11	0	0	0	0	

Defencemen

Season	Surname	First name	P	GP	G	A	PTS	PIM	
1975-82	Vadnais	Carol	D	485	56	190	246	690	
1973-76	Marotte	Gilles	D	180	10	66	76	131	
1977-81	Marois	Mario	D	166	15	52	67	356	
1987-89	Petit	Michel	D	133	17	49	66	377	
1987-93	Hardy	Mark	D	284	7	52	59	409	
1978-85	Doré	André	D	139	8	38	46	153	
1972-76	Harris	Ron	D	146	6	30	36	64	
1999-2003	Lefebvre	Sylvain	D	229	4	30	34	131	
1988-92	Rochefort	Normand	D	112	7	15	22	108	
2002-04	Bouchard	Joël	D	55	6	14	20	24	
1999-2000	Quintal	Stéphane	D	75	2	14	16	77	
1979-80	Guèvremont	Jocelyn	D	20	2	5	7	6	
1970-71	Dupont	André	D	7	1	2	3	21	
1988-89	Brochu	Stéphane	D	1	0	0	0	0	

Goalies

Season	Surname	First name	P	GP	W	L	T	AV.	%
1970-75	Villemure	Gilles	G	171	95	48	19	2.27	
2001-03	Blackburn	Dan	G	63	20	32	6	3.22	.894
1976-77	Gratton	Gilles	G	41	11	18	7	4.22	
1997-99	Cloutier	Dan	G	34	10	13	4	2.62	.912
1999-2000	Labbé	Jean-François	G	1	0	1	0	3.00	.864

OAKLAND SEALS 1970 to 1976				102 Players			8 QC		7.84%

Forwards

Season	Surname	First name	P	GP	G	A	PTS	PIM	
1975-76	Girard	Bob	W	80	16	26	42	54	
1970-71	Hardy	Joe	C	40	4	10	14	31	
1973-74	Monahan	Hartland	W	1	0	0	0	0	

➤

Defencemen

Season	Surname	First name	P	GP	G	A	PTS	PIM	
1970-72	Vadnais	Carol	D	94	24	36	60	197	
1972-75	Murray	Terry	D	90	0	17	17	60	

Goalies

Season	Surname	First name	P	GP	W	L	T	AV.	%
1971-76	Meloche	Gilles	G	250	58	140	48	3.83	
1973-74	Champoux	Bob	G	17	2	11	3	5.20	

OTTAWA SENATORS 1992 to 2009				257 Players			30 QC		11.67%

Forwards

Season	Surname	First name	P	GP	G	A	PTS	PIM	
1993-98	Daigle	Alexandre	W	301	74	98	172	119	
2003-09	Vermette	Antoine	C	359	80	87	167	205	
1992-95	Turgeon	Sylvain	W	152	47	41	88	185	
1999-2000	Juneau	Joé	C	65	13	24	37	22	
1999-2002	Roy	André	W	193	13	16	29	462	
1994-96	Picard	Michel	W	41	7	14	21	24	
1998-2006	Martins	Steve	C	70	9	7	16	24	
1994-95	Larouche	Steve	C	18	8	7	15	6	
1999-2000	Dineen	Kevin	W	67	4	8	12	57	
2001-02	Brunet	Benoit	W	13	5	3	8	0	
2003-07	Hamel	Denis	W	52	5	3	8	10	
2007-08	Lapointe	Martin	W	18	3	3	6	23	
1996-97	Chassé	Denis	W	22	1	4	5	19	
1998-2000	Sarault	Yves	W	22	0	3	3	11	
1993-95	Boivin	Claude	W	18	1	1	2	44	
1995-96	Roy	Jean-Yves	W	4	1	1	2	2	
2000-01	Lacroix	Éric	W	9	0	1	1	4	
1992-93	Fortier	Marc	C	10	0	1	1	6	
1994-95	Guérard	Daniel	W	2	0	0	0	0	
1992-93	St-Amour	Martin	W	1	0	0	0	2	

Defencemen

Season	Surname	First name	P	GP	G	A	PTS	PIM	
1995-97	Duchesne	Steve	D	140	31	52	83	80	
1995-2000	Traverse	Patrick	D	117	7	26	33	45	
2008-09	Picard	Alexandre	D	47	6	8	14	8	
1994-96	Laperrière	Daniel	D	19	1	1	2	4	
1992-93	Lavoie	Dominic	D	2	0	1	1	0	
1993-94	Leroux	François	D	23	0	1	1	70	
1999-2000	Dollas	Bobby	D	1	0	0	0	0	

Goalies										
Season	Surname	First name	P	GP	W	L	T	AV.	%
1999-2004	Lalime	Patrick	G	283	146	100	46	2.32	.908
1992-94	Berthiaume	Daniel	G	26	2	17	3	4.39	.869
2001-02	Lajeunesse	Simon	G	1	0	0	0	0.00	1.000

PHILADELPHIA FLYERS 1970 to 2009					491 Players		64 QC		13.03%
Forwards									
Season	Surname	First name	P	GP	G	A	PTS	PIM
1999-09	Gagné	Simon	W	606	242	242	484	231
1985-91	Mellanby	Scott	W	355	83	114	197	694
1991-96	Dineen	Kevin	W	284	88	88	176	533
1970-74	Nolet	Simon	W	263	67	76	143	83
1971-75	Clément	Bill	C	229	53	52	105	166
2007-09	Brière	Daniel	C	108	42	55	97	94
1970-72	Bernier	Serge	W	121	35	39	74	138
2001-06	Brashear	Donald	W	270	22	44	66	648
1970-72	Gendron	Jean-Guy	W	132	26	29	55	82
1970-71	Lacroix	André	C	78	20	22	42	12
1989-91	Lacombe	Normand	W	92	11	22	33	34
1997-99	Daigle	Alexandre	W	68	12	19	31	8
1998-2004	White	Peter	C	104	10	21	31	24
1991-94	Boivin	Claude	W	114	11	18	29	320
1992-94	Faust	André	W	47	10	7	17	14
1998-2000	Bureau	Marc	W	125	6	8	14	20
1971-72	Parizeau	Michel	W	37	2	12	14	10
1996-98	Lacroix	Daniel	W	130	8	5	13	298
2002-04	Lapointe	Claude	C	56	7	5	12	48
2002-06	Chouinard	Éric	C	46	7	4	11	10
1978-81	Preston	Yves	W	28	7	3	10	4
1991-93	Kasper	Steve	W	37	4	5	9	12
1999-2001	Odjick	Gino	W	30	4	4	8	38
1994-96	Dionne	Gilbert	W	22	0	7	7	2
1971-72	Sarrazin	Dick	W	28	3	4	7	4
2000-01	Picard	Michel	W	7	1	4	5	0
1971-73	Plante	Pierre	W	26	1	3	4	15
2000-01	Stock	P.-J.	W	31	1	3	4	78
2006-07	Meloche	Éric	W	13	1	2	3	4
1991-96	Dupré	Yanick	W	35	2	0	2	16
1974-75	Sirois	Bob	W	4	1	0	1	4
1974-75	Boland	Mike	W	2	0	0	0	0
1971-72	Drolet	René	W	1	0	0	0	0

➤

1986-87	Gillis	Jerry	W	1	0	0	0	0	
2006-07	Hamel	Denis	W	7	0	0	0	0	
2001-03	Lefebvre	Guillaume	W	17	0	0	0	4	
1976-77	Ritchie	Robert	W	1	0	0	0	0	
1993-94	Vilgrain	Claude	W	2	0	0	0	0	

Defencemen

Season	Surname	First name	P	GP	G	A	PTS	PIM	
1994-06	Desjardins	Éric	D	738	93	303	396	406	
1972-80	Dupont	André	D	549	42	135	177	1505	
1991-95	Galley	Garry	D	236	28	144	172	260	
1991-99	Duchesne	Steve	D	89	20	43	63	88	
1994-2000	Dykhuis	Karl	D	227	13	41	54	211	
1993-94	Racine	Yves	D	67	9	43	52	48	
1975-81	Murray	Terry	D	115	1	30	31	69	
1986-88	Daigneault	Jean-Jacques	D	105	8	18	26	68	
2005-08	Picard	Alexandre	D	72	3	19	22	23	
1993-95	Zettler	Rob	D	65	0	5	5	103	
2005-07	Gauthier	Denis	D	60	0	4	4	82	
1996-97	Petit	Michel	D	20	0	3	3	51	
2006-07	Grenier	Martin	D	3	0	0	0	0	
1973-75	Lajeunesse	Serge	D	6	0	0	0	2	
2001-03	St-Jacques	Bruno	D	13	0	0	0	4	

Goalies

Season	Surname	First name	P	GP	W	L	T	AV.	%
1970-79	Parent	Bernard	G	328	225	129	80	2.45	
1991-96	Roussel	Dominic	G	139	62	49	21	3.18	.895
2006-09	Biron	Martin	G	133	65	47	16	2.71	.915
1979-81	Myre	Philippe	G	57	24	12	19	3.71	
1972-73	Belhumeur	Michel	G	23	9	7	3	3.22	
1992-93	Beauregard	Stéphane	G	16	3	9	0	4.41	.854
1993-94	Chabot	Frédéric	G	4	0	1	2	4.26	.875
1982-83	Larocque	Michel	G	2	0	1	1	4.00	
2000-01	Ouellet	Maxime	G	2	0	1	0	2.38	.889
2006-07	Houle	Martin	G	1	0	0	0	27.27	.667
1998-99	Pelletier	Jean-Marc	G	1	0	1	0	5.00	.828

PHOENIX COYOTES 1996 to 2009					230 Players			22 QC	9.57%

Forwards

Season	Surname	First name	P	GP	G	A	PTS	PIM	
1997-2003	Brière	Daniel	C	258	70	76	146	146	
2000-03	Lemieux	Claude	W	164	32	49	81	158	
2000-01	Juneau	Joé	C	69	10	23	33	28	
2006-07	Perreault	Yanic	C	49	19	14	33	30	

2006-07	Laraque	Georges	W	56	5	17	22	52	
2005-09	Perrault	Joël	C	76	11	14	25	68	
2002-03	Abid	Ramzi	W	30	10	8	18	30	
1999-2000	Hogue	Benoit	C	27	3	10	13	10	
1996-98	Lemieux	Jocelyn	W	32	4	3	7	27	
2005-07	Lehoux	Yanick	C	10	2	2	4	6	
2001-02	Bordeleau	Sébastien	C	6	0	0	0	0	
1998-99	Jomphe	Jean-François	C	1	0	0	0	2	
2005-06	Rhéaume	Pascal	C	1	0	0	0	0	

Defencemen

Season	Surname	First name	P	GP	G	A	PTS	PIM	
1998-2000	Daigneault	J.-Jacques	D	88	1	13	14	54	
2005-06	Gauthier	Denis	D	45	2	9	11	61	
1997-98	Petit	Michel	D	32	4	2	6	77	
2000-01	Bouchard	Joé	D	32	1	2	3	22	
1997-99	Doig	Jason	D	13	0	2	2	22	
2001-03	Grenier	Martin	D	8	0	0	0	5	

Goalies

Season	Surname	First name	P	GP	W	L	T	AV.	%
1997-99	Waite	Jimmy	G	33	11	11	5	2.45	.903
2002-04	Pelletier	Jean-Marc	G	6	1	3	1	3.68	.864
2005-06	Sauvé	Philippe	G	5	1	5	1	5.46	.867
2008-09	Torsman	Josh	G	2	0	2	0	4.08	.871

| PITTSBURGH PENGUINS 1970 to 2009 | | | | 526 Players | | 62 QC | | 11.79% | |

Forwards

Season	Surname	First name	P	GP	G	A	PTS	PIM	
1984-2006	Lemieux	Mario	C	915	690	1033	1723	834	
1970-78	Pronovost	Jean	W	605	280	241	521	220	
1983-93	Erry	Bob	W	572	132	140	272	651	
1974-78	Larouche	Pierre	C	240	119	134	253	99	
2005-07	Ouellet	Michel	W	123	35	45	80	46	
2005-09	Talbot	Maxime	W	261	42	38	80	228	
1994-95	Robitaille	Luc	W	46	23	19	42	37	
2007-09	Dupuis	Pascal	W	87	14	26	40	38	
1981-84	St-Laurent	André	C	96	23	14	37	130	
2001-02	Richer	Stéphane	W	58	13	12	25	14	
1981-83	Simpson	Bobby	W	30	10	9	19	4	
1999-2001	Corbet	René	W	47	9	9	18	57	
1971-72	Robert	René	W	49	7	11	18	42	
2001-04	Meloche	Éric	W	61	8	9	17	32	
1975-76	Nolet	Simon	W	39	9	8	17	2	

➤

2006-08	Laraque	Georges	W	88	4	11	15	159	
1975-79	Cossette	Jacques	W	64	8	6	14	29	
2002-03	Daigle	Alexandre	C	33	4	3	7	8	
2002-06	Lefebvre	Guillaume	W	21	2	4	6	9	
2002-04	Abid	Ramzi	W	19	3	2	5	29	
1970-73	Burns	Robin	W	41	0	5	5	32	
2005-07	Roy	André	W	47	2	1	3	128	
1977-78	Monahan	Hartland	W	7	2	0	2	2	
1998-99	Lebeau	Patrick	W	8	1	0	1	2	
1974-77	Bergeron	Yves	W	3	0	0	0	0	
1987-88	Mann	Jimmy	W	9	0	0	0	53	
1986-87	Lemieux	Alain	C	1	0	0	0	0	

Defencemen

Season	Surname	First name	P	GP	G	A	PTS	PIM	
1974-82	Faubert	Mario	D	231	21	90	111	222	
2006-09	Letang	Kristopher	D	144	18	34	52	51	
1978-80	Tallon	Dale	D	95	10	33	43	53	
1995-97	Daigneault	J.-Jacques	D	66	6	17	23	59	
1970-75	Lagacé	Jean-Guy	D	89	4	19	23	105	
2000-04	Bergevin	Marc	D	157	4	17	21	89	
1994-97	Leroux	François	D	165	2	14	16	356	
1989-90	Delorme	Gilbert	D	54	3	7	10	44	
1998-2001	Dollas	Bobby	D	75	2	8	10	64	
2003-04	Boileau	Patrick	D	16	3	4	7	8	
2008-09	Boucher	Philippe	D	25	3	3	6	24	
1982-83	Meighan	Ron	D	41	2	6	8	16	
2005-08	Nasreddine	Alain	D	56	1	4	5	30	
1984-85	Weir	Wally	D	14	0	3	3	34	
2002-03	Bouchard	Joël	D	7	0	1	1	0	
1991-93	Chychrun	Jeff	D	18	0	1	1	37	
1980-81	Lupien	Gilles	D	31	0	1	1	34	
1982-83	Turnbull	Ian	D	6	0	0	0	4	

Goalies

Season	Surname	First name	P	GP	W	L	T	AV.	%
1972-86	Herron	Denis	G	290	88	133	44	3.88	
2003-09	Fleury	Marc-André	G	235	111	85	28	2.87	.907
1998-2004	Aubin	J.-Sébastien	G	168	63	72	21	2.92	.901
1981-85	Dion	Michel	G	151	42	79	20	4.28	
1982-94	Romano	Roberto	G	125	42	62	8	3.96	
1985-88	Meloche	Gilles	G	104	34	43	18	3.65	
2002-06	Caron	Sébastien	G	90	24	47	14	3.49	.892
1974-76	Plasse	Michel	G	75	33	24	14	3.59	
1979-81	Holland	Robbie	G	44	11	22	9	4.08	
2005-09	Sabourin	Dany	G	44	16	18	3	2.88	.899

1996-97	Lalime	Patrick	G	39	21	12	4	2.95	.913
2005-07	Thibault	Jocelyn	G	38	8	17	5	3.52	.894
1975-79	Laxton	Gord	G	17	4	9	0	5.55	
2008-09	Garon	Mathieu	G	4	2	1	0	2.91	.894
1983-84	Tremblay	Vincent	G	4	0	4	0	6.00	
1994-97	Derouville	Philippe	G	3	1	2	0	3.16	.903
2003-04	Brochu	Martin	G	1	0	0	0	1.84	.947
2000-01	Parent	Rich	G	7	1	1	3	3.08	.887

QUÉBEC NORDIQUES 1979 À 1995				245 Players			75 QC		30.61%
Forwards									
Season	Surname	First name	P	GP	G	A	PTS	PIM	
1979-90	Goulet	Michel	W	813	456	489	945	613	
1979-89	Côté	Alain	W	696	103	190	293	383	
1979-83	Cloutier	Réal	W	236	122	162	284	94	
1979-83	Tardif	Marc	W	272	116	128	244	154	
1979-83	Richard	Jacques	W	186	79	103	182	126	
1984-93	Hough	Mike	W	363	68	97	165	461	
1983-91	Mckegney	Tony	C	203	69	63	132	124	
1983-87	Sauvé	Jean-François	C	192	41	89	130	47	
1990-95	Lapointe	Claude	C	253	40	73	113	299	
1987-92	Fortier	Marc	C	196	42	59	101	124	
1987-89	Duchesne	Gaétan	W	150	32	44	76	139	
1983-85	Savard	André	C	95	29	34	63	46	
1989-91	Lafleur	Guy	W	98	24	38	62	6	
1979-85	Sleigher	Louis	W	111	30	32	62	81	
1979-81	Leduc	Richard	C	97	24	34	58	55	
1987-88	Haworth	Alan	W	72	23	34	57	112	
1989-92	Morin	Stéphane	C	84	15	37	52	46	
1980-84	Aubry	Pierre	W	163	18	23	41	92	
1979-81	Bernier	Serge	W	78	10	22	32	49	
1984-86	Lemieux	Alain	C	37	11	11	22	14	
1989-91	Deblois	Lucien	W	84	11	10	21	58	
1979-80	Plante	Pierre	W	69	4	14	18	68	
1993-94	Gélinas	Martin	W	31	6	6	12	8	
1983-86	Mann	Jimmy	W	82	1	8	9	244	
1979-83	David	Richard	W	31	4	4	8	10	
1979-80	Smrke	John	W	30	3	5	8	2	
1993-94	Savage	Réginald	C	17	3	4	7	16	
1993-95	Corbet	René	W	17	1	4	5	2	
1989-91	Dore	Daniel	W	17	2	3	5	59	
1984-85	Dufour	Luc	W	30	2	3	5	27	

➤

Season	Surname	First name	P	GP	G	A	PTS	PIM	
1979-80	Cloutier	Roland	C	14	2	3	5	0	
1981-82	Gillis	Jere	W	12	2	1	3	0	
1989-91	Vincelette	Daniel	W	27	0	2	2	63	
1979-80	Bilodeau	Gilles	W	9	0	1	1	25	
1988-89	Baillargeon	Joël	W	5	0	0	0	4	
1991-92	Charbonneau	Stéphane	W	2	0	0	0	0	
1986-87	Héroux	Yves	W	1	0	0	0	0	
1988-89	Mailhot	Jacques	W	5	0	0	0	33	
1990-91	Roberge	Serge	W	9	0	0	0	24	
1989-90	Routhier	Jean-Marc	W	8	0	0	0	9	
1981-82	Tanguay	Christian	W	2	0	0	0	0	

Defencemen

Season	Surname	First name	P	GP	G	A	PTS	PIM	
1980-90	Marois	Mario	D	403	38	162	200	778	
1980-88	Rochefort	Normand	D	480	32	104	136	452	
1985-90	Picard	Robert	D	289	25	79	104	299	
1985-95	Finn	Steven	D	605	29	73	102	1514	
1979-83	Lacroix	Pierre	D	218	18	82	100	179	
1992-93	Duchesne	Steve	D	82	20	62	82	57	
1979-84	Weir	Wally	D	272	19	39	58	535	
1989-91	Petit	Michel	D	82	16	31	47	262	
1980-83	Dupont	André	D	169	12	32	44	262	
1985-87	Delorme	Gilbert	D	83	4	18	22	65	
1983-89	Donnelly	Gord	D	213	10	12	22	668	
1983-84	Doré	André	D	25	1	16	17	25	
1981-83	Hamel	Jean	D	91	3	13	16	70	
1990-91	Anderson	Shawn	D	31	3	10	13	21	
1994-95	Lefebvre	Sylvain	D	48	2	11	13	17	
1980-83	Therrien	Gaston	D	22	0	8	8	12	
1982-86	Gaulin	Jean-Marc	D	26	4	3	7	8	
1985-88	Poudrier	Daniel	D	25	1	5	6	10	
1989-91	Doyon	Mario	D	21	2	3	5	10	
1987-89	Dollas	Bobby	D	25	0	3	3	18	
1987-90	Richard	Jean-Marc	D	5	2	1	3	2	
1981-83	Bolduc	Michel	D	10	0	0	0	6	
1993-94	Côté	Alain	D	6	0	0	0	4	
1987-90	Guérard	Stéphane	D	34	0	0	0	40	
1979-80	Lacombe	François	D	3	0	0	0	2	

Goalies

Season	Surname	First name	P	GP	W	L	T	AV.	%
1980-85	Bouchard	Daniel	G	225	107	79	36	3.59	
1983-89	Gosselin	Mario	G	193	79	83	12	3.67	
1989-95	Fiset	Stéphane	G	151	62	61	15	3.42	.891
1979-81	Dion	Michel	G	62	15	33	9	4.02	

1990-94	Cloutier	Jacques	G	58	12	26	7	3.92	.881
1993-95	Thibault	Jocelyn	G	47	20	15	5	2.95	.901
1980-82	Plasse	Michel	G	41	12	17	10	3.96	
1987-90	Brunetta	Mario	G	40	12	17	1	3.92	.871
1984-87	Sévigny	Richard	G	35	13	13	3	3.71	

SAN JOSE SHARKS 1991 to 2009					236 Players		17 QC		7.20%
Forwards									
Season	Surname	First name	P	GP	G	A	PTS	PIM	
1998-2004	Damphousse	Vincent	C	385	92	197	289	316	
2005-08	Bernier	Steve	W	160	42	39	81	126	
1993-97	Errey	Bob	W	107	17	26	43	173	
1993-95	Duchesne	Gaétan	W	117	14	25	39	44	
1998-2000	Stern	Ronnie	W	145	11	14	25	309	
1991-93	Courtenay	Ed	W	44	7	13	20	10	
2007-08	Mitchell	Torrey	C	82	10	10	20	50	
1991-93	Quintin	Jean-François	W	22	5	5	10	4	
2000-01	Montgomery	Jim	C	28	1	6	7	19	
1992-93	Picard	Michel	W	25	4	0	4	24	
2008-09	Lemieux	Claude	W	18	0	1	1	21	
2006-07	Darche	Mathieu	W	2	0	0	0	0	
Defencemen									
Season	Surname	First name	P	GP	G	A	PTS	PIM	
1997-2002	Matteau	Stéphane	D	345	55	64	119	241	
2006-09	Vlasic	M.-Édouard	D	245	11	65	76	84	
1991-94	Zettler	Rob	D	196	1	18	19	351	
1995-96	Racine	Yves	D	32	1	16	17	28	
2000-01	Dollas	Bobby	D	16	1	1	2	14	

ST. LOUIS BLUES 1970 to 2009					548 Players		63 QC		11.50%
Forwards									
Season	Surname	First name	P	GP	G	A	PTS	PIM	
1996-2001	Turgeon	Pierre	C	327	134	221	355	117	
1972-77	Plante	Pierre	W	357	104	112	216	420	
2000-04	Mellanby	Scott	W	235	62	75	137	370	
1987-89	Mckegney	Tony	W	151	65	55	120	140	
1988-97	Momesso	Sergio	W	222	44	70	114	506	
2007-09	Perron	David	C	143	28	49	77	88	
1970-72	Bordeleau	Christian	C	119	29	41	70	54	
1981-85	Lemieux	Alain	C	81	17	33	50	24	
1997-2004	Rhéaume	Pascal	C	148	19	31	50	74	

➤

1983-84	Chouinard	Guy	C	64	12	34	46	10	
1993-96	Laperrière	Ian	W	71	16	20	36	172	
1997-99	Picard	Michel	W	61	12	19	31	45	
1999-2000	Richer	Stéphane	W	36	8	17	25	14	
2000-03	Corso	Daniel	C	70	14	10	24	20	
1979-81	Monahan	Hartland	W	97	9	14	23	40	
1989-92	Mongeau	Michel	C	50	5	18	23	8	
1993-96	Chassé	Denis	W	92	10	10	20	256	
1993-94	Montgomery	Jim	C	67	6	14	20	44	
1986-88	Lemieux	Jocelyn	W	76	11	8	19	136	
1994-95	Carbonneau	Guy	C	42	5	11	16	16	
1994-96	Tardif	Patrice	C	50	6	10	16	41	
1984-86	Cyr	Denis	W	40	8	7	15	2	
1974-75	Dupéré	Denis	W	22	3	6	9	8	
2007-09	Stastny	Yan	C	46	4	5	9	29	
2005-06	Gamache	Simon	W	15	3	4	7	10	
1979-80	Simpson	Bobby	W	18	2	2	4	0	
1984-85	Dufour	Luc	C	23	1	3	4	18	
1971-72	Parizeau	Michel	W	21	1	2	3	8	
1985-86	Baron	Normand	W	23	2	0	2	39	
2006-07	Perreault	Joël	C	11	0	0	0	0	

Defencemen									
Season	Surname	First name	P	GP	G	A	PTS	PIM	
1993-98	Duchesne	Steve	D	163	38	87	125	82	
1995-97	Matteau	Stéphane	D	120	23	33	56	115	
1987-89	Gingras	Gaston	D	120	10	32	42	24	
1981-83	Lapointe	Guy	D	72	3	29	32	47	
1996-2002	Bergevin	Marc	D	328	5	23	28	319	
1971-73	Dupont	André	D	85	4	16	20	198	
1983-85	Delorme	Gilbert	D	118	2	17	19	94	
1970-73	Picard	Noël	D	106	5	13	18	179	
1990-92	Marois	Mario	D	81	.2	15	17	119	
1991-93	Quintal	Stéphane	D	101	1	16	17	132	
2001-04	Laflamme	Christian	D	71	0	11	11	69	
1972-74	Hamel	Jean	D	78	3	8	11	30	
1981-83	Vigneault	Alain	D	42	2	5	7	82	
1976-77	Marotte	Gilles	D	47	3	4	7	26	
2002-04	Martins	Steve	D	53	4	3	7	40	
1988-92	Lavoie	Dominic	D	26	2	4	6	28	
1992-95	Laperrière	Daniel	D	29	1	4	5	23	
1995-96	Daigneault	J.-Jacques	D	37	1	3	4	24	
1994-96	Dufresne	Donald	D	25	0	3	3	14	
1989-90	Plavsic	Adrien	D	4	0	1	1	2	

1970-71	Talbot	Jean-Guy	D	5	0	0	0	6	
2003-04	Pollock	James	D	9	0	0	0	6	
1972-73	Lafrenière	Roger	D	10	0	0	0	0	

Goalies

Season	Surname	First name	P	GP	W	L	T	AV.	%
1988-92	Riendeau	Vincent	G	122	58	45	20	3.34	.883
1974-78	Johnston	Eddie	G	118	41	52	20	3.36	
1977-79	Myre	Philippe	G	83	20	47	16	3.96	
1971-73	Caron	Jacques	G	58	22	22	10	3.02	
1974-78	Bélanger	Yves	G	48	19	23	3	3.66	
2005-06	Lalime	Patrick	G	31	4	18	16	3.64	.881
1993-94	Hrivnac	Jim	G	23	4	10	0	4.27	.877
1997-99	Parent	Rich	G	11	4	3	2	2.49	.887
1975-76	Gratton	Gilles	G	6	2	0	2	2.49	
1983-84	Larocque	Michel	G	5	0	5	0	6.20	
1970-71	Plasse	Michel	G	1	1	0	0	3.00	

TAMPA BAY LIGHTNING 1992 to 2009				288 Players			39 QC		13.54%

Forwards

Season	Surname	First name	P	GP	G	A	PTS	PIM	
1998-2009	Lecavalier	Vincent	C	787	302	367	669	561	
2000-09	St-Louis	Martin	W	621	234	331	565	194	
1997-2000	Richer	Stéphane	W	110	28	37	65	62	
1993-95	Savard	Denis	C	105	24	39	63	116	
1992-95	Bureau	Marc	W	186	20	40	60	171	
2007-08	Ouellet	Michel	W	64	17	19	36	12	
2003-07	Perrin	Éric	C	86	13	23	36	30	
1995-98	Poulin	Patrick	C	125	14	22	36	75	
2001-08	Roy	André	W	218	17	14	31	484	
1998-99	Hogue	Benoit	C	62	11	14	25	50	
2007-08	Darche	Mathieu	W	73	7	15	22	20	
1992-93	Maltais	Steve	W	63	7	13	20	35	
1999-2001	Martins	Steve	C	77	6	8	14	50	
1998-99	Daigle	Alexandre	W	32	6	6	12	2	
1992-93	Kasper	Steve	C	47	3	4	7	18	
1996-98	Brousseau	Paul	W	17	0	2	2	27	
2007-08	Lessard	Junior	W	19	1	1	2	9	
1992-93	Mongeau	Michel	C	4	1	1	2	2	
2001-02	Royer	Gaétan	W	3	0	0	0	2	
1992-93	Simard	Martin	W	7	0	0	0	11	
1998-99	Delisle	Xavier	C	2	0	0	0	0	

➤

Defencemen

Season	Surname	First name	P	GP	G	A	PTS	PIM	
1992-2003	Bergevin	Marc	D	206	5	31	36	204	
1997-99	Dykhuis	Karl	D	111	7	10	17	128	
1993-99	Ciccone	Enrico	D	135	5	9	14	604	
1995-96	Petit	Michel	D	45	4	7	11	108	
1993-94	Dufresne	Donald	D	51	2	6	8	48	
1997-98	Racine	Yves	D	60	0	8	8	41	
2007-08	Picard	Alexandre	D	20	3	3	6	8	
1993-96	Charron	Éric	D	63	1	4	5	46	
1992-93	Côté	Alain	D	2	0	0	0	0	
1995-96	Finn	Steven	D	16	0	0	0	24	
1998-99	Larocque	Mario	D	5	0	0	0	16	
1992-93	Richer	Stéphane	D	3	0	0	0	0	
1993-94	Rochefort	Normand	D	6	0	0	0	10	

Goalies

Season	Surname	First name	P	GP	W	L	T	AV.	%
1999-2001	Cloutier	Daniel	G	76	12	43	16	3.50	.887
2006-08	Denis	Marc	G	54	18	23	2	3.32	.879
1992-96	Bergeron	Jean-Claude	G	53	14	26	5	3.65	.867
1996-99	Wilkinson	Derek	G	22	3	12	4	3.67	.874
1999-2000	Parent	Rich	G	14	2	7	2	3.70	.878

TORONTO MAPLE LEAFS 1970 to 2009				498 Players			45 QC		9.04%

Forwards

Season	Surname	First name	P	GP	G	A	PTS	PIM	
1986-91	Damphousse	Vincent	C	394	118	211	329	262	
1970-75	Keon	Dave	C	376	134	175	309	21	
1982-90	Daoust	Dan	C	518	87	166	253	540	
1987-92	Marois	Daniel	W	285	106	80	186	346	
1993-2007	Perreault	Yanic	C	176	54	69	123	90	
1970-74	Dupéré	Denis	W	192	29	44	73	26	
1971-74	Jarry	Pierre	W	104	24	30	54	65	
1970-82	Robert	René	W	74	19	31	50	45	
1970-72	Trottier	Guy	W	113	28	17	45	37	
1994-96	Hogue	Benoit	C	56	15	28	43	68	
1990-92	Deblois	Lucien	W	92	18	23	41	69	
1975-77	Garland	Scott	W	85	13	23	36	91	
1981-83	Aubin	Norm	C	69	18	13	31	30	
1989-91	Thibaudeau	Gilles	C	41	9	18	27	17	
1991-94	Larose	Guy	C	53	10	7	17	45	
1995-96	Momesso	Sergio	W	54	7	8	15	112	

1987-90	Mckenna	Sean	W	48	5	6	11	32	
2007-08	Gamache	Simon	W	11	2	2	4	6	
1982-83	Boisvert	Serge	W	17	0	2	2	4	
1977-78	Bélanger	Alain	W	9	0	1	1	6	
1993-94	Lacroix	Éric	W	3	0	0	0	2	
1986-87	James	Val	W	4	0	0	0	14	
1995-96	White	Peter	C	1	0	0	0	0	

Defencemen

Season	Surname	First name	P	GP	G	A	PTS	PIM	
1973-82	Turnbull	Ian	D	580	112	302	414	651	
1982-85	Gingras	Gaston	D	109	17	40	57	26	
1990-92	Petit	Michel	D	88	10	32	42	217	
1997-2000	Côté	Sylvain	D	94	8	31	39	34	
1992-94	Lefebvre	Sylvain	D	164	4	21	25	169	
1980-81	Picard	Robert	D	59	6	19	25	68	
1995-98	Zettler	Rob	D	136	2	20	22	207	
1996-99	Tremblay	Yannick	D	78	4	11	15	22	
1979-80	Mulhern	Richard	D	26	0	10	10	11	
1979-80	Carriere	Larry	D	2	0	1	1	0	
1976-77	Mackasey	Blair	D	1	0	0	0	2	

Goalies

Season	Surname	First name	P	GP	W	L	T	AV.	%
1991-99	Potvin	Félix	G	369	160	149	53	2.87	.908
1970-73	Plante	Jacques	G	106	48	38	15	2.46	
1972-78	Mcrae	Gord	G	71	30	22	10	3.49	
1980-83	Larocque	Michel	G	74	16	35	13	4.79	
1970-72	Parent	Bernard	G	65	24	25	12	2.59	
1979-83	Tremblay	Vincent	G	54	12	22	8	4.59	
2005-07	Aubin	J.-Sébastien	G	31	12	5	4	2.88	.899
1973-74	Johnston	Ed	G	26	12	9	4	3.09	
1996-98	Cousineau	Marcel	G	15	3	5	1	3.19	.905
1974-79	Hamel	Pierre	G	5	1	2	0	5.51	
2001-02	Centomo	Sébastien	G	1	0	0	0	4.50	.750

VANCOUVER CANUCKS
1970 to 2009

| | | | | 473 Players | | | 44 QC | | 9.30% |

Forwards

Season	Surname	First name	P	GP	G	A	PTS	PIM	
1970-76	Boudrias	André	W	458	121	267	388	140	
1971-77	Lalonde	Bobby	C	353	72	117	189	185	
1993-98	Gélinas	Martin	W	258	90	81	171	173	
1990-95	Momesso	Sergio	W	269	68	73	141	655	
1977-85	Gillis	Jere	W	309	63	75	138	210	

➤

Season	Surname	First name	P	GP	G	A	PTS	PIM	
1996-2002	Brashear	Donald	W	388	50	53	103	1159	
2005-09	Burrows	Alexandre	W	288	50	53	103	483	
1990-98	Odjick	Gino	W	444	46	52	98	2127	
1971-74	Lemieux	Richard	W	129	29	61	90	68	
1973-76	Bordeleau	Paulin	W	183	33	56	89	47	
1977-79	Martin	Hubert Pit	C	131	27	45	72	60	
1971-72	Connelly	Wayne	C	53	14	20	34	12	
1983-88	Lanthier	Jean-Marc	W	105	16	16	32	29	
1974-76	Rochefort	Léon	W	87	18	14	32	2	
2008-09	Bernier	Steve	W	81	15	17	32	27	
1988-95	Charbonneau	José	W	46	8	8	16	55	
1987-91	Stern	Ronnie	W	97	5	6	11	480	
2006-07	Chouinard	Marc	C	42	2	2	4	10	
1995-96	Bélanger	Jesse	C	9	3	0	3	4	
1992-94	Morin	Stéphane	C	6	1	2	3	6	
1987-88	Vilgrain	Claude	C	6	1	1	2	0	
2008-09	Ouellet	Michel	W	3	0	0	0	0	

Defencemen

Season	Surname	First name	P	GP	G	A	PTS	PIM	
1970-73	Tallon	Dale	D	222	44	93	137	219	
1971-75	Guèvremont	Jocelyn	D	227	44	88	132	124	
1982-88	Petit	Michel	D	226	24	57	81	373	
1984-86	Daigneault	J.-Jacques	D	131	9	46	55	114	
1980-81	Marois	Mario	D	50	4	12	16	115	
1976-78	Carriere	Larry	D	56	1	12	13	66	
1979-81	Logan	Dave	D	40	1	5	6	122	
2006-07	Tremblay	Yannick	D	12	1	2	3	12	
2003-04	Bergevin	Marc	D	9	0	2	2	2	
1997-98	Ciccone	Enrico	D	13	0	1	1	47	
2006-07	Coulombe	Patrick	D	7	0	1	1	4	
2003-04	Grenier	Martin	D	7	1	0	1	9	
1973-74	Folco	Peter	D	2	0	0	0	0	

Goalies

Season	Surname	First name	P	GP	W	L	T	AV.	%
1980-88	Brodeur	Richard	G	377	126	173	62	3.87	
2000-06	Cloutier	Dan	G	208	109	68	29	2.42	.906
2006-09	Luongo	Roberto	G	203	115	64	22	2.32	.920
1999-2001	Potvin	Félix	G	69	26	30	17	2.84	.897
1970-71	Hodge	Charlie	G	35	10	13	5	3.42	
1973-74	Caron	Jacques	G	10	2	5	1	4.90	
2006-07	Sabourin	Dany	G	9	2	4	1	2.63	.906
2001-02	Brochu	Martin	G	6	0	3	0	4.16	.856
2005-06	Ouellet	Maxime	G	4	0	2	1	3.25	.894

WASHINGTON CAPITALS 1974 to 2009				450 Players			52 QC		11.56%
Forwards									
Season	Surname	First name	P	GP	G	A	PTS	PIM	
1976-81	Charron	Guy	C	320	118	156	274	54	
1982-87	Haworth	Alan	C	346	129	139	268	249	
1993-99	Juneau	Joé	C	312	62	172	234	98	
1981-87	Duchesne	Gaétan	W	451	87	138	225	251	
1975-80	Sirois	Bob	W	282	91	120	211	38	
1975-85	Currie	Glen	W	307	38	77	115	91	
1975-76	Monahan	Hartland	W	159	40	56	96	72	
1981-84	Valentine	Chris	W	105	43	52	95	127	
1980-82	Pronovost	Jean	W	90	23	38	61	65	
1977-80	Girard	Bob	W	132	18	29	47	42	
1974-75	Dupéré	Denis	W	53	20	15	35	8	
1975-76	Clément	Bill	C	46	10	17	27	20	
2006-09	Brashear	Donald	W	220	10	15	25	396	
1977-79	Forbes	Dave	W	79	11	12	23	121	
1978-79	Bergeron	Michel	W	30	7	6	13	7	
1977-79	Godin	Eddie	W	27	3	6	9	12	
1997-99	Gratton	Benoit	C	22	4	4	8	22	
1994-96	Gendron	Martin	W	26	4	2	6	10	
1990-93	Savage	Réginald	C	17	2	3	5	12	
2006-07	Giroux	Alexandre	C	9	2	2	4	2	
2001-02	Hogue	Benoit	C	9	0	1	1	4	
1995-96	Chassé	Denis	W	3	0	0	0	5	
1989-91	Maltais	Steve	W	15	0	0	0	4	
2005-06	Robitaille	Louis	W	2	0	0	0	5	
1998-99	Lefebvre	Patrice	C	3	0	0	0	2	
1974-75	Peloffy	André	C	9	0	0	0	0	
Defencemen									
Season	Surname	First name	P	GP	G	A	PTS	PIM	
1991-2003	Côté	Sylvain	D	622	75	195	270	336	
1977-80	Picard	Robert	D	230	42	114	156	308	
1986-88	Galley	Garry	D	76	8	33	41	54	
1975-78	Lemieux	Jean-Luc	D	64	13	25	38	4	
1981-82	Murray	Terry	D	74	3	22	25	60	
1978-82	Bouchard	Pierre	D	106	8	16	24	54	
1992-94	Anderson	Shawn	D	110	2	15	17	30	
2005-06	Biron	Mathieu	D	52	4	9	13	50	
1999-2002	Zettler	Rob	D	90	1	10	11	130	
2001-04	Fortin	Jean-François	D	71	1	4	5	42	
1993-99	Ciccone	Enrico	D	89	3	1	4	277	

➤

1995-97	Charron	Éric	D	29	1	2	3	24	
1996-2002	Boileau	Patrick	D	7	0	1	1	4	
2003-04	Grand-Pierre	Jean-Luc	D	13	1	0	1	14	
1978-80	Tremblay	Brent	D	10	1	0	1	6	
1985-88	Beaudoin	Yves	D	11	0	0	0	5	
1989-90	Côté	Alain	D	2	0	0	0	7	

Goalies

Season	Surname	First name	P	GP	W	L	T	AV.	%
1975-79	Wolfe	Bernie	G	120	20	61	21	4.17	
2008-09	Théodore	José	G	57	32	17	5	2.85	.901
1974-76	Belhumeur	Michel	G	42	0	29	4	5.32	
2002-04	Charpentier	Sébastien	G	26	6	14	4	2.93	.902
2003-04	Ouellet	Maxime	G	6	2	3	1	3.12	.910
2005-07	Cassivi	Frédéric	G	5	0	2	1	3.04	.886
2003-04	Yeats	Matthew	G	5	1	3	0	3.03	.908
1998-99	Brochu	Martin	G	2	0	2	0	3.01	.891
1987-88	Raymond	Alain	G	1	0	1	0	3.06	.900

Winnipeg Jets 1979 À 1996				243 Players			30 QC		12.35 %

Forwards

Season	Surname	First name	P	GP	G	A	PTS	PIM	
1981-92	Deblois	Lucien	W	235	87	101	188	208	
1980-83	Dupont	Normand	W	181	47	67	114	36	
1986-89	Hamel	Gilles	W	143	35	32	67	59	
1980-82	Geoffrion	Daniel	W	79	20	26	46	87	
1979-81	Drouin	Jude	W	85	8	16	24	54	
1979-84	Mann	Jimmy	W	202	9	12	21	598	
1986-87	Baillargeon	Joël	W	15	0	2	2	27	
1979-81	Daley	Patrick	W	12	1	0	1	13	
1979-80	Guindon	Bob	W	6	0	1	1	2	
1988-91	Larose	Guy	C	10	0	1	1	14	
1995-96	Chassé	Denis	W	15	0	0	0	12	
1979-80	Tomalty	Glen	W	1	0	0	0	0	

Defencemen

Season	Surname	First name	P	GP	G	A	PTS	PIM	
1985-92	Marois	Mario	D	255	17	116	133	378	
1983-86	Picard	Robert	D	160	20	43	63	158	
1993-95	Quintal	Stéphane	D	124	14	35	49	197	
1988-92	Donnelly	Gord	D	173	12	17	29	726	
1981-83	Savard	Serge	D	123	6	21	27	55	
1983-86	Dollas	Bobby	D	56	0	5	5	66	
1980-81	Mulhern	Richard	D	19	0	4	4	14	

1995-96	Doig	Jason	D	15	1	1	2	28	
1988-89	Fletcher	Steven	D	3	0	0	0	5	
1979-80	Maciver	Don	D	6	0	0	0	2	
Goalies									
Season	**Surname**	**First name**	**P**	**GP**	**W**	**L**	**T**	**AV.**	**%**
1985-90	Berthiaume	Daniel	G	120	50	45	13	3.63	
1989-94	Beauregard	Stéphane	G	74	16	30	11	3.48	.885
1979-81	Hamel	Pierre	G	64	12	39	7	4.34	
1885-86	Bouchard	Daniel	G	32	11	14	2	3.79	
1986-88	Penney	Steve	G	15	3	8	2	4.64	
1980-81	Dion	Michel	G	14	3	6	3	4.83	
1998-96	Draper	Tom	G	9	3	5	0	4.80	
1995-96	Roussel	Dominic	G	7	2	2	0	3.37	.881

Chapter 4

Quebecers in the NHL

This chapter provides a statistical summary of all the Quebec hockey players who played in the National Hockey League since its inception in 1917. The players are divided into two groups: hockey players who started playing in the 1970-71 season or after, and those who started playing between the 1917-18 and the 1969-70 seasons.

The tables are numbered as follows:

· Centres: Tables 4.5 and 4.6
· Wingers: Tables 4.7 and 4.8
· Goalies: Tables 4.9 and 4.10
· Defencemen: Tables 4.11 and 4.12

Centres (1970-2009)

· Between the 1970-71 and 2008-09 seasons, 107 Quebec centres played at least one game in the NHL.
· In forty years, forty-six centres played more than two hundred games (three years).
· Of the forty-six centres, thirty-nine were French-speaking.
· 44.31 percent of the French-speaking centres played more than two hundred games.

Wingers (1970-2009)

· Between the 1970-71 and 2008-09 seasons, 199 Quebec wingers played at least one game in the NHL.
· In forty years, seventy-seven wingers played more than two hundred games (three years).
· Of the seventy-seven wingers, sixty were French-speaking
· 37.97 percent of the French-speaking wingers played more than two hundred games.

Goalies (1970-2009)

· Between the 1970-71 and 2008-09 seasons, ninety-six Quebec goalies played at least one game in the NHL.
· In forty years, thirty-one French-speaking goalies played more than two hundred games (three years). Not one English-speaking goalie played more than two hundred games.
· 39.24 percent of the French-speaking goalies played more than two hundred games.

Defencemen (1970-2009)

· Between the 1970-71 and 2008-09 seasons, 119 Quebec defencemen played at least one game in the NHL.
· In forty years, sixty-four defencemen played more than two hundred games (three years).
· Forty-six defencemen were French-speaking.
· 50.54 percent of the French-speaking defencemen played more than two hundred games.

TABLE 4.1

**Comparison by position of French-speaking Quebec hockey players
who played more than two hundred games (1970-2009)**

POSITIONS	TOTAL	PERRCENTAGE
Centres	39/88	44.31%
Wingers	60/158	37.97%
Goalies	31/79	39.24%
Defencemen	46/91	50.54%
TOTAL	176/416	42.31%

Conclusions for Table 4.1

Table 4.1 shows that French-speaking Quebec defencemen were proportionally the most successful in attaining more than two hundred games played in the NHL during their careers.

Although the English-Canadian hockey world broadly claimed that French-speaking Quebec hockey players lacked the defensive hockey skills necessary for success in the NHL, the theory obviously does not hold water. If French-speaking Quebec defencemen didn't have what it takes to play the game, there wouldn't have been as many who succeeded in playing more than two hundred NHL games. What is also surprising is the high percentage of French-speaking defencemen compared to the other three positions.

TABLE 4.2

Comparison of the Quebecers who participated by year*

QUEBEC PLAYERS	DECADE 1970-1979										AVERAGE
	1970	1971	1972	1973	1974	1975	1976	1977	1978	1979	
FR. 154	53	62	64	65	74	71	64	68	68	89	67.8
ENG. 53	17	11	15	14	15	17	18	16	14	21	15.8
TOTAL 207	70	73	79	79	89	88	82	84	82	110	83.6

QUEBEC PLAYERS	DECADE 1980-1989										AVERAGE
	1980	1981	1982	1983	1984	1985	1986	1987	1988	1989	
FR. 173	78	82	73	62	62	60	57	63	60	69	66.6
ENG. 47	16	17	15	14	15	16	19	21	23	23	17.9
TOTAL 220	94	99	88	76	77	76	76	84	83	92	84.5

QUEBEC PLAYERS	DECADE 1990-1999										AVERAGE
	1990	1991	1992	1993	1994	1995	1996	1997	1998	1999	
FR. 185	74	75	80	83	77	79	86	79	97	94	82.4
ENG. 43	23	25	25	27	19	23	16	17	18	15	20.8
tOTAL 228	97	100	105	110	96	102	102	96	115	109	103.2

QUEBEC PLAYERS	DECADE 2000-2008										AVERAGE
	2000	2001	2002	2003	2004	2005	2006	2007	2008	2009	
FR. 178	86	88	81	80	NIL	83	76	70	67	—	78.9
ENG. 23	14	11	11	10	NIL	7	6	6	4	—	8.6
TOTAL 201	100	99	92	90	nil	90	82	77	71	—	87.5

* Note: The numbers included under each year represent the number of players who participated in at least one game.

TABLE 4.3

Comparison of the Quebecers who participated by decade

DECADE	TOTAL BY DECADE	FRENCH-SPEAKING PLAYERS	%	ENGLISH-SPEAKING PLAYERS	%
1970-1979	207	154	74.40%	53	25.60%
1980-1989	220	173	78.64%	47	21.36%
1990-1999	228	185	81.14%	43	18.86%
2000-2008	201	178	87.00%	23	13.00%

The disappearance of English-speaking Quebecers!

On Monday, June 23, 2008, a *Journal de Montreal* sports reporter writing in *ruefrontenac.com* asked, "Why are the numbers of Quebec hockey players in the NHL dropping?" As Table 4.2 shows, his observation is accurate, but only partially since the drop in Quebecers in the NHL stems from decreasing numbers of English-speaking Quebec hockey players. In previous decades English-speaking Quebecers represented on average between 19 percent and 28 percent of the players from Quebec, which is relatively high considering English-speaking population accounts for only 8.5 percent of the total Quebec population. Today those figures are down to 5.63 percent, with only four English-speaking Quebec hockey players playing in the 2008-09 season. English-speaking Quebecers are now realizing what it means to be a Quebecer in the National Hockey League. Sixty-seven French-speaking Quebecers were playing in the NHL during the same period, which is higher than the average of 65.5 players who played in the league in the 70s and 80s.

The NHL All-Star Game

The NHL All-Star Game honours the best players from each NHL team. It is often said in the Quebec hockey world that the majority of French-speaking Quebecers who succeed in the NHL are stars. Table 4.4 proves that observation to be accurate. Sixty-eight French-speaking Quebecers have played in NHL All-Star Games since the 1970 season. This number represents almost 40 percent of the French-speaking Quebecers who played more than two hundred games in the NHL.

TABLE 4.4

Participation of Quebec Hockey Players in NHL All-Star Games

	PLAYER	YEAR OF PARTICIPATION								TOTAL
1	Hubert (Pit) Martin	1971	1972	1973	1974					4
2	Gilles Villemure	1971	1972	1973						3
3	Jean-Claude Tremblay	1971	1972							2
4	Jean Ratelle	1971	1972	1973	1980					4
5	Gilbert Perreault	1971	1972	1977	1978	1980	1984			6
6	Yvan Cournoyer	1971	1972	1973	1974	1978				5
7	Dale Tallon	1971	1972							2
8	Richard Martin	1972	1973	1974	1975	1976	1977	1978		7
9	Simon Nolet	1972	1975							2
10	Carol Vadnais	1972	1975	1976	1978					4
11	Lorne Worsley	1972								1
12	Rodrigue Gilbert	1972	1975	1977						3
13	Dave Keon	1973								1
14	Guy Lapointe	1973	1975	1976						3
15	Jacques Lemaire	1973								1
16	René Robert	1973	1975							2
17	Serge Savard	1973	1977	1978						3
18	Bob Berry	1973								1
19	Gilles Marotte	1973								1
20	Rogatien Vachon	1973	1975	1978						3
21	Bernard Parent	1974	1975	1977						3
22	Henri Richard	1974								1
23	Denis Potvin	1974	1975	1976	1977	1978	81-83	84-87		11
24	Jocelyn Guèvremont	1974								1
25	Gilles Gilbert	1974								1
26	Marcel Dionne	1975	1976	1977	1978	1980	1981	83-85		9
27	Denis Dupéré	1975								1
28	Guy Lafleur	1975	1976	1977	1978	1980	1991			6
29	Jean Pronovost	1975	1976	1977	1978					4
30	Bill Clément	1976	1978							2
31	Pierre Larouche	1976	1984							2
32	André Dupont	1976								1
33	Guy Charron	1977								1
34	Ian Turnbull	1977								1
35	Bob Sirois	1978								1
36	Michael Bossy	1978	1980	1981	1982	1983	1985	1986		7
37	Réal Cloutier	1980								1
38	Gilles Meloche	1980	1982							2
39	Robert Picard	1980	1981							2

➤

PLAYER		YEAR OF PARTICIPATION									TOTAL
40	Mario Lessard	1981									1
41	Raymond Bourque	1981-86. 1988-94. 1996-2001									19
42	Michel Dion	1982									1
43	Marc Tardif	1982									1
44	Denis Savard	1982	1983	1984	1986	1988	1991	1996			7
45	Michel Goulet	1983	1984	1985	1986	1988					5
46	Kevin Lowe	1984	1985	1986	1988	1989	1990				6
47	Mario Lemieux	1985-1987		1989-1990		1992	1996-1997		2001-2002		10
48	Mario Gosselin	1986									1
49	Sylvain Turgeon	1986									1
50	Patrick Roy	1988	1990-1994		1997-1998		2001-2003				11
51	Kevin Dineen	1985	1989								2
52	Luc Robitaille	1988-1993		1999	2001						8
53	Steve Duchesne	1989	1990	1993							3
54	Réjean Lemelin	1989									1
55	Stéphane Richer	1990									1
56	Pierre Turgeon	1990	1993	1994	1996						4
57	Vincent Damphousse	1991	1992	2002							3
58	Garry Galley	1991	1994								2
59	Éric Desjardins	1992	1996	2000							3
60	Félix Potvin	1994									2
61	Martin Brodeur	1996-1999		2000-2001		2003-2004		2007			9
62	Donald Audette	2001									1
63	Simon Gagné	2001	2007								2
64	José Théodore	2002	2004								2
65	Éric Dazé	2002									1
66	Jocelyn Thibault	2003									1
67	Martin St-Louis	2003	2004	2007	2008	2009					5
68	Vincent Lecavalier	2003	2006	2008	2009						4
69	Patrick Lalime	2003									1
70	Roberto Luongo	2004	2007	2009							3
71	Alex Tanguay	2004									1
72	Philippe Boucher	2007									1
73	Yanic Perreault	2007									1
74	Daniel Brière	2007									1
75	Mike Ribeiro	2008									1
76	Stéphane Robidas	2009									1
77	Jean-Sébastien Giguère	2009									1

NHL Individual Trophy Winners

Individual NHL player trophies are awarded at a gala event at the end of the each hockey season. The NHL's leading sponsors and team managers all attend the event.

The Hart Trophy is awarded to the player adjudged the most valuable to his team.

Quebecers who have won the Hart Trophy

1976-1977: Guy Lafleur	1995-1996: Mario Lemieux
1977-1978: Guy Lafleur	2001-2002: José Théodore
1987-1988: Mario Lemieux	2003-2004: José Théodore
1992-1993: Mario Lemieux	

The Art Ross Trophy is awarded to the player with the most points in regular season play.

Quebecers who have won the Art Ross Trophy

1975-1976: Guy Lafleur	1988-1989: Mario Lemieux
1976-1977: Guy Lafleur	1991-1992: Mario Lemieux
1977-1978: Guy Lafleur	1992-1993: Mario Lemieux
1979-1980: Marcel Dionne	1996-1997: Mario Lemieux
1987-1988: Mario Lemieux	2003-2004: Martin St-Louis

The Maurice Richard Trophy is awarded the leading goal scorer in regular season play. Vincent Lecavalier won the trophy in the 2006-07 season.

The Calder Trophy is awarded to the best rookie.
Quebecers who have won the Calder Trophy

1970-1971: Gilbert Perreault	1984-1985: Mario Lemieux
1973-1974: Denis Potvin	1986-1987: Luc Robitaille
1977-1978: Michael Bossy	1993-1994: Martin Brodeur
1979-1980: Raymond Bourque	

From 1926-27 to 1981-82, the Vézina Trophy was awarded to the goaltender of the team that allowed the fewest number of goals. Since 1982-83, the trophy has been given to the best goaltender based on a vote by NHL General Managers.

Quebecers who have won the Vézina Trophy

1970-1971 : Gilles Villemure	1988-1989 : Patrick Roy
1973-1974 : Bernard Parent	1989-1990 : Patrick Roy
1974-1975 : Bernard Parent	1991-1992 : José Théodore
1976-1977 : Michel Larocque	2002-2003 : Martin Brodeur
1977-1978 : Michel Larocque	2003-2004 : Martin Brodeur
1978-1979 : Michel Larocque	2006-2007 : Martin Brodeur
1979-1980 : Robert Sauvé	2007-2008 : Martin Brodeur
1980-1981 : Richard Sévigny. Michel Larocque et Denis Herron	

The Conn Smythe Trophy is awarded to the player judged to be most valuable to his team during the playoffs.

Quebecers who have won the Conn Smythe Trophy

1972-1973 : Yvan Cournoyer	1990-1991 : Mario Lemieux
1973-1974 : Bernard Parent	1991-1992 : Mario Lemieux
1974-1975 : Bernard Parent	1994-1995 : Claude Lemieux
1976-1977 : Guy Lafleur	2000-2001 : Patrick Roy
1981-1982 : Michael Bossy	2002-2003 : Jean-Sébastien Giguère
1985-1986 : Patrick Roy	

The James Norris Trophy is awarded to the best defenceman.

Quebecers who have won the James Norris Trophy

1975-1976 : Denis Potvin	1987-1988 : Raymond Bourque
1977-1978 : Denis Potvin	1989-1990 : Raymond Bourque
1978-1979 : Denis Potvin	1990-1991 : Raymond Bourque
1986-1987 : Raymond Bourque	1993-1994 : Raymond Bourque

The Frank J. Selke Trophy is awarded
to the best defensive forward.

Quebecers who have won the Frank J. Selke Trophy

1981-1982: Steve Kasper	1987-1988: Guy Carbonneau
1986-1987: Guy Carbonneau	1991-1992: Guy Carbonneau

The Lester B. Pearson Award, now the Ted Lindsay Award,
is awarded to the most outstanding player as judged
by members of the NHL Players Association.

Quebecers who have won
the Lester B. Pearson/Ted Lindsay Award

1971-1972: Jean Ratelle	1985-1986: Mario Lemieux
1975-1976: Guy Lafleur	1987-1988: Mario Lemieux
1976-1977: Guy Lafleur	1992-1993: Mario Lemieux
1977-1978: Guy Lafleur	1995-1996: Mario Lemieux
1978-1979: Marcel Dionne	2003-2004: Martin St-Louis
1979-1980: Marcel Dionne	

The Bill Masterton Trophy is awarded to the player
who best exemplifies perseverance, sportsmanship,
and dedication to hockey.

Quebecers who have won the Bill Masterton Trophy

1970-1971: Jean Ratelle	1978-1979: Serge Savard
1973-1974: Henri Richard	1992-1993: Mario Lemieux
1975-1976: Rodrigue Gilbert	

The King Clancy Trophy is awarded for a player's leadership qualities and contribution to the community.
Raymond Bourque won it in 1991-92
and Vincent Lecavalier in 2007-2008.

The Jennings Trophy is awarded to the goaltender who had the fewest goals scored against him.

Quebecers who have won the Jennings Trophy

1981-1982 : Denis Herron	1996-1997 : Martin Brodeur
1984-1985 : Robert Sauvé	1997-1998 : Martin Brodeur
1986-1987 : Patrick Roy	2001-2002 : Patrick Roy
1988-1989 : Patrick Roy	2002-2003 : Martin Brodeur
1989-1990 : Réjean Lemelin	2003-2004 : Martin Brodeur

The Roger Crozier Saving Grace Award is awarded to the goaltender with the best save percentage.
José Théodore won it in 2001-02.

The Plus-Minus Award is awarded to the player with the best +/- ratio regular season play.
Martin St-Louis won the award in 2003-2004.

The Lady Bing Trophy is awarded to the most gentlemanly player.

Quebecers who have won the Lady Bing Trophy

1971-1972 : Jean Ratelle	1982-1983 : Michael Bossy
1972-1973 : Gilbert Perreault	1983-1984 : Michael Bossy
1974-1975 : Marcel Dionne	1985-1986 : Michael Bossy
1975-1976 : Jean Ratelle	1992-1993 : Pierre Turgeon
1976-1977 : Marcel Dionne	

Equal talent, unequal treatment!

Discrimination is based on unequal treatment. 176 French-speaking Quebec hockey players played more than two hundred games between 1970-71 and 2008-09 in the National Hockey League. Seventy-four of those 176 French-speaking players or 42 percent were awarded NHL individual trophies or awards. It is clear therefore that only the most talented French-speaking Quebec hockey players managed to have careers of more than two hundred games in the National Hockey League. The other Quebec players were quickly eliminated from the league.

Guy Lafleur was well aware of this phenomenon in both National Hockey League and Team Canada circles, as reported in Marc Lavoie's book *Désavantage numérique, Les francophones dans la LNH* (page 80). Speaking to the Ottawa French-language daily *Le Droit* in 1994, he said, "It has been known for a long time that Team Canada, whose offices are in Calgary, is not interested in including third and fourth-line Quebec hockey players. Those positions are reserved for their disciplined and obedient English-speaking players." In the same article Lafleur declared that the same mentality prevails in the National Hockey League. He added that the Boston Bruins star defenceman and captain Raymond Bourque told him that he would never have been able to pursue his career in Boston if he had not been a first-line hockey player.

TABLE 4.5

Centres 1970 to 2009*

	SURNAME	FIRST NAME	SEASON	GP	G	A	PTS	PIM.
1	Dionne	Marcel	1971-89	1348	731	1040	1771	600
2	Lemieux	Mario	1984-06	915	690	1033	1723	834
3	Savard	Denis	1980-97	1196	473	865	1338	1336
4	Turgeon	Pierre	1987-07	1294	515	812	1327	452
5	Perreault	Gilbert	1970-87	1191	512	814	1326	500
6	Damphousse	Vincent	1986-04	1378	432	773	1205	1190
7	Larouche	Pierre	1974-88	812	395	427	822	237
8	Lecavalier	Vincent	1998-09	787	302	367	669	561
9	Carbonneau	Guy	1980-00	1318	260	403	663	820
10	Chouinard	Guy	1974-84	578	205	370	575	120
11	Juneau	Joé	1991-04	828	156	416	572	272
12	Krushelnysky	Mike	1981-95	897	241	328	569	699
13	Perreault	Yannick	1993-08	859	247	269	516	402
14	Savard	André	1973-84	790	211	271	482	411
15	Brière	Daniel	1997-09	591	204	269	473	459
16	Kasper	Steve	1980-93	821	177	291	468	554
17	Mondou	Pierre	1977-85	548	194	262	456	179
18	Haworth	Allan	1980-88	524	189	211	400	425
19	Ribeiro	Mike	1999-09	515	117	256	373	212
20	Clement	Bill	1971-82	719	148	208	356	383
21	Richard	Jacques	1972-83	556	160	187	347	307
22	Lalonde	Bobby	1971-82	641	124	210	334	298
23	St-Laurent	André	1973-84	644	129	187	316	749
24	Laperrière	Ian	1993-09	1001	118	198	316	1794
25	Lapointe	Claude	1990-04	879	127	178	305	721
26	Lebeau	Stéphane	1988-95	373	118	159	277	105
27	Bouchard	Pierre-Marc	2002-09	425	77	190	267	136
28	Bélanger	Éric	2000-09	557	106	152	258	251
29	Daoust	Dan	1982-90	522	87	167	254	544
30	Comeau	Reynald	1971-80	564	98	141	239	175
31	Bergeron	Patrice	2003-09	303	80	148	228	88
32	Sauvé	Jean-François	1980-87	290	65	138	203	114
33	Statsny	Paul	2006-09	193	63	122	185	88
34	Lombardi	Matthew	2003-09	366	70	113	183	239

* Classification based on number of points in career.

	SURNAME	FIRST NAME	SEASON	GP	G	A	PTS	PIM.
35	Vermette	Antoine	2003-09	376	87	93	180	213
36	Bureau	Marc	1989-00	567	55	83	138	327
37	Bélanger	Jesse	1991-01	246	59	76	135	56
38	Lemieux	Richard	1971-76	274	39	82	121	132
39	Perrin	Éric	2003-09	245	32	72	104	92
40	Fortier	Marc	1997-93	212	42	60	102	135
41	Bordeleau	Sébastien	1995-02	251	37	61	98	118
42	Valentine	Chris	1981-84	105	43	52	95	127
43	Rhéaume	Pascal	1996-06	318	39	52	91	144
44	Bordeleau	Paulin	1973-76	183	33	56	89	47
45	Talbot	Maxime	2005-09	261	42	38	80	228
46	Chouinard	Marc	2000-07	320	37	41	78	123
47	Perron	David	2007-09	143	28	49	77	88
48	Lemieux	Alain	1981-87	119	28	44	72	38
49	Dubinsky	Steve	1993-03	375	25	45	70	164
50	Leduc	Richard	1972-83	130	28	38	66	69
51	Thibodeau	Gilles	1986-91	119	25	37	62	40
52	White	Peter	1993-04	220	23	37	60	36
53	Lapierre	Maxim	2005-09	179	28	30	58	160
54	Morin	Stéphane	1989-94	90	16	39	55	52
55	St-Sauveur	Claude	1975-76	79	24	24	48	23
56	Martins	Steve	1995-06	267	21	25	46	142
57	Guité	Ben	2005-09	169	19	26	45	93
58	Orlando	Gates	1984-87	98	18	26	44	51
59	Pouliot	Marc-Antoine	2005-09	141	14	25	39	53
60	Jomphe	Jean-François	1995-99	111	10	29	39	102
61	Montgomery	Jim	1993-03	122	9	25	34	80
62	Brady	Neil	1989-94	89	9	22	31	95
63	Aubin	Normand	1981-83	69	18	13	31	30
64	Mongrain	Robert	1979-86	81	13	14	27	14
65	Brassard	Dérick	2007-09	48	11	16	27	23
66	Perreault	Joël	2005-09	87	11	14	25	68
67	Corso	Daniel	2000-04	77	14	11	25	20
68	Mongeau	Michel	1989-93	54	6	19	25	10
69	Chouinard	Éric	2000-06	90	11	11	22	16
70	Murphy	Rob	1987-94	125	9	12	21	152

➤

	SURNAME	FIRST NAME	SEASON	GP	G	A	PTS	PIM.
71	Mitchell	Tory	2007-08	82	10	10	20	50
72	Larose	Guy	1988-94	70	10	9	19	63
73	Savard	Jean	1977-80	43	7	12	19	29
74	Tardif	Patrice	1994-96	65	7	11	18	78
75	Larouche	Steve	1994-96	26	9	9	18	10
76	Galarneau	Michel	1980-83	78	7	10	17	34
77	Parizeau	Michel	1971-72	58	3	14	17	18
78	Faust	André	1992-94	47	10	7	17	14
79	Cloutier	Roland	1977-80	34	8	9	17	2
80	Gratton	Benoit	1997-04	58	6	10	16	58
81	Statsny	Yan	2005-09	87	5	10	15	58
82	Landry	Éric	1997-02	68	5	9	14	47
83	Stewart	Anthony	2005-09	105	4	8	12	38
84	Savage	Réginald	1990-94	34	5	7	12	28
85	Couturier	Sylvain	1988-92	33	4	5	9	4
86	Verret	Claude	1983-85	14	2	5	7	2
87	Reid	Brandon	2002-07	13	2	4	6	0
88	Houde	Éric	1996-99	30	2	3	5	4
89	Delisle	Xavier	1998-01	16	3	2	5	6
90	Lehoux	Yanick	2006-07	10	2	2	4	6
91	Dubé	Christian	1996-99	33	1	1	2	4
92	Grenier	Richard	1972-73	10	1	1	2	2
93	Desjardins	Martin	1989-90	8	0	2	2	2
94	Yates	Ross	1983-84	7	1	1	2	4
95	Walter	Ben	2005-09	9	1	0	1	4
96	Roy	Stéphane	1987-88	7	1	0	1	0
97	Bolduc	Alexandre	2008-09	4	0	1	1	4
98	Dupuis	Philippe	2008-09	8	0	0	0	4
99	Holts	Greg	1975-78	11	0	0	0	0
100	Péloffy	André	1974-75	9	0	0	0	0
101	Cloutier	Sylvain	1998-99	7	0	0	0	0
102	Thyer	Mario	1989-90	5	0	0	0	0
103	Dusablon	Benoit	2003-04	3	0	0	0	2
104	Richer	Bob	1972-73	3	0	0	0	0
105	Hughes	Ryan	1995-96	3	0	0	0	0
106	Guay	François	1989-90	1	0	0	0	0
107	Vachon	Nicholas	1996-97	1	0	0	0	0

TABLE 4.6

Centres whose careersbegan before the 1970-71 season*

	SURNAME	FIRST NAME	SEASON	GP	G	A	PTS	PIM.
1	Ratelle	Jean	1960-81	1281	491	776	1267	276
2	Béliveau	Jean	1950-71	1125	507	712	1219	1029
3	Richard	Henri	1955-75	1256	358	688	1046	928
4	Keon	Dave	1961-82	1296	396	590	986	117
5	Lemaire	Jacques	1968-79	853	366	469	835	217
6	Martin	Hubert (Pit)	1961-79	1101	324	485	809	609
7	Goyette	Philippe	1956-72	941	207	467	674	131
8	Cowley	Bill	1934-47	549	195	353	548	143
9	Charron	Guy	1969-81	730	221	309	530	146
10	Henry	Camille	1953-70	727	279	249	528	88
11	Stewart	Nels	1925-40	650	324	191	515	953
12	Boudrias	André	1963-76	662	151	340	491	216
13	Sloan	Todd	1947-61	745	220	262	482	831
14	Drouin	Jude	1969-81	666	151	305	456	346
15	Watson	Phil	1935-48	590	144	265	409	532
16	O'connor	Buddy	1941-51	509	140	257	397	34
17	Barry	Marty	1927-40	509	195	192	387	231
18	Mackell	Fleming	1947-60	665	149	220	369	562
19	Mosdell	Ken	1941-58	693	141	168	309	475
20	Connelly	Wayne	1960-72	543	133	174	307	156
21	Lépine	Pit	1925-38	526	143	98	241	392
22	Lacroix	André	1968-80	325	79	119	198	44
23	Haynes	Paul	1930-41	391	61	134	195	164
24	Blinco	Russ	1933-39	268	59	66	125	24
25	Bordeleau	Christian	1969-72	205	38	65	103	82
26	Peters	Jimmy	1964-75	309	37	36	73	48
27	Leclair	Jackie	1954-57	160	20	40	60	56
28	Thurier	Fred	1940-45	80	25	27	52	18
29	Keats	Duke	1926-29	82	30	19	49	113
30	Brière	Michel	1969-70	76	12	32	44	20
31	Leblanc	J.-P.	1969-79	153	14	30	44	87
32	Mahaffy	John	1942-44	37	11	25	36	4
33	Hardy	Joe	1969-71	63	9	14	23	51
34	Rozzini	Gino	1944-45	31	5	10	15	20

* Classification based on number of points in career.

➤

	SURNAME	FIRST NAME	SEASON	GP	G	A	PTS	PIM.
35	Campeau	Todd	1943-49	42	5	9	14	16
36	Boileau	Marc	1961-62	54	5	6	11	8
37	Crutchfield	Nels	1934-35	41	5	5	10	20
38	Lépine	Hector	1925-26	33	5	2	7	2
39	Broden	Connie	1955-58	6	2	1	3	2
40	Desaulniers	Gérard	1950-54	8	0	2	2	4
41	Gilbert	Jeannot	1962-65	22	0	1	1	4
42	Dineen	Gary	1968-69	12	0	1	1	0
43	White	Moe	1945-46	4	0	1	1	2
44	Burnett	Kelly	1952-53	3	1	0	1	0
45	Tremblay	Nils	1945-46	3	0	1	1	0
46	Joanette	Rosario	1944-45	2	0	1	1	4
47	Haworth	Gord	1952-53	2	0	1	1	0
48	Boileau	René	1925-26	7	0	0	0	0
49	Bourcier	Conrad	1935-36	6	0	0	0	0
50	Buchanan	Ron	1966-70	5	0	0	0	0
51	Burchell	Fred	1950-54	4	0	0	0	2
52	Lee	Bobby	1942-43	1	0	0	0	0
53	Read	Mel	1946-47	1	0	0	0	0

TABLE 4.7

Wingers 1970 to 2009*

	SURNAME	FIRST NAME	SEASON	GP	G	A	PTS	PIM.
1	Robitaille	Luc	1986-06	1431	668	726	1394	1177
2	Lafleur	Guy	1971-91	1127	560	793	1353	399
3	Goulet	Michel	1979-94	1089	548	604	1152	825
4	Bossy	Michael	1977-87	752	573	553	1126	210
5	Mellanby	Scott	1985-07	1431	364	476	840	2479
6	Richer	Stéphane	1984-02	1054	421	398	819	614
7	Lemieux	Claude	1983-09	1215	379	407	786	1777
8	Dineen	Kevin	1984-03	1188	355	405	760	2229
9	Robert	René	1970-82	744	284	418	702	597
10	Martin	Richard	1971-82	685	384	317	701	477
11	Gélinas	Martin	1988-08	1273	309	351	660	820
12	Mckegney	Tony	1978-91	912	320	319	639	517
13	St-Louis	Martin	1998-09	690	238	347	585	226
14	Tremblay	Mario	1974-86	852	258	326	584	1043
15	Tanguay	Alex	1999-09	659	193	387	580	345
16	Hogue	Benoit	1987-02	863	222	321	543	877
17	Deblois	Lucien	1977-92	993	249	276	525	814
18	Audette	Donald	1990-2004	735	260	249	509	584
19	Turgeon	Sylvain	1983-95	669	269	226	495	691
20	Gagné	Simon	2000-09	606	242	242	484	231
21	Lambert	Yvon	1972-82	683	206	273	479	340
22	Dumont	Jean-Pierre	1998-09	678	187	272	459	328
23	Duchesnes	Gaétan	1981-95	1028	179	254	433	617
24	Dazé	Éric	1994-06	601	226	172	398	176
25	Errey	Bobby	1983-98	895	170	212	382	1005
26	Lapointe	Martin	1991-08	991	181	200	381	1417
27	Mckay	Randy	1997-03	932	162	201	363	1731
28	Momesso	Sergio	1983-97	710	152	193	345	1557
29	Cloutier	Réal	1979-85	317	146	198	344	119
30	Daigle	Alexandre	1993-06	616	129	198	327	186
31	Matteau	Stéphane	1990-03	848	144	172	316	742
32	Plante	Pierre	1971-80	599	125	172	297	599
33	Côté	Alain	1979-89	696	103	190	293	383
34	Hamel	Gilles	1980-89	519	127	147	274	276

* Classification based on number of points in career.

►

	SURNAME	FIRST NAME	SEASON	GP	G	A	PTS	PIM.
35	Brunet	Benoit	1988-02	539	101	161	262	229
36	Hough	Mike	1986-99	707	100	156	256	675
37	Pominville	Jason	2003-09	304	99	145	244	90
38	Poulin	Patrick	1991-02	634	101	134	235	299
39	Bordeleau	Jean-Pierre	1971-80	519	97	126	223	143
40	Sirois	Bob	1974-80	286	92	120	212	42
41	Marois	Daniel	1988-96	350	117	93	210	419
42	Jarry	Pierre	1971-78	344	88	117	205	142
43	Brashear	Donald	1993-09	989	85	119	204	2561
44	Dupuis	Pascal	2000-09	506	95	107	202	228
45	Smith	Derek	1976-83	335	78	116	194	60
46	Dupéré	Denis	1970-78	421	80	99	179	66
47	Gillis	Jere	1977-87	386	78	95	173	230
48	Lemieux	Jocelyn	1986-98	598	80	84	164	740
49	Mckenna	Sean	1981-90	414	82	80	162	181
50	Stern	Ronnie	1987-00	638	75	86	161	2077
51	Laraque	Georges	1997-09	667	52	98	150	1098
52	Gagnon	Germain	1971-76	259	40	101	141	72
53	Monahan	Hartland	1973-81	334	61	80	141	163
54	Dionne	Gilbert	1990-96	223	61	79	140	108
55	Dupont	Normand	1979-84	256	55	85	140	52
56	Bergeron	Michel	1974-79	229	80	58	138	165
57	Lacroix	Éric	1993-01	472	67	70	137	361
58	Odjick	Gino	1990-02	605	64	73	137	2567
59	Corbet	René	1993-01	362	58	74	132	420
60	Forbes	Dave	1973-79	363	64	64	128	341
61	Milks	Hib	1925-33	317	87	41	128	179
62	Sheppard	Johnny	1926-34	308	68	58	126	224
63	Bernier	Steve	2005-09	258	60	62	122	155
64	Currie	Glen	1979-88	326	39	79	118	100
65	Ouellet	Michel	2005-09	190	52	64	116	58
66	Lacombe	Normand	1984-91	319	53	62	115	196
67	Girard	Robert	1975-80	305	45	69	114	140
68	Aubin	Serge	1998-06	374	44	64	108	361
69	Daigle	Alain	1974-80	389	56	50	106	122
70	Burrows	Alexandre	2005-09	288	50	53	103	483

	SURNAME	FIRST NAME	SEASON	GP	G	A	PTS	PIM.
71	Sleigher	Louis	1979-86	194	46	53	99	146
72	Veilleux	Stéphane	2002-09	361	43	47	90	254
73	Bégin	Steve	1997-09	409	47	39	86	482
74	Cyr	Denis	1980-86	193	41	43	84	36
75	Gratton	Normand	1971-76	201	39	44	83	64
76	Latendresse	Guillaume	2006-09	209	46	36	82	133
77	Picard	Michel	1990-01	166	28	42	70	103
78	Burns	Robin	1970-76	190	31	38	69	139
79	Roy	André	1995-09	515	35	33	68	1169
80	Simpson	Bobby	1976-83	175	35	29	64	98
81	Dagenais	Pierre	2000-06	142	35	23	58	58
82	Vilgrain	Claude	1987-94	89	21	32	53	78
83	Geoffrion	Daniel	1979-82	111	20	32	52	99
84	Aubry	Pierre	1980-85	202	24	26	50	133
85	Worrel	Peter	1997-04	391	19	27	46	1554
86	Dufour	Luc	1982-85	167	23	21	44	199
87	Léveillé	Normand	1981-83	75	17	25	42	49
88	Vincelette	Daniel	1987-92	193	20	22	42	351
89	Leroux	Jean-Yves	1996-01	220	16	22	38	146
90	Garland	Scott	1975-79	91	13	24	37	115
91	Sullivan	Bob	1982-83	62	18	19	37	18
92	Lanthier	Jean-Marc	1983-88	105	16	16	32	29
93	Boivin	Claude	1991-95	132	12	19	31	364
94	Hamel	Denis	1999-07	192	19	12	31	77
95	Mann	Jimmy	1979-88	293	10	20	30	895
96	Abid	Ramzi	2002-07	68	14	16	30	78
97	Smrke	John	1977-80	103	11	17	28	33
98	Roy	Jean-Yves	1994-98	61	12	16	28	26
99	Shank	Daniel	1989-92	77	13	14	27	175
100	Maltais	Steve	1989-01	120	9	18	27	53
101	Stock	P.-J.	1997-04	235	5	21	26	523
102	Chassé	Denis	1993-97	132	11	14	25	292
103	Darche	Mathieu	2000-08	101	8	16	24	26
104	Grenier	Lucien	1970-72	128	12	11	23	16
105	Charbonneau	José	1987-95	71	9	13	22	67

➤

	SURNAME	FIRST NAME	SEASON	GP	G	A	PTS	PIM.
106	Courteney	Ed	1991-93	44	7	13	20	10
107	Meloche	Éric	2001-07	74	9	11	20	36
108	Sarault	Yves	1994-02	106	10	10	20	51
109	Fontaine	Len	1972-74	46	8	11	19	10
110	Dubé	Normand	1974-76	57	8	10	18	54
111	Lacroix	Daniel	1993-00	188	11	7	18	379
112	Logan	Robert	1986-89	42	10	5	15	0
113	Goneau	Daniel	1996-00	53	12	3	15	14
114	Cossette	Jacques	1975-79	64	8	6	14	29
115	Roberge	Mario	1990-95	112	7	7	14	314
116	Gamache	Simon	2002-08	48	6	7	13	18
117	Ritchie	Robert	1976-78	29	8	4	12	10
118	Boisvert	Serge	1982-88	46	5	7	12	8
119	Leblanc	Fernand	1976-79	34	5	6	11	0
120	Larose	Claude	1979-80	25	4	7	11	2
121	Quintin	Jean-François	1991-93	22	5	5	10	4
122	Preston	Yves	1978-81	28	7	3	10	4
123	Godin	Eddy	1977-79	27	3	6	9	12
124	Nantais	Richard	1974-77	63	5	4	9	79
125	Sévigny	Pierre	1993-98	78	4	5	9	64
126	Langlais	Alain	1973-75	25	4	4	8	10
127	David	Richard	1979-83	31	4	4	8	10
128	Courteau	Yves	1984-87	22	2	5	7	4
129	Gaulin	Jean-Marc	1982-86	26	4	3	7	8
130	Blouin	Sylvain	1996-03	115	3	4	7	336
131	Giroux	Alexandre	2005-09	22	3	3	6	12
132	Bréault	François	1990-93	27	2	4	6	42
133	Gendron	Martin	1994-98	30	4	2	6	10
134	Lefebvre	Guillaume	2001-06	38	2	4	6	13
135	Simard	Martin	1990-93	44	1	5	6	183
136	Lebeau	Patrick	1990-99	15	3	2	5	6
137	Doré	Daniel	1989-91	17	2	3	5	59
138	Matte	Christian	1996-01	25	2	3	5	12
139	Langevin	Christian	1983-86	22	3	1	4	22
140	Brousseau	Paul	1995-01	26	1	3	4	29
141	Lessard	Junior	2005-08	27	3	1	4	23

	SURNAME	FIRST NAME	SEASON	GP	G	A	PTS	PIM.
142	Lessard	Francis	2001-06	91	1	3	4	268
143	Heindl	Bill	1970-73	18	2	1	3	0
144	Gosselin	David	1999-02	13	2	1	3	11
145	Rioux	Pierre	1982-83	14	1	2	3	4
146	Chicoine	Daniel	1977-80	31	1	2	3	12
147	Côté	Patrick	1995-01	105	1	2	3	377
148	Dupré	Yannick	1991-96	35	2	0	2	16
149	Gainey	Steve	2000-06	33	0	2	2	34
150	Baron	Normand	1983-86	27	2	0	2	51
151	Rodgers	Marc	1999-00	21	1	1	2	10
152	Baillargeon	Joël	1986-89	20	0	2	2	31
153	Bethel	John	1979-80	17	0	2	2	4
154	Picard	Alexandre	2005-09	58	0	2	2	48
155	Létourneau Leblond	Pierre-Luc	2008-09	8	0	1	1	22
156	Daley	Patrick	1979-81	12	1	0	1	13
157	Saunders	Bernie	1979-81	10	0	1	1	8
158	Bilodeau	Gilles	1979-80	9	0	1	1	25
159	Bélanger	Alain	1977-78	9	0	1	1	0
160	Ferland	Jonathan	2005-06	7	1	0	1	2
161	Guindon	Bob	1979-80	6	0	1	1	0
162	Giroux	Pierre	1982-83	6	1	0	1	17
163	Parenteau	P.-A.	2006-07	5	0	1	1	2
164	Jacques	Jean-François	2005-09	60	1	0	1	44
165	L'abbe	Moe	1972-73	5	0	1	1	0
166	Bertrand	Éric	1999-01	15	0	0	0	4
167	Lafrenière	Roger	1972-73	10	0	0	0	0
168	James	Val	1981-87	11	0	0	0	30
169	Fleming	Gerry	1993-95	11	0	0	0	42
170	Morissette	Dave	1998-00	11	0	0	0	57
171	Bélanger	Francis	2000-01	10	0	0	0	29
172	Labelle	Marc	1996-97	0	0	0	0	46
173	Roberge	Serge	1990-91	9	0	0	0	24
174	Routhier	Jean-Marc	1989-90	8	0	0	0	9
175	Gosselin	Benoit	1977-78	7	0	0	0	33
176	Gauthier	Daniel	1994-95	5	0	0	0	0

➤

	SURNAME	FIRST NAME	SEASON	GP	G	A	PTS	PIM.
177	Mailhot	Jacques	1988-89	5	0	0	0	33
178	Audet	Philippe	1998-99	4	0	0	0	0
179	Forey	Connie	1973-74	4	0	0	0	2
180	Bergeron	Yves	1974-77	3	0	0	0	0
181	Fletcher	Steven	1988-89	3	0	0	0	5
182	Johnson	Brian	1983-84	3	0	0	0	5
183	Royer	Gaétan	2001-02	3	0	0	0	2
184	Archambault	Michel	1976-77	3	0	0	0	0
185	Drouin	P.-C.	1996-97	3	0	0	0	0
186	Lefebvre	Patrice	1998-99	3	0	0	0	2
187	Carter	Ron	1979-80	2	0	0	0	0
188	Boland	Mike	1974-75	2	0	0	0	0
189	Brulé	Steve	2002-03	2	0	0	0	0
190	Guérard	Daniel	1994-95	2	0	0	0	0
191	Charbonneau	Stéphane	1991-92	2	0	0	0	0
192	Drolet	René	1971-75	2	0	0	0	0
193	Tanguay	Christian	1981-82	2	0	0	0	0
194	Robitaille	Louis	2005-06	2	0	0	0	5
195	Héroux	Yves	1986-87	1	0	0	0	0
196	St-Amour	Martin	1992-93	1	0	0	0	2
197	Delisle	Jonathan	1998-99	1	0	0	0	0
198	Ratwell	Jake	1974-75	1	0	0	0	0
199	Tomalty	Greg	1979-80	1	0	0	0	0

TABLE 4.8

Wingers whose careers began before the season 1970-71*

	SURNAME	FIRST NAME	SEASON	GP	G	A	PTS	PIM.
1	Gilbert	Rodrigue	1960-78	1065	406	615	1021	508
2	Richard	Maurice	1942-60	978	544	421	965	1285
3	Cournoyer	Yvan	1963-79	968	428	435	863	255
4	Geoffrion	Bernard	1950-68	883	393	429	822	689
5	Pronovost	Jean	1969-82	998	391	383	774	413
6	Rousseau	Bobby	1960-75	942	245	458	703	359
7	Moore	Dickie	1951-68	719	261	347	608	652
8	Provost	Claude	1955-70	1005	254	335	589	469
9	Marshall	Don	1951-72	1176	265	324	589	127
10	Marcotte	Don	1965-82	868	230	254	484	317
11	Houle	Réjean	1969-83	635	161	247	408	395
12	Tardif	Marc	1969-83	517	194	207	401	443
13	Gendron	Jean-Guy	1956-72	863	182	201	383	701
14	Berry	Bob	1969-77	541	159	191	350	344
15	Nolet	Simon	1968-77	562	150	182	332	187
16	Tremblay	Gilles	1960-69	509	168	162	330	161
17	Peters	Jimmy	1945-54	574	125	150	275	186
18	Chamberlain	Murph	1937-49	510	100	175	275	769
19	Bonin	Marcel	1952-62	454	97	175	272	336
20	Rochefort	Léon	1960-76	617	121	147	268	93
21	Gagnon	Johnny	1930-40	454	120	141	261	295
22	Fleming	Reggie	1960-71	749	108	132	240	1468
23	Finnigan	Frank	1923-37	553	115	88	203	407
24	Pronovost	André	1956-68	556	94	104	198	408
25	Bernier	Serge	1969-81	302	78	119	197	234
26	Mantha	Georges	1928-41	488	89	102	191	148
27	Robinson	Earl	1928-40	417	83	98	181	133
28	Malone	Joe	1917-24	126	143	32	175	57
29	Lemieux	Réal	1967-74	456	51	104	155	262
30	Cleghorn	Odie	1918-28	181	95	34	129	142
31	Mondou	Armand	1928-40	386	47	71	118	99
32	Fillion	Bob	1943-50	327	42	61	103	84
33	Pitre	Didier	1917-23	127	64	33	97	87
34	Gauthier	Fern	1943-49	229	46	50	96	35

* Classification based on number of points in career. ➤

	SURNAME	FIRST NAME	SEASON	GP	G	A	PTS	PIM.
35	Dineen	Bill	1953-58	323	51	44	95	122
36	Sinclair	Reg	1950-53	208	49	43	92	139
37	Gravelle	Léo	1946-51	223	44	34	78	42
38	Berlinguette	Louis	1917-26	193	45	33	78	129
39	Drouin	Polly	1934-41	160	23	50	73	80
40	Heffernan	Gerry	1941-44	83	33	35	68	27
41	Lorrain	Rod	1935-42	179	28	39	67	30
42	Bartlett	Jim	1954-61	191	34	23	57	273
43	Laforge	Claude	1957-69	193	24	35	57	82
44	Sarrazin	Dick	1968-72	100	20	35	55	22
45	Gray	Terry	1961-70	147	26	28	54	64
46	Majeau	Fern	1943-45	56	22	24	46	43
47	Trottier	Guy	1969-72	115	28	17	45	37
48	Bouchard	Edmond	1921-29	211	19	21	40	117
49	Mcinenly	Bert	1930-36	166	19	15	34	144
50	Aubuchon	Ossie	1942-43	50	20	12	32	4
51	Bellefeuille	Pete	1925-30	92	26	4	30	58
52	Connelly	Bert	1934-38	87	13	15	28	37
53	Langlois	Charlie	1924-28	151	22	5	27	189
54	Gaudreault	Armand	1944-45	44	15	9	24	27
55	Morin	Pete	1941-42	31	10	12	22	7
56	Caron	Alain	1967-69	60	9	13	22	18
57	Leclerc	René	1969-71	87	10	11	21	105
58	Gladu	Jean-Paul	1944-45	40	6	14	20	2
59	Plamondon	Gerry	1945-51	74	7	13	20	10
60	Rivard	Bob	1967-68	27	5	12	17	4
61	Locas	Jacques	1947-49	59	7	8	15	66
62	Gaudreault	Léo	1927-33	67	8	4	12	30
63	Raymond	Paul	1932-39	76	2	3	5	6
64	Cline	Bruce	1956-57	30	2	3	5	10
65	Bell	Billy	1917-24	66	3	2	5	14
66	Ramsey	Les	1944-45	11	2	2	4	2
67	Picard	Roger	1967-68	15	2	2	4	21
68	Dubé	Gilles	1949-50	12	1	2	3	2
69	Toupin	Jacques	1943-44	8	1	2	3	0
70	Sheppard	Frank	1927-28	8	1	1	2	0

	SURNAME	FIRST NAME	SEASON	GP	G	A	PTS	PIM.
71	Finnigan	Ed	1934-36	15	1	1	2	2
72	Denis	Jean-Paul	1946-50	10	0	2	2	2
73	Lafrance	Léo	1926-28	33	2	0	2	6
74	Alexandre	Art	1931-33	11	0	2	2	8
75	Dufour	Marc	1963-69	14	1	0	1	2
76	Robert	Claude	1950-51	23	1	0	1	9
77	Corriveau	André	1953-54	3	0	1	1	0
78	Bourcier	Jean	1935-36	9	0	1	1	0
79	Rousseau	Guy	1954-57	4	0	1	1	0
80	Perreault	Fern	1947-50	3	0	0	0	0
81	Malone	Cliff	1951-52	3	0	0	0	0
82	Mcdonagh	Bill	1949-50	4	0	0	0	2
83	Mcnaughton	Georges	1919-20	1	0	0	0	0
84	Hinse	André	1967-68	4	0	0	0	0
85	Imlach	Brent	1965-67	3	0	0	0	0
86	Fillion	Marcel	1944-45	1	0	0	0	0
87	Harnott	Walter	1933-34	6	0	0	0	2
88	Cormier	Roger	1925-26	1	0	0	0	0
89	Cusson	Jean	1967-68	2	0	0	0	0
90	Davis	Bob	1932-33	3	0	0	0	0
91	Labadie	Mike	1952-53	3	0	0	0	0
92	Latreille	Phil	1960-61	4	0	0	0	2
93	Buchanan	Bucky	1948-49	2	0	0	0	0
94	Cardin	Claude	1967-68	1	0	0	0	0

TABLE 4.9

Goalies 1970 to 2009*

	SURNAME	FIRST NAME	SEASON	GP	W	L	T	AV.	%
1	Roy	Patrick	1984-03	1029	551	315	131	2.54	.910
2	Brodeur	Martin	1991-09	999	557	299	128	2.21	.914
3	Meloche	Gilles	1970-88	788	270	351	131	3.64	.875
4	Bouchard	Dan	1972-86	655	286	232	113	3.26	.876
5	Potvin	Félix	1991-04	635	266	260	85	276	.905
6	Thibeault	Jocelyn	1993-08	586	238	238	75	2.75	.904
7	Luongo	Roberto	1999-09	544	230	232	64	2.57	.919
8	Lemelin	Réjean	1978-93	507	236	162	63	3.46	.884
9	Théodore	José	1995-09	501	215	214	45	2.67	.908
10	Herron	Denis	1972-86	462	146	203	76	3.70	.879
11	Giguère	J.-Sébastien	1996-09	457	210	169	56	2.49	.914
12	Biron	Martin	1995-09	433	199	162	45	2.59	.911
13	Lalime	Patrick	1996-09	421	196	161	46	2.57	.905
14	Sauvé	Robert	1976-89	420	182	154	54	3.48	.876
15	Gilbert	Gilles	1969-83	416	192	143	60	3.27	
16	Fiset	Stéphane	1989-02	390	164	153	44	3.07	.899
17	Brodeur	Richard	1979-88	385	131	175	62	3.85	.864
18	Cloutier	Dan	1997-08	351	139	142	37	2.77	.899
19	Denis	Marc	1996-09	349	112	179	31	3.02	.902
20	Fernandez	Emmanuel	1994-09	325	143	123	35	2.50	.912
21	Larocque	Michel	1973-84	312	160	89	45	3.33	.811
22	Plasse	Michel	1970-82	299	92	136	54	3.79	
23	Cloutier	Jacques	1981-94	255	82	102	24	3.64	.874
24	Gosselin	Mario	1983-94	242	91	107	14	3.74	.871
25	Lessard	Mario	1978-84	240	92	97	39	3.74	.838
26	Fleury	Marc-André	2003-09	235	111	85	26	2.87	.907
27	Dion	Michel	1979-85	227	60	118	32	4.24	.856
28	Aubin	Sébastien	1998-08	218	80	83	16	2.93	.900
29	Berthiaume	Daniel	1986-94	215	81	90	21	3.67	.878
30	Roussel	Dominic	1991-01	205	77	70	23	3.12	.895
31	Garon	Mathieu	2000-09	204	94	83	13	2.84	.905
32	Riendeau	Vincent	1987-95	184	85	65	20	3.30	.880
33	Sévigny	Richard	1979-87	176	80	54	20	3.21	.867
34	Romano	Roberto	1982-94	126	46	63	8	3.97	.881

* Classification based on number of games played in career.

	SURNAME	FIRST NAME	SEASON	GP	W	L	T	AV.	%
35	Leclaire	Pascal	2003-09	125	45	55	12	2.82	.907
36	Wolfe	Bernard	1975-79	120	20	61	21	4.17	
37	Micalef	Corado	1981-86	113	26	59	15	4.24	.858
38	Waite	Jimmy	1988-99	106	28	41	12	3.35	.871
39	Fichaud	Éric	1995-01	95	22	47	10	3.14	.897
40	Caron	Sébastien	2003-07	92	25	47	12	3.45	.892
41	Penney	Steve	1983-88	91	35	38	12	3.62	.859
42	Beauregard	Stéphane	1989-94	90	19	39	11	3.65	.879
43	Baron	Marco	1979-85	86	34	38	9	3.63	.861
44	Hrivnac	Jim	1989-94	85	34	30	3	3.73	.877
45	Bélanger	Yves	1974-80	78	29	33	6	3.76	
46	Bergeron	Jean-Claude	1990-97	72	21	33	7	3.69	.866
47	McRae	Gord	1972-78	71	30	22	10	3.49	
48	Hamel	Pierre	1974-81	69	13	41	7	4.40	
49	Racicot	André	1989-94	68	26	23	8	3.50	.880
50	Belhumeur	Michel	1972-76	65	9	36	7	4.61	
51	Blackburn	Dan	2001-03	63	20	32	4	3.22	.894
52	Tremblay	Vincent	1979-84	58	12	26	8	4.80	8.31
53	Sabourin	Dany	2004-09	57	18	25	4	2.87	.898
54	Draper	Tom	1988-96	53	19	23	5	3.70	.877
55	Gratton	Gilles	1975-77	47	13	18	9	4.02	
56	Holland	Robbie	1979-81	44	11	22	9	4.08	
57	Brunetta	Mario	1987-90	40	12	17	1	3.90	.871
58	Dannis	Yan	2005-09	37	13	19	3	2.84	.910
59	Sauvé	Philippe	2004-07	32	10	14	3	3.45	.888
60	Chabot	Frédéric	1990-99	32	4	8	4	2.95	.894
61	Parent	Rich	1997-01	32	7	11	5	3.15	.882
62	Cousineau	Marcel	1996-00	26	4	10	1	2.92	.900
63	Corsi	Jim	1979-80	26	8	14	3	3.63	
64	Charpentier	Sébastien	2001-04	26	6	14	1	2.93	.902
65	St-Laurent	Sam	1985-90	22	3	12	3	3.67	.874
66	Wilkinson	Derek	1995-99	22	3	12	3	3.67	.874
67	O'neill	Mike	1991-97	21	0	9	2	4.28	.859
68	Champoux	Bob	1973-74	17	2	11	3	5.20	
69	Laxton	Gord	1975-79	17	4	9	0	5.55	
70	Labbé	Jean-François	1999-03	15	3	6	0	3.44	.889

➤

	SURNAME	FIRST NAME	SEASON	GP	W	L	T	AV.	%
71	Cassivi	Frédéric	2001-07	13	3	6	9	3.63	.892
72	Ouellet	Maxime	2000-06	12	2	6	2	3.08	.903
73	Deslauriers Drouin Jeff		2008-09	10	4	3	0	3.33	.901
74	Brochu	Martin	1998-04	9	0	5	0	3.58	.876
75	Dumas	Michel	1974-77	8	2	1	2	3.98	
76	Pelletier	J.-M.	1999-04	7	1	4	0	3.90	.857
77	Crawford	Corey	2005-08	7	1	2	1	2.52	.915
78	Damphousse	J.-F.	2001-02	6	1	3	0	2.45	.896
79	Sneddon	Bob	1970-71	5	0	2	0	5.60	
80	Yeats	Matthew	2003-04	5	1	3	0	3.20	.908
81	Bernier	Jonathan	2007-08	4	1	3	0	4.03	
82	Legris	Claude	1980-82	4	0	1	1	2.64	
83	Derouville	Philippe	1994-97	3	1	2	0	3.16	.903
84	Larocque	Michel	2000-01	3	0	2	0	3.55	.847
85	Tordjman	Josh	2008-09	2	0	2	0	4.07	.871
86	Labrecque	Patrick	1995-96	2	0	1	0	4.29	.851
87	Levasseur	Jean-Louis	1979-80	1	0	1	0	7.00	
88	Chouinard	Mathieu	2003-04	1	0	0	0	.00	1.000
89	Houle	Martin	2006-07	1	0	0	0	30.00	.667
90	Lajeunesse	Simon	2001-02	1	0	0	0	.00	1.000
91	Pageau	Paul	1980-81	1	0	1	0	8.00	
92	Raymond	Alain	1987-88	1	0	1	0	3.00	.900
93	Soucy	Christian	1993-94	1	0	0	0	.00	
94	Centomo	Sébastien	2001-02	1	0	0	0	4.50	.750
95	Michaud	Olivier	2001-02	1	0	0	0	.00	1.000
96	Sharples	Scott	1991-92	1	0	0	1	3.69	.900

TABLE 4.10

Goalies whose careers began before the season 1970-71*

	SURNAME	FIRST NAME	SEASON	GP	W	L	T	AV.	%
1	Worsley	Lorne Gump	1952-74	861	335	352	150	2.88	
2	Plante	Jacques	1952-73	837	437	246	145	2.38	
3	Vachon	Rogatien	1966-82	795	355	291	127	2.99	
4	Parent	Bernard	1965-79	608	271	198	121	2.55	
5	Johnston	Eddie	1962-78	592	234	257	80	3.25	
6	Myre	Phil	1969-83	439	149	198	76	3.53	
7	Chabot	Lorne	1927-37	411	201	147	52	2.03	
8	Hodge	Charlie	1954-71	358	150	125	61	2.70	
9	Dejordy	Denis	1962-74	316	124	128	51	3.13	
10	McNeil	Gerry	1947-57	276	119	105	52	2.36	
11	Bibeault	Paul	1940-47	214	81	107	25	3.65	
12	Villemure	Gilles	1963-77	205	100	64	29	2.81	
13	Vézina	Georges	1917-26	190	103	81	5	3.28	
14	Paille	Marcel	1957-65	107	32	52	22	3.42	
15	Caron	Jacques	1967-74	72	24	29	11	3.29	
16	Gardner	George	1965-72	66	16	30	6	3.75	
17	Rivard	Fern	1968-75	55	9	27	11	3.98	
18	Dion	Connie	1943-45	38	23	11	4	3.13	
19	Perreault	Bob	1955-63	31	8	16	7	3.38	
20	Rhéaume	Herb	1925-26	31	10	20	1	2.92	
21	Brophy	Frank	1919-20	21	3	18	0	7.11	
22	Pelletier	Marcel	1950-63	8	1	6	0	4.86	
23	Courteau	Maurice	1943-44	6	2	4	0	5.50	
24	Evans	Claude	1954-58	5	1	2	1	3.69	
25	Gill	André	1967-68	5	3	2	0	2.89	
26	Boisvert	Gilles	1959-60	3	0	3	0	3.00	
27	Marois	Jean	1943-44	3	1	2	0	5.00	
28	Pronovost	Claude	1955-59	3	1	1	0	3.50	
29	Cyr	Claude	1958-59	1	0	0	0	3.00	
30	Murphy	Hal	1952-53	1	1	0	0	4.00	
31	Ouimet	Ted	1968-69	1	0	1	0	2.00	
32	Binette	André	1954-55	1	0	0	0	4.00	

* Classification based on number of games played in career.

TABLE 4.11

Defencemen 1970 to 2009*

	SURNAME	FIRST NAME	SEASON	GP	G	A	PTS	PIM.
1	Bourque	Raymond	1979-01	1612	410	1169	1579	1141
2	Potvin	Denis	1973-88	1060	310	742	1052	1356
3	Duschesne	Steve	1986-02	1113	227	525	752	824
4	Galley	Gary	1984-01	1149	125	475	600	1218
5	Desjardins	Éric	1988-06	1143	136	439	575	757
6	Turnbull	Ian	1973-83	628	123	317	440	736
7	Côté	Sylvain	1984-03	1171	122	313	435	545
8	Marois	Mario	1977-92	955	76	357	433	1746
9	Lowe	Kevin	1979-98	1254	84	348	432	1498
10	Picard	Robert	1977-90	899	104	319	423	1025
11	Brisebois	Patrice	1990-09	1009	98	322	420	623
12	Hardy	Marc	1979-94	915	62	306	368	1293
13	Tallon	Dale	1970-80	642	98	238	336	568
14	Petit	Michel	1982-98	827	90	238	328	1839
15	Guèvremont	Jocelyn	1971-80	571	84	223	307	319
16	Boucher	Philippe	1992-09	748	94	206	300	702
17	Daigneault	Jean-Jacques	1984-01	899	53	197	250	687
18	Dupont	André	1970-83	800	59	185	244	1986
19	Quintal	Stéphane	1988-04	1037	63	180	243	1320
20	Gingras	Gaston	1979-89	476	61	174	235	161
21	Racine	Yves	1989-98	508	37	194	231	439
22	Dandenault	Mathieu	1995-09	868	68	135	203	516
23	Lefebvre	Sylvain	1989-03	945	30	154	184	674
24	Bergevin	Marc	1984-04	1191	36	145	181	1090
25	Bergeron	Marc-André	2002-09	339	62	98	160	161
26	Rochefort	Normand	1980-94	598	39	119	158	570
27	Dollas	Bobby	1983-01	646	42	96	138	467
28	Robidas	Stéphane	1999-09	561	30	105	135	418
29	Dykhus	Karl	1991-04	644	42	91	133	495
30	Lacroix	Pierre	1979-83	274	24	108	132	197
31	Tremblay	Yannick	1996-07	390	38	87	125	178
32	Delorme	Gilbert	1981-90	541	31	92	123	520
33	Hamel	Jean	1972-84	699	26	95	121	766
34	Mulhern	Richard	1975-81	303	27	93	120	217
35	Finn	Steven	1985-97	725	34	78	112	1724
36	Faubert	Mario	1974-82	231	21	90	111	292
37	Bouchard	Pierre	1970-82	595	24	82	106	433
38	Bouillon	Francis	1999-09	485	21	81	102	371
39	Velischek	Randy	1982-92	509	21	76	97	401
40	Doré	André	1978-85	257	14	81	95	261
41	Carriere	Larry	1972-80	367	16	74	90	462
42	Beauchemin	François	2002-09	246	21	69	90	172
43	Lemieux	Jean	1973-78	204	23	63	86	39
44	Murray	Terry	1972-82	302	4	76	80	199
45	Gauthier	Denis	1997-09	554	17	60	77	748

* Classification based on number of points in career.

	SURNAME	FIRST NAME	SEASON	GP	G	A	PTS	PIM.
46	Vlasic	Marc-Édouard	2006-09	245	11	65	76	84
47	Bouchard	Joël	1994-06	364	22	53	75	264
48	Messier	Éric	1996-04	406	25	50	75	146
49	Plavsic	Adrien	1989-97	214	16	56	72	161
50	Zettler	Rob	1988-02	569	5	65	70	920
51	Donnely	Gord	1983-95	554	28	41	69	2069
52	Weir	Wally	1979-85	320	21	45	66	625
53	Traverse	Patrick	1995-06	279	14	51	65	113
54	Anderson	Shawn	1986-95	255	11	51	62	117
55	Letang	Kristopher	2006-09	144	18	34	52	51
56	Laflamme	Christian	1996-04	324	2	45	47	282
57	Gervais	Bruno	2005-09	207	6	39	45	103
58	Girard	Jonathan	1998-03	150	10	34	44	46
59	Biron	Mathieu	1999-06	253	12	32	44	177
60	Dufresne	Donald	1988-97	268	6	36	42	258
61	Picard	Alexandre	2005-09	139	12	30	42	39
62	Logan	Dave	1975-81	218	5	29	34	470
63	Trépanier	Pascal	1997-03	229	12	22	34	252
64	Lupien	Gilles	1977-82	226	5	25	30	416
65	Ciccone	Enrico	1991-01	374	10	18	28	1469
66	Chychrun	Jeff	1986-94	262	3	22	25	744
67	Doig	Jason	1995-04	158	6	18	24	285
68	Leroux	François	1988-98	249	3	20	23	577
69	Grand-Pierre	Jean-Luc	1998-04	269	7	13	20	311
70	Côté	Alain	1985-94	119	2	18	20	124
71	Boileau	Patrick	1996-04	48	5	11	16	26
72	Lavoie	Dominic	1988-94	38	5	8	13	32
73	Hynes	Gord	1991-93	52	3	9	12	22
74	St-Jacques	Bruno	2001-06	67	3	7	10	47
75	Meighan	Ron	1981-83	48	3	7	10	18
76	Charron	Éric	1992-00	130	2	7	9	127
77	Houde	Claude	1974-76	59	3	6	9	40
78	Therrien	Gaston	1980-83	22	0	8	8	12
79	Doyon	Mario	1988-91	28	3	4	7	16
80	Vigneault	Alain	1981-83	42	2	5	7	82
81	Laperriere	Daniel	1992-96	48	2	5	7	27
82	Poudrier	Daniel	1985-88	25	1	5	6	10
83	Richer	Stéphane	1992-95	27	1	5	6	20
84	Fortin	J.-F.	2001-04	71	1	4	5	42
85	Nasreddine	Alain	1998-08	74	1	4	5	84
86	Lajeunesse	Serge	1970-75	103	1	4	5	103
87	Lachance	Michel	1978-79	21	0	4	4	22
88	Roy	Mathieu	2005-08	30	2	1	3	57
89	Proulx	Christian	1993-94	7	1	2	3	20
90	Richard	Jean-Marc	1987-90	5	2	1	3	2

➤

	SURNAME	FIRST NAME	SEASON	GP	G	A	PTS	PIM.
91	Descoteaux	Mathieu	2000-01	5	1	1	2	4
92	Cloutier	Réjean	1979-82	5	0	2	2	2
93	Poulin	Daniel	1981-82	3	1	1	2	2
94	Tremblay	Brent	1978-80	10	1	0	1	6
95	Groleau	François	1995-98	8	0	1	1	6
96	Grenier	Martin	2001-07	18	1	0	1	14
97	Coulombe	Patrick	2006-07	7	0	1	1	4
98	Germain	Éric	1987-88	4	0	1	1	13
99	Guérard	Stéphane	1987-90	34	0	0	0	40
100	Royer	Rémi	1998-99	18	0	0	0	67
101	Beaudoin	Yves	1985-88	11	0	0	0	5
102	Bolduc	Michel	1981-83	10	0	0	0	6
103	Pollock	James	2003-04	9	0	0	0	6
104	Côté	J.-Philippe	2005-06	8	0	0	0	4
105	Cornforth	Mark	1995-96	6	0	0	0	4
106	Maciver	Don	1979-80	6	0	0	0	2
107	Larocque	Mario	1998-99	5	0	0	0	16
108	Allan	Jeff	1977-78	4	0	0	0	2
109	Beaudoin	Serge	1979-80	3	0	0	0	0
110	Gauthier	Luc	1990-91	3	0	0	0	2
111	Gaul	Michael	1998-01	3	0	0	0	4
112	Gragnani	M.-A.	2007-09	6	0	0	0	6
113	Gauvreau	Jocelyn	1983-84	2	0	0	0	0
114	Folco	Peter	1973-74	2	0	0	0	0
115	Bisaillon	Sébastien	2006-07	2	0	0	0	0
116	Brochu	Stéphane	1988-89	1	0	0	0	0
117	Lavigne	Éric	1994-95	1	0	0	0	0
118	Mackasey	Blair	1976-77	1	0	0	0	2
119	Mormina	Joey	2007-08	1	0	0	0	0

TABLE 4.12

Defencemen whose careers began before the season 1970-71*

	SURNAME	FIRST NAME	SEASON	GP	G	A	PTS	PIM.
1	Lapointe	Guy	1968-84	884	171	451	622	893
2	Vadnais	Carol	1966-83	1087	169	418	587	1813
3	Harvey	Doug	1947-69	1113	88	452	540	1216
4	Pilote	Pierre	1955-69	890	80	418	498	1251
5	Savard	Serge	1966-83	1040	106	333	439	592
6	Tremblay	Jean-Claude	1959-72	794	57	306	363	204
7	Pronovost	Marcel	1950-70	1206	88	257	345	851
8	Marotte	Gilles	1965-77	808	56	265	321	919
9	Talbot	Jean-Guy	1954-71	1056	43	242	285	1006
10	Laperriere	Jacques	1962-74	691	40	242	282	674
11	Vasko	Moose	1956-70	786	34	166	200	719
12	Morrison	Jim	1951-71	704	40	160	200	542
13	Bouchard	Émile Butch	1941-56	785	49	144	198	863
14	St-Laurent	Dollard	1950-62	652	29	133	162	496
15	Mantha	Sylvio	1923-37	542	63	78	141	671
16	Cleghorn	Sprague	1918-28	259	83	55	138	538
17	Langlois	Albert Junior	1957-66	497	21	91	112	488
18	Harris	Ron	1962-76	476	20	91	111	474
19	Leduc	Albert	1925-35	383	57	35	92	614
20	Mcmahon	Mike	1963-72	224	15	68	83	171
21	Buller	Hy	1943-54	188	22	58	80	215
22	Picard	Noël	1964-73	335	12	63	75	616
23	Léger	Roger	1943-50	187	18	53	71	71
24	Eddolls	Frank	1944-52	317	23	43	66	114
25	Buswell	Walt	1932-40	368	10	40	50	164
26	Lagacé	Jean-Guy	1968-76	197	9	39	48	251
27	Goupille	Red	1935-43	222	12	28	40	256
28	Gauthier	Jean	1960-70	166	6	29	35	150
29	Orlando	Jimmy	1936-43	199	6	25	31	375
30	Watson	Jim	1963-72	221	4	19	23	345
31	Wilcox	Archie	1929-35	208	8	14	22	158
32	Ritchie	Dave	1917-26	58	15	6	21	50
33	Blackburn	Bob	1968-71	135	8	12	20	105
34	Gorman	Ed	1924-28	111	14	6	20	108

* Classification based on number of points in career.

	SURNAME	FIRST NAME	SEASON	GP	G	A	PTS	PIM.
35	Lacombe	François	1968-80	78	2	17	19	54
36	Zeidel	Larry	1951-69	158	3	16	19	198
37	Hollingworth	Gord	1954-58	163	4	14	18	201
38	Labrie	Guy	1943-45	42	4	9	13	16
39	Lamirande	Jean-Paul	1946-55	49	5	5	10	26
40	Campbell	Earl	1923-26	76	6	3	9	14
41	Hicks	Henry	1928-31	96	7	2	9	72
42	Johnstone	Ross	1943-45	42	5	4	9	14
43	Fortin	Raymond	1968-70	92	2	6	8	33
44	Pusie	Jean	1930-36	61	1	4	5	28
45	Lemieux	Jacques	1967-70	19	0	4	4	8
46	Lemieux	Bob	1967-68	19	0	1	1	12
47	Paulhus	Rollie	1925-26	33	0	0	0	0
48	Croghan	Maurice	1937-38	16	0	0	0	4
49	O'grady	George	1917-18	4	0	0	0	0
50	Manastersky	Tom	1950-51	6	0	0	0	0
51	Campbell	Dave	1920-21	2	0	0	0	0
52	Deslauriers	Jacques	1955-56	2	0	0	0	0
53	Leroux	Gaston	1935-36	2	0	0	0	0
54	Jacobs	Paul	1918-19	1	0	0	0	0
55	Laforce	Ernie	1942-43	1	0	0	0	0
56	Mailley	Frank	1942-43	1	0	0	0	0
57	Patrick	Lester	1926-27	1	0	0	0	2
58	Pelletier	Roger	1967-68	1	0	0	0	0
59	Roche	Ernie	1950-51	4	0	0	0	2
60	Rousseau	Roland	1952-53	2	0	0	0	0

Chapter 5

Coaches

Most Quebec coaches who started out in the Quebec Major Junior Hockey League have experienced what Jacques Laporte described when quoted in the *ruefrontenac.com* on April 2, 2009. "The key to a career in the National Hockey League is first and foremost to have a solid network of contacts in the English-speaking hockey world. Therefore it is much better to coach a university team anywhere in Canada, but not in Quebec." Jacques Laporte is coach of the Patriotes of the Université du Québec à Trois-Rivières. The network of contacts for Quebec university coaches has been limited to two teams: the Montreal Canadiens and the Quebec Nordiques. However, the Nordiques moved to Colorado. As a result, the only team that might need French-speaking coaches from the Quebec Major Junior Hockey League and the Quebec university league is the Montreal Canadiens.

The only other person in professional hockey who has given Quebec coaches a chance is Jacques Martin who began coaching the Montreal Canadiens on June 1, 2009. This makes it very challenging for Quebec coaches to advance in their careers. Jacques Laporte is on the mark when he talks about networking. That is exactly how things played out in the following months when the Canadiens hired Guy Boucher on June 29, 2009. Guy Boucher was chosen from a long list of candidates to replace Don Lever as the head coach for the Canadiens' farm team in Hamilton, Ontario. Media pressure may have been instrumental in the hiring of a French-speaking Quebec coach. It certainly didn't hurt. Guy Boucher needed assistants and so he turned to his network of contacts and thus gave the same opportunity to two other Quebec coaches, Daniel Lacroix and Martin Raymond, both of whom were highly skilled and qualified to coach in the professional leagues. That is how the NHL operates and, once in a while, enables a Quebec coach to seize the opportunity to reach the big leagues and show that he is qualified to coach in the NHL. That visibility also explains why Guy Boucher was hired as head coach of the Tampa Bay Lighning.

Following the publication of this book in French, Michel Bergeron, who coached the Quebec Nordiques and the New York Rangers from 1981 through 1990 declared: "I agree with Bob Sirois' conclusions. The many statistics are interesting and troubling. With firsthand experience, I can say that it reflects reality exactly. What's more, if the Quebec Nordiques had not existed, I would never have coached a National Hockey League team. The same can be said for all those who came after me, Jacques Demers, Alain Vigneault, Michel Therrien, and more."

Thirty-two Quebec coaches have worked as head coach in the National Hockey League. Eighteen of them participated in more than two hundred games. Table 5.1 lists all the Quebec coaches with their first teams and their main statistics since the 1970 season.

The great coaches obtained amazing, even phenomenal, results. When I decided to include coaches in this book, I never expected to find such impressive results. Though I knew they were all qualified and competent, their results greatly exceed my expectations. A list of the Quebec coaches who won the Jack Adams Award is provided first. The Jack Adams Award has been presented annually since 1974 to the NHL coach who has contributed the most to his team's success of his team. The winner is chosen based on a vote by the NHL Broadcasters' Association.

The Jack Adams Award has been presented thirty-five times since 1974 and eight Quebec coaches have won it a total of fourteen times. This means that seven of the eighteen Quebec coaches won the trophy, or 44 percent. By winning this honour fourteen times, these coaches only left the award open for their English Canadian or American counterparts on twenty-one other occasions. Here is the list of Jack Adams Award winners:

1977: Scotty Bowman of the Montreal Canadiens
1983: Orval Tessier of the Chicago Blackhawks
1984: Bryan Murray of the Washington Capitals
1987: Jacques Demers of the Detroit Red Wings
1988: Jacques Demers of the Detroit Red Wings
1989: Pat Burns of the Montreal Canadiens
1993: Pat Burns of the Toronto Maple Leafs

TABLE 5.1

RANK	SEASON	NAME	TEAM	GAMES PLAYED	WINS	LOSSES	TIES	POINTS	% AVERAGE
1	1968-2002	Scotty Bowman	St. Louis	2141	1244	573	324	2812	.657
2	1981-2008	Bryan Murray	Washington	1239	620	465	154	1394	.563
3	1983-2009	Jacques Lemaire	Montréal	1131	540	414	177	1257	.556
4	1989-2004	Pat Burns	Montréal	1019	501	353	165	1167	.573
5	1979-1999	Jacques Demers	Québec	1007	409	468	130	948	.471
6	1979-1994	Bob Berry	Los Angeles	860	384	355	121	889	.517
7	1989-2009	Terry Murray	Washington	819	394	314	111	899	.549
8	1981-1990	Michel Bergeron	Québec	792	338	350	104	780	.492
9	1988-1998	Pierre Pagé	Minnesota	636	253	301	82	588	.462
10	1998-2009	Alain Vigneault	Montréal	512	242	204	66	550	.537
11	2001-2009	Michel Therrien	Montréal	462	212	182	68	492	.532
12	2002-2009	Claude Julien	Montréal	402	213	134	55	481	.598
13	1969-1981	Claude Ruel	Montréal	305	172	82	51	395	.648
14	1985-1989	Jean Perron	Montréal	287	142	110	35	319	.556
15	1969-1980	Bernard Geoffrion	NY Rangers	281	114	119	48	276	.491
16	2007-2009	Guy Carbonneau	Montréal	230	124	83	23	271	.589
17	1983-1985	Orval Tessier	Chicago	213	99	93	21	219	514
18	1972-1978	Jean-Guy Talbot	St. Louis	200	82	90	28	192	.480
19	1996-1997	Mario Tremblay	Montréal	159	71	63	25	167	.525
20	1974-1976	Marc Boileau	Pittsburgh	151	66	61	24	156	.517
21	2007-2009	Denis Savard	Chicago	147	65	66	16	146	.497
22	1977-1979	Marcel Pronovost	Buffalo	104	52	29	23	127	.611
23	1987-1989	Ron Lapointe	Québec	89	33	50	6	72	.404
24	1999-2000	Kevin Lowe	Edmonton	82	32	26	24	88	.537
25	1987-1988	Pierre Creamer	Pittsburgh	80	36	35	9	81	.506
26	1992-2001	Guy Charron	Calgary	65	20	33	12	52	.400
27	1972-1973	Phil Goyette	NY Islanders	48	6	38	4	16	.167
28	1977-1978	André Beaulieu	Minnesota	32	6	23	3	15	.234
29	1987-1988	André Savard	Québec	24	10	13	1	21	.438
30	1984-1995	Rogatien Vachon	Los Angeles	10	4	3	3	11	.550
31	1981	Maurice Fillion	Québec	6	1	3	2	4	.333
32	1996	Jacques Laperrière	Montréal	1	–	–	–	–	.000

1994: Jacques Lemaire of the New Jersey Devils
1996: Scotty Bowman of the Detroit Red Wings
1998: Pat Burns of the Boston Bruins
2003: Jacques Lemaire of the Minnesota Wild
2007: Alain Vigneault of the Vancouver Canucks
2009: Claude Julien of the Boston Bruins

Coaches also win other honours besides the Jack Adams Award. Since the 1970-71 season, the Stanley Cup has been won thirty-eight times. That prestigious cup has been won thirteen times by teams with Quebec coaches. This is the list of the cup winners:

1972-73: Scotty Bowman of the Montreal Canadiens
1975-76: Scotty Bowman of the Montreal Canadiens
1976-77: Scotty Bowman of the Montreal Canadiens
1977-78: Scotty Bowman of the Montreal Canadiens
1978-79: Scotty Bowman of the Montreal Canadiens
1985-86: Jean Perron of the Montreal Canadiens
1991-92: Scotty Bowman of the Pittsburgh Penguins
1992-93: Jacques Demers of the Montreal Canadiens
1994-95: Jacques Lemaire of the New Jersey Devils
1996-97: Scotty Bowman of the Detroit Red Wings
1997-98: Scotty Bowman of the Detroit Red Wings
2001-02: Scotty Bowman of the Detroit Red Wings
2002-03: Pat Burns of the New Jersey Devils

Canada has had many English and French-speaking prime ministers from Quebec. If the country accepts having a Prime Minister from Quebec, perhaps—I don't want to sound pushy—the time has come for Hockey Canada choose a head coach from Quebec to lead Team Canada at the Olympics or the World Championships.

Chapter 6
Conclusion

Statistics can reveal many things depending on the questions asked. Yet they cannot be made to say absolutely everything. The figures must be carefully scrutinized in order to obtain straight-forward and accurate answers that are unswayed by emotion.

This book provides many lists and tables. Any number of questions can be asked and clear unambiguous answers can be obtained. All that is required is a pen, a piece of paper, and a calculator. The figures cannot be twisted to say something that doesn't bear out. They will always provide honest answers.

The French-speaking population in Canada comprises an ethnic minority, and in the NHL French-speaking Quebecers are even more of a minority. Although some discriminatory practices have been denounced, the participation of Quebecers in Canadian and American hockey has never really been analysed. The Quebec media through its close contact with Quebec hockey players and certain members of NHL teams has led the way in documenting and revealing these discriminatory practices. One persistent question will just not go away. Are Quebec hockey players in the NHL treated equally or unequally during the Entry Draft? When national teams are chosen? When a head coach is chosen for Team Canada at the Olympics? The same question is asked with regards to Hockey Canada and the formation of Junior Team Canada. Inevitably, in all these situations the old question of "equal talent and unequal treatment" is raised.

This is a very serious issue. Several academics in North America have examined the possibility that French-speaking players in the NHL experience discrimination. In 1975 the first sociologist to study the question, an American named David Marple, reached conclusions that were both surprising and shocking.[1] After studying the

---

1. Marc Lavoie, *Désavantage numérique, Les francophones dans la LNH,* Éditions Vents d'Ouest, 1997, p. 29.

situation of African Americans in basketball in the 1970s, he examined whether French-speaking hockey players in the NHL experienced analogous conditions. David Marple was the first to analyse the numbers of players and their productivity in the NHL from the standpoint of ethnicity. Marple concluded that French-speaking players suffered discrimination because, like African Americans in basketball, French-speaking players were more productive yet played fewer games. His conclusions left room for doubt however because they were based on only one hockey season.

Yet his study opened new ground. After he made those observations other academics looked into the question from different angles between 1970 and 2009.[2] If Marple's observations were to bear out over several seasons, it would be proof of a very unhealthy sociological phenomenon.

The following pages present the quantitative findings of several academics over the past forty years. Their research contradicts the myths and stereotypes so often repeated about French-speaking Quebecers. Moreover, the conclusions drawn in this book corroborate their conclusions. Some readers are bound to be surprised.

Marc Lavoie is a Professor of Economics at the University of Ottawa and also an elite athlete. He has won the Canadian Individual Fencing Championship seven times, brought home silver from Commonwealth Games, and competed in the Olympics twice. He has also published two books on hockey in the NHL: *Avantage numérique: l'argent et la Ligue nationale de hockey* and *Désavantage numérique: les francophones dans la NHL*.

Marc Lavoie was particularly upset when he read an article by Guy Robillard of the Canadian Press on March 6, 1990. Robillard asked, "When will a serious study be conducted on French-speaking hockey players in professional hockey?" That is when he decided to undertake his study. My conclusion begins with a myth that Professor Lavoie analysed concerning the size of French-speaking Quebecers.

---

2. Marc Lavoie, *op. cit.;* Neil Longley, "The underrepresentation of French Canadians on English Canadian NHL Teams: Evidence from 1943 to 1998," *Journal of Sports Economics*, vol. 1, No. 3, March 2001, pp. 236-256.

Are French-speaking players really smaller than their English counterparts?

Hockey players have grown in size over the past twenty years. We often hear that Quebec juniors are smaller than juniors in Ontario and in the West. This is not myth or prejudice. According to Table 6.1, Quebec hockey players are in fact smaller and weigh less than juniors in other Canadian junior leagues. Yet it should be added that statistically the gap is almost insignificant.

TABLE 6.1

Comparison of the average height and weight of Canadian major junior hockey league players according to their positions (1984-88)

PLAYERS	FORWARDS		DEFENCEMEN		GOALIES	
	HEIGHT (in)	WEIGHT (lb)	HEIGHT (in)	WEIGHT (lb)	HEIGHT (in	WEIGHT (lb)
LHJMQ	70.9	180.1	71.9	187.2	69.9	167.4
OHL	71.7	184.5	72.7	191.3	70.5	170.2
WHL	71.3	182.4	72.5	190.5	70.3	171.3

LHJMQ – OHL	- 0.8	- 4.4	- 0.8	- 4.1	- 0.6	- 2.8
LHJMQ – WHL	- 0.4	- 2.1	- 0.2	- 0.8	- 0.2	- 1.1

Quebec hockey players are 0.7 in or 1.76 cm shorter than those from Ontario.
Quebec hockey players are 4.2 lbs or 1.93 kg lighter than those from Ontario.
Quebec hockey players are 0.45 in or 1.01 cm shorter than those from the West.
Quebec hockey players are 1.45 lbs or 0.66 kg lighter than those from the West.

Players' heights were studied further to determine whether those differences were the same in the NHL. It was found that English-speaking players were bigger than French-speaking players in the NHL, but the difference was rarely significant in comparison with what was found in junior hockey. In the 1993-94 season, French-speaking forwards were bigger than English-speaking forwards. The same went for French-speaking defencemen who were bigger than the English-speaking defencemen in 1977-78 and 1983-84,. Therefore, when people say that French-speaking Quebec hockey players are smaller than their English-speaking counterparts, it should be remembered that the difference is only about half an inch and three pounds (1 cm, 1.4 kg).

Do French-speaking players lack defensive skills?

It is often said that the Quebec Major Junior Hockey League focuses only on offence and as a result French-speaking players always like to be attacking and consider defensive play to be less important. Is this a stereotype or is it based on fact? The only way to determine whether offensive play is the priority in Quebec junior hockey is to compare the number of goals scored per season in the country's three junior leagues. The league in which offence is the most important should register the most goals in a season while the league that focuses most on defensive play should logically register the least number of goals per season

Table 6.2 presents data gathered by Marc Lavoie of the University of Ottawa for his 1998 book *Désavantage numérique*, and the results are astounding. They cover the Canadian junior hockey leagues for eighteen seasons from 1979 to 1997. They show that hockey players in the Quebec Major Junior Hockey League did not score any more goals per season than the other two Canadian junior hockey leagues. Moreover between 1990 and 1997 fewer goals per season were scored in the Quebec league than in Ontario and the West. Some people will reply gratuitously that the goalies in the other two junior leagues were not as good as Quebec goalies. Yet these statistics show that NHL scouts and many Canadian junior hockey analysts will no longer have grounds to claim that French-speaking hockey players lack defensive skills compared to junior hockey players from the rest of Canada.

The statistics in Table 6.2 clearly debunk the myth perpetuated by many in Canada, and even in Quebec, about the poor defensive play of Quebecers. The myth is shown to be based only on prejudice, but It comes in handy when the time comes to justify biased choices made by NHL scouts and Junior Team Canada decision-makers.

TABLE 6.2

**Average number of goals per season and per team
in the Canadian major junior hockey leagues (1979-97)**

SEASON	LEAGUE			STANDING OF THE LHJMQ
	OHL	WHL	LHJMQ	
1979-80	4.85	4.7	5.11	3
1980-81	4.84	4.89	4.7	1
1981-82	4.5	5.1	4.92	2
1982-83	4.81	5.16	5.4	3
1983-84	4.62	5.06	5.04	2
1984-85	4.56	4.91	4.97	3
1985-86	4.43	4.97	5	3
1986-87	4.46	4.94	5.14	3
1987-88	4.47	4.76	4.87	3
1988-89	4.55	4.72	4.6	3
1989-90	4.38	4.8	4.22	1
1990-91	4.47	4.71	3.86	1
1991-92	4.45	4.14	4.21	2
1992-93	4.48	4.15	4.4	2
1993-94	4.37	4.24	4.13	1
1994-95	4.03	3.92	3.96	2
1995-96	4.09	4	4.01	2
1996-97	4.01	3.85	3.76	1
AVERAGE				
1979-83	4.75	4.96	5.03	3
1983-90	4.5	4.88	4.83	2
1990-97	4.31	4.19	4.01	1
AVERAGE				
1979-97	4.37	4.68	4.62	2
2007-08	3.45	3	3.42	2

Are Quebec goaltenders the best in the NHL?

NO. The proportion of French-speaking goalies is high in relation to the number of French-speaking defencemen and forwards. That's why people believe that French-speaking goalies are so good.

The average performance of French-speaking goalies, however, is almost identical to that of English-speaking goalies. Marc Lavoie reached that conclusion after compiling all the statistics concerning Canadian and Quebec goalies.

Is the career offensive performance of French-speaking players superior to that of English-speaking players?

YES. All researchers, be it Marple (1975), Longley (2001), Coulombe and Lavoie (1985) or Lavoie (1998), have concluded that the average performance of French-speaking forwards is between 17 and 26 percent superior to that of English Canadians depending on the season. Furthermore, the performance of French-speaking defencemen surpasses that of English-Canadian defencemen by between 11 percent and 41 percent.

This observation made by all the academics who have examined the issue does not prove that French-speaking Quebec hockey players are better at offensive play than English-Canadian players. It does however corroborate the hypothesis first advanced in 1975 by University of Cincinnati sports sociologist David Marple. Marple had first studied the situation of African-American basketball players compared to that of whites. He was immediately struck by the similarity between those results and the ones he had compiled for professional hockey. He concluded his study by asking whether French-speaking hockey players had to be more talented than the others to be drafted by the NHL. He was right on the mark.

Table 4.4 and the section entitled "NHL Individual Trophy Winners" show that a total of seventy-four of the 176 French-speaking Quebec hockey players who played more than two hundred games in the NHL between the 1970-71 and 2008-09 won a league individual trophy or participated in an NHL All-Star Game. It also shows that more than 42 percent of French-speaking Quebec hockey players won honours from the NHL, which proves that they were top-level players on their teams. It is understandable, therefore, that academics found the performance of French-speaking hockey players to be superior to that of the English Canadian players. "Only top-level French-speaking Quebec hockey players can hope to have a career in the NHL." That statement, which often appears in Quebec media, is thus shown to be true and based on fact.

The facts on discrimination against French-speaking Quebecers in the NHL (1970-2009)

·   17.06 percent of Quebec players drafted between 1970 and 2009 were English-speaking Quebecers, which is twice the percentage of the English-speaking population in Quebec (8.5 percent).

·   19.80 percent of Quebec players who were drafted and played at least one game in the NHL were English-speaking Quebecers, which is slightly more than twice the percentage of the English-speaking population in Quebec. Furthermore, 21.08 percent of Quebec hockey players who played more than two hundred games were English-speaking Quebecers, which is two-and-a-half times the percentage of the English-speaking population in Quebec.

· Ten percent of the hockey players who played in the NHL were never drafted =, whereas 19.06 percent of Quebec hockey players who played in the league were never drafted (almost twice as many).

· Young English-speaking midget hockey players from Quebec have twice as much chance of being drafted three years later by an NHL team than French-speaking midgets in Quebec. French-speaking midgets had one chance in 618 whereas English-speaking midgets had one chance in 334.

· Table 2.16 shows that there is an enormous difference between teams at the top and those in the cellar.

· In thirteen seasons, only one French-speaking Quebecer played more than one season (80 games) with the Carolina Hurricanes.

· More than 42 percent of French-speaking Quebecers who played more than two hundred games in the NHL between 1970 and 2009 won individual honours. This proves that Quebecers must be better than other players to make it in the NHL.

Discrimination towards French-speaking Quebecers in the NHL has an impact in Quebec. The facts leave no doubt: at equal talent in Quebec, English-speaking Quebecers are favoured.

There are few solutions to this problem, but I propose two: bring an NHL team to Quebec City and create a Quebec junior team.

Time has come for an NHL team to return to Quebec City

The rivalry between the Montreal Canadiens and Quebec Nordiques played out over the course of sixteen seasons and gave 124 Quebec hockey players tremendous visibility in the NHL (See Appendix, Table I). Many players benefited from this visibility and were able to show managers of other NHL teams that Quebec produces many excellent hockey players.

Since the Nordiques left for Colorado, Quebec players have been on the verge of extinction with the Montreal Canadiens (See Appendix, Table I) and elsewhere in the NHL (See Table 4.2). If the rivalry between Quebec and Montreal could be revived, hockey fans would be happy and more Quebec players would inevitably make it to the NHL. That's the first solution. It would provide the visibility that most Quebec hockey players now lack.

The other way to increase the visibility of Quebec hockey players is to establish a Junior Team Quebec to represent Quebec during the World Hockey Championships on an equal footing the Junior Team Canada.

Quebec is a nation

Every year during Christmas holidays people can be heard asking, why are Quebecers unable to make Junior Team Canada? Many say that a different style of hockey is played in Quebec compared to the other Canadian junior leagues. When the final line-up for Junior Team Canada is announced, Quebec hockey players are unfailingly few and far between. Canada has earned the reputation as a junior hockey powerhouse, yet many young Canadian and Quebec players who could be facing off in the World Championships are excluded. On the other hand, Quebec hockey certainly has what is needed to form a good team for each World Junior Hockey Championship. A glance at all the English and French-speaking players who are drafted each year by the NHL will give you an idea how well Quebec would be represented if it had a team at the World Junior Championships.

How does Quebec rank as a nation based on the National Hockey League draft and what was the representation of Quebec players in the NHL during 2008-09 hockey season?

Table 6.3 shows that for the last sixteen years Quebec has ranked fourth in the number of hockey players drafted. For the number of active NHL players during the 2008-09 season, Quebec ranked third just behind the United States and Canada without Quebec. The vast majority of players who now play in the NHL were rejected by Hockey Canada team managers when they were juniors. Despite their being snubbed, Quebecers like David Perron, Marc-Édouard

TABLE 6.3

Results of NHL player draft by nation between 1994 and 2009

NATION	1994	1995	1996	1997	1998	1999	2000	2001	2002	2003	2004	2005	2006	2007	2008	2009	TOTAL DRAFTED	AVERAGE DRAFTED	AVERAGE ACTIVE PLAYERS	NUMBER ACTIVE PLAYERS
Canada*	118	105	109	109	100	91	77	91	90	101	107	92	64	91	99	81	1527	37.55%	44.97%	438
United States	48	16	29	39	40	50	56	41	60	59	64	61	60	63	46	55	787	19.36%	22.17%	216
Russia	30	24	20	19	25	27	39	36	33	29	18	11	15	8	9	7	350	8.60%	3.28%	32
Québec	33	33	31	20	29	16	19	15	17	28	18	18	17	11	21	21	346	8.51%	7.29%	71
Sweden	17	8	15	15	17	22	23	17	20	16	19	12	18	17	17	24	277	6.81%	5.44%	53
Czech Rep.	16	21	11	16	21	18	24	31	26	18	21	12	8	5	3	3	254	6.25%	5.85%	57
Finland	7	13	8	12	12	18	19	23	25	13	14	9	13	4	7	10	207	5.09%	4.31%	42
Slovakia	4	7	7	6	6	12	16	15	3	10	10	8	4	3	0	5	116	2.85%	1.85%	18
Switzerland	1	0	1	3	2	2	6	5	5	5	4	0	3	2	2	0	41	1.00%	0.51%	5
Germany	2	2	3	2	0	0	1	6	0	4	2	1	3	3	1	1	31	0.76%	0.92%	9
Kazakhstan	1	1	1	0	2	5	6	3	0	2	3	0	0	1	0	0	25	0.61%	0.20%	2
Ukraine	4	3	3	1	1	1	1	1	1	1	0	0	0	1	0	0	18	0.44%	0.41%	4
Latvia	0	0	0	1	1	2	2	1	3	2	1	1	2	0	0	0	16	0.39%	0.10%	1
Belarus	1	0	1	1	0	2	0	0	1	2	4	1	0	0	1	1	15	0.37%	0.31%	3
Austria	0	1	0	1	1	2	1	2	1	1	0	0	2	2	0	0	12	0.30%	0.31%	3
Other	3	0	2	1	1	4	3	2	5	1	6	3	2	2	6	3	44	1.08%	2.05%	20
TOTAL	285	234	241	246	258	272	293	289	290	292	291	229	213	211	211	211	4066			974

* Excluding Québec.

Vlasic, and others who now play in the NHL managed to adapt their style of play to professional hockey. Hockey Canada always blames Quebecers for their supposed inability to adapt to the Canadian style of play when they announce their choices. Hockey Canada even claimed that Mario Lemieux would not be able to adapt. Somebody who is in the know please tell me exactly what the Quebec style of hockey is!

Photo: Victor Charbonneau

Hockey Canada even failed to include Mario Lemieux on Junior Team Canada in 1983. Picture taken when Mario Lemieux received the Maurice Richard Award from the Société Saint-Jean-Baptiste in 2002.

Over the last ten years an average of 1.8 Quebec hockey player a year has made Junior Team Canada. This is very disappointing indeed. The Quebec Major Junior Hockey League and Hockey Quebec are wrongly blamed for the problems faced by our talented young hockey players. The facts tell a totally different story.

Quebec's young players either lack the talent or fail the litmus test for being Canadian as required to make Junior Team Canada. Yet they often have the talent required to play in the NHL, sometimes even before players who made Junior Team Canada. Something other than talent must come into play.

The time has come to move on and demand that decision-makers in Quebec form a Junior Team Quebec as soon as possible so that our talented youth can participate in the World Junior Hockey Championships. Despite the contempt that Hockey Canada brass has for Quebec hockey players, Table 6.3 shows that Quebec as a nation has always played a leading role in the National Hockey league. Quebec's withdrawal from Junior Team Canada should not be seen as an insult to Canada. Quebec is a nation as stated by Prime Minister Harper and voted in the Parliament of Canada, and this means that Quebec is perfectly justified in having its own team in the next World Junior Hockey Championships.

When Quebec has its own team, we might finally grasp what actually is the mysterious Quebec style of play that leading Canadian hockey analysts have attributed to Quebecers, often with contempt. Strange events that poisoned Mario Lemieux's relationship with Junior Team Canada in 1983 will no longer occur. Our junior hockey players will be able to play with the best in the world and obtain the visibility needed to avoid being underrated.

Hockey Quebec ratified its general by-laws on June 10, 2007. Chapter 1 provides the general provisions while Section 1.3.1 is entitled: "The mission of Hockey Quebec: provide supervision for ice hockey in order to promote human development." Further on in the first chapter under the heading "Jurisdiction," it is stated that:

1.3.2a)   The jurisdiction of the corporation covers all Quebec.

1.3.2b)   The corporation should also encourage the development of networks fostering the participation of its members in Canadian hockey.

1.3.2c)   The corporation should also encourage the development of networks to foster the participation of its members in international hockey.

Would it be naïve to ask Hockey-Quebec decision-makers to use section 1.3.2c of their Charter to establish Junior Team Quebec so that members of Hockey Quebec will no longer be sidelined by the great minds who run Hockey Canada? Starting up such a team is an expensive undertaking. Fundraising campaigns will be necessary to get it going. The other very delicate but important aspect will be the negotiations involving governments, Hockey Canada, and the International Ice Hockey Federation. Who will take the lead?

Leadership is required

Quebec's minister for Education, Sports, Recreation, and the Family proposed a series of measures to eliminate violence in Quebec junior hockey in March 2008. Her stated aim was to protect young Quebec hockey players from the gratuitous violence that occurs mainly in junior hockey. As a former Quebec Major Junior Hockey League player, I applaud the minister's efforts. To be consistent with her desire to defend Quebec's young hockey players, the minister and her successors should throw their support behind Hockey Quebec's efforts to defend young Quebecers against the discrimination they suffer from Hockey Canada officials each time the line-up of Junior Team Canada is decided. It is my hope that Hockey Quebec managers will officially demand to be disassociated from Hockey Canada as regards the World Junior Hockey Championships. Quebec's best junior hockey players will then have the opportunity to play with other great hockey players from throughout the world.

The media is looking for the guilty parties

A journalist's work is to gather, examine, and comment facts and bring them to public attention through the media. Quebec sportswriters regularly report quotes and facts about Quebec players in the National Hockey League or in Quebec junior hockey. The facts they report often set North America's metaphoric Gallic village ablaze. It has yet to be confirmed whether René Goscinny, creator of the *Astérix* and *Obélix* comic books, ever spent a hockey season in Quebec, but it would surprise nobody to learn that Quebec was inspired his fifteenth album, *La Zizanie* (*Asterix and the Roman Agent*).

Asterix, Obelix and The Roman Agent

Julius Caesar decided to finish off the Gallic villagers once and for all because of their resistance to colonization by the Romans. He decided to send a renowned trouble-maker by the name of Detritus to the Gauls' village. Detritus, who had a gift for provoking fights, wreaked havoc in streets and homes.

No Julius Caesar rules over English-Canadian hockey culture but, come to think of it, one name springs to mind—no I'll stop there. Unfortunately, Detritus-type characters abound in English-Canadian hockey. They whisper myths and falsehoods about Quebec junior hockey players in the ears of the NHL and Hockey Canada brass. When the media report what is being said at the top, havoc is wreaked throughout our village. Hockey Quebec authorities are dragged over the coals on radio hotlines. Quebec Major Junior Hockey League coaches are accused of being incompetent. Hockey analysts and TV sports pundits go for the jugular. The tribe joins the fight which, unlike the comic book characters in the mythical village of the Gauls, does not end with a great village feast and celebration. The main difference between that Gallic village and Quebec is that in the comic book version Asterix and Obelix always end up solving the problem.

Where are Quebec's Asterix and Obelix? The answer is that they roam all over North America in the large hockey temples looking for the magic potion. When summer reaches the Gallic village, they return to their families and friends. That is exactly what I did as a professional during summer holidays.

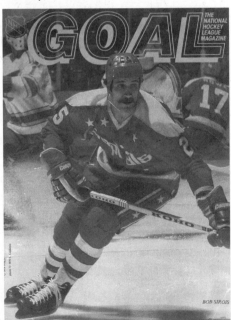

Author Bob Sirois played in the 1978 NHL All-Star Game representing the Washington Capitals.

Don't bother looking for those who let Detritus do his work in the English-Canadian hockey world. I'll tell you who they are. They are our own incarnations of Asterix and Obelix and I know them well because I was one of them. Every time someone called us "fucking frogs" or "fucking Frenchmen," we would play it down and trivialize the insult, not wanting to appear to be whiners or cry babies. The problem is that many players who used racial slurs against us are now employed by NHL teams. They hold strategic positions as scouts, coaches, and assistant coaches in the minor professional leagues and the NHL. It is doubtful that they have become more civilized with time. In fact, they have become to be the Detritus characters of our time.

The "invaders" are to blame

More than 90 percent of the players on National Hockey League teams from the 1917-18 season until the mid-70s were Canadian citizens. Until the first expansion in 1967, French-speaking Quebec hockey players played almost exclusively for the Montreal Canadiens. The five other NHL teams were made up of English Canadians, except for the odd French-Canadian player. When six new teams joined the NHL in 1967, demand for hockey players shot up and everybody was happy. The same thing occurred when the World Hockey Association was created. But even after those two events, French-speaking hockey players continued to be perceived as job thieves, poaching other people's rightful positions. Many English Canadians considered that the only place for French-speaking Quebecers was with the Montreal Canadiens. Toward the end of the 1970s when players from Sweden and Finland began to arrive, they too were seen as thieves stealing other players' jobs. Quebecers tended to react the same way as English Canadians. This mindset is very ingrained among English Canadians and probably explains discrimination that NHL players from other nations suffer. Quebecers are in fact included in the "other nations" because that's exactly how we are perceived, namely as invaders from another hockey planet.

All players from other countries who play for American teams in the NHL must obtain an H-1B visa from the American government. To obtain that visa, no other American citizen can be able do the work. That is exactly what happens in the National Hockey League. If foreign players are better than English Canadians, they will be able to play in the NHL. That means there is no place for any other category of player. In the NHL, when talent is equal an English Canadian will get the job. It is an employment protectionist measure. One of the ways that English Canadians in the NHL protect their jobs from the "invaders" is to discriminate against foreign hockey players. Quebec hockey players are treated in exactly the same way, as players from another nation. The Prime Minister of Canada and the Canadian Parliament are right: Canada is in fact comprised of two nations.

Summary

This recap will help readers draw their own conclusions regarding the current and past situation for French-speaking hockey players in the NHL.

- The myth about French-speaking Quebec hockey players is in fact true according to Marc Lavoie of the University of Ottawa. However, we are only talking about a half-inch and three-pound difference (1 cm, 1.4 kg).
- The myth about French-speaking hockey players' weakness in defensive hockey is disproven by Marc Lavoie in his book entitled, *Désavantage numérique*. Marc Lavoie analysed and compared the average number of goals by game, by team and by junior league in Canada. On many occasions, the Quebec Major Junior Hockey League registered the fewest goals scored per game.
- Table 4.1 shows that Quebec defencemen adapt the most quickly to the NHL style of play. Moreover, all things being equal and for all positions, they had the best results. Almost 51 percent of French-speaking Quebec defencemen played more than two hundred games, compared to 39 percent for wingers and goalies and 44 percent who for centres. This confirms that French-speaking Quebec hockey players are systematically underrated by NHL teams because of the myths and stereotypes spread by scouts from those same teams.

· The section entitled, "Equal talent, unequal treatment!" in Chapter 4 shows that 42 percent of French-speaking Quebec hockey players who played more than three seasons (two hundred games) in the NHL won individual honours. This proves that French-speaking Quebec hockey players have to be better than the others in order to succeed in the NHL. At equal talent, an English Canadian will be chosen.

· Chapter 2 provides facts proving that in Quebec when talent is equal an English-speaking Quebec hockey player will be chosen.

Taken together these facts corroborate conclusions reached by academics who, for more than forty years, have investigated the possibility that French-speaking Quebecers suffer discrimination in the National Hockey League. They found that French-speaking hockey players had to be much more talented than others to be drafted.

Recognizing discrimination, addressing the source, and taking steps to eradicate it is very important for everybody. Discrimination is alive and well in the English-Canadian National Hockey League.

Now is the time for people who hold authority to take action.

Epilogue

Quebecers are not alone

I wrote this book because, in Quebec, rarely does a day go by when the issue of the number of Quebec hockey players in the NHL compared to those from elsewhere in Canada is not discussed in the media. But are Quebecers the only ones being discriminated against? Do people from other nations have reasons to complain?

The only way to determine whether English Canadian hockey players have an advantage over people from other countries is to examine the number of registered minor hockey players in each major hockey nation and the number of hockey players from those nation who make it to the NHL.

This book deals specifically with the facts on hockey players from Quebec and from English-speaking Canada. It shows that the National Hockey League is in fact the English Canadian National League. The league allows the best players from other nations to play in their league, but when talent is equal or comparable, they will not choose a Quebecer, a European, or even an American. They will inevitably choose a "good ol' Canadian boy." Why, in a league with more than twenty-four teams in the United States, would they not favour an American hockey player who is equally talented? Though

TABLE 6.4

Registered Minor Hockey Players by Nation and Presence in the NHL (2009-10) *

Nation	Hockey players registered in minor leagues	Percent of registered players	Number drafted	Percent drafted	Number in NHL	Percent in NHL
Canada **	409,000	36.9	89	47.8	436	56.9
USA	465,000	41.9	59	31.7	189	24.5
Quebec	90,000	8.1	10	5.4	63	8.2
Russia	84,500	7.7	8	4.3	29	4
Sweden	60,000	5.4	20	10.8	49	6.5
TOTAL	1,108,500	100%	186	100%	766	100%

* Source: NHL.com, International Ice Hockey Federation
** Figures for Canada exclude Quebec.

the answer is not simple, it is not necessary to call on Albert Einstein for help. Who has not heard some of the following slurs in the past two decades? "The chicken Swedes." "The French wimps with their visors." "Those Europeans takin' jobs from good ol' Canadian boys." This talk never stops. As for the Americans, it is said that they don't play enough in their college schedules and cannot handle the harsh NHL schedule.

The prejudice among some scouts about how European, French Canadian, and Americans play hockey explains the glaring discrepancy between the number of young Americans and young Canadians who play minor hockey and the number who are drafted. In the past ten years, almost as many people play hockey in the United States as in Canada (without Quebec), yet NHL teams have drafted 1539 Canadians compared to 790 Americans, for a 2-to-1 ratio. In the 2009-10 season, the NHL had 436 Canadian hockey players and 189 Americans. That is two and half times more Canadian-born hockey players than American-born players.

These figures reflect the influence of the stereotypes created by the Canadian media and Canadian hockey brass on National Hockey League Teams in the United States. Ownership of the NHL teams in the United States is American, but their hockey operations are seventy percent Canadian.

Is this prejudice against American-born hockey players intentional? In my opinion it is not. But is it any wonder that many of the twenty-four teams in the United States are struggling. The question deserves to be addressed, just as discrimination against Quebec hockey players MUST be addressed. Our great sport of hockey can only stand to gain.

Appendix

TABLE I

Quebecers who played for the Montreal Canadiens
Number of games played per season

| PLAYERS | | DECADE 1970-79 | | | | | | | | | | | TOTAL |
SURNAME	FIRST NAME	70-71	71-72	72-73	73-74	74-75	75-76	76-77	77-78	78-79	79-80	TOTAL	SEASON
		***					***	***	***	***			
Béliveau	Jean	70											1
Cournoyer	Yvan	65	73	67	67	71	60	68	15				8
Tremblay	Jean-Claude	76	76										2
Lemaire	Jacques	78	77	77	66	80	61	75	76	50			9
Tardif	Marc	76	75	76									3
Richard	Henri	75	75	71	75	16							5
Lapointe	Guy	78	69	75	71	80	77	77	49	69	45		10
Houle	Réjean	66	77	72				65	76	66	60		7
Laperrière	Jacques	49	73	57	42								4
Rochefort	Léon	57											1
Savard	Serge	37	23	74	67	80	71	78	77	80	46		10
Charron	Guy	15											1
Bouchard	Pierre	51	60	41	60	79	66	73	59				8
Lafleur	Guy		73	69	73	70	80	80	78	80	74		9
Comeau	Reynald		4										1
Gagnon	Germain		4										1
Vachon	Rogatien	47	1										2
Myre	Philippe	30	9										2
Dejordy	Denis		7										1
Lambert	Yvon			1	60	80	80	79	77	79	77		8
Plasse	Michel			17	15								2
Larocque	Michel				27	25	22	26	30	34	39		7
Tremblay	Mario					63	71	74	56	76	77		6
Mondou	Pierre								71	77	75		3
Larouche	Pierre								44	36	73		3
Lupien	Gilles								46	72	56		3
Gingras	Gaston										34		1
Geoffrion	Daniel										32		1
Dupont	Normand										35		1
Herron	Denis										34		1
Sévigny	Richard										11		1
TOTAL: FRENCH-SPEAKING QUEBECERS		15	16	12	11	10	9	10	13	11	15	122	12.2
TOTAL PLAYERS USED		30	28	27	25	26	25	22	27	26	28	264	26.4
YEARLY AVERAGE		50%	57%	44%	44%	38%	36%	45%	48%	42%	53%	46%	46%

*** : Stanley Cup

PLAYERS		DECADE 1980-89											TOTAL
SURNAME	FIRST NAME	80-81	81-82	82-83	83-84	84-85	85-86	86-87	87-88	88-89	89-00	TOTAL	SEASON
							***						
Lafleur	Guy	51	66	68	80	19							5
Tremblay	Mario	77	80	80	67	75	56						6
Houle	Réjean	77	51	16									3
Lambert	Yvon	73											1
Larouche	Pierre	61	22										2
Mondou	Pierre	57	73	76	52	67							5
Gingras	Gaston	55	34	22			34	66	2				6
Savard	Serge	77											1
Lapointe	Guy	33	47										2
Picard	Robert	8	62	64	7								4
Carbonneau	Guy	2		77	78	79	80	79	80	79	68		9
Sévigny	Richard	33	19	38	40								4
Larocque	Michel	28											1
Herron	Denis	25	27										2
Delorme	Gilbert		60	78	27								3
Daoust	Daniel			4									1
Hamel	Jean				79								1
Lemieux	Claude				8	1	10	76	78	69	39		7
Baron	Normand				4								1
Gauvreau	Jocelyn				2								1
Momesso	Sergio				1		24	59	53				4
Penney	Steve				4	54	18						3
Roy	Patrick					1	47	46	45	48	54		6
Deblois	Lucien					51	61						2
Boisvert	Serge					14	9	1	5				4
Richer	Stéphane					1	65	57	72	68	51		6
Thibaudeau	Gilles							9	17	32			3
Charbonneau	José							16	9				2
Riendeau	Vincent							1					1
Desjardins	Éric									36	55		2
Dufresne	Donald									13	18		2
Brunet	Benoit									2			1
Lebeau	Stéphane									1	57		2
Lemieux	Jocelyn									1	34		2
Lefebvre	Sylvain									68			1
Daigneault	Jean-Jacques									36			1
Desjardins	Martin									8			1
Racicot	André									1			1
TOTAL: FRENCH-SPEAKING QUEBECERS		14	11	10	13	10	10	8	10	11	12	109	10.9
TOTAL PLAYERS USED		30	29	29	41	34	31	29	31	32	34	320	32
YEARLY AVERAGE		47%	38%	34%	32%	29%	32%	28%	32%	34%	35%	34%	34%

PLAYERS		DECADE 1990-1999											TOTAL
SURNAME	FIRST NAME	90-91	91-92	92-93	93-94	94-95	95-96	96-97	97-98	98-99	99-00	TOTAL	Season
				***									
Richer	Stéphane	75						63	14				3
Savard	Denis	70	77	63									3
Lebeau	Stéphane	73	77	71	34								4
Carbonneau	Guy	78	72	61	79								4
Desjardins	Éric	62	77	82	84	9							5
Lefebvre	Sylvain	63	69										2
Daigneault	Jean-Jacques	51	79	66	68	45	7						6
Dufresne	Donald	53	3	32									3
Turgeon	Sylvain	19	56										2
Côté	Alain	28	13										2
Brunet	Benoit	17	18	47	71	45	26	39	68	60	50		10
Brisebois	Patrice	10	26	70	53	35	69	49	79	54	54		10
Lebeau	Patrick	2											1
Roberge	Mario	5	20	50	28	9							5
Gauthier	Luc	3											1
Dionne	Gilbert	2	39	75	74	6							5
Roy	Patrick	48	67	62	68	43	22						6
Racicot	André	21	9	26	11								4
Bergeron	Jean-Claude	18											1
Chabot	Frédéric	3		1	1					11			4
Bélanger	Jesse		4	19							16		3
Damphousse	Vincent			84	84	48	80	82	76	65			7
Charron	Éric			3									1
Sévigny	Pierre				43	19		13					3
Brashear	Donald				14	20	67	10					4
Proulx	Christian				7								1
Turgeon	Pierre					15	80	9					3
Racine	Yves					47	25						2
Sarault	Yves					8	14						2
Quintal	Stéphane						68	71	71	82			4
Bureau	Marc						65	43	74				3
Groleau	François						2	5	1				3
Bordeleau	Sébastien						4	28	53				3
Thibault	Jocelyn						40	61	47	10			4
Labrecque	Patrick						2						1
Théodore	José						1	16		18	30		4
Houde	Éric							13	9	8			3
Poulin	Patrick								34	81	82		3
Morissette	Dave									10	1		2
Nasreddine	Alain									8			1
Jomphe	Jean-François									6			1
Blouin	Sylvain									5			1
Delisle	Jonathan									1			1
Bouillon	Francis										74		1
Ribeiro	Mike										19		1
Laflamme	Christian										15		1
Robidas	Stéphane										1		1
TOTAL: FRENCH-SPEAKING QUEBECERS		20	16	16	15	13	16	14	11	14	10	145	14.5
TOTAL PLAYERS USED		36	34	34	37	39	40	37	35	40	38	370	37
YEARLY AVERAGE		56%	47%	47%	41%	33%	40%	38%	31%	35%	26%	39%	39%

| PLAYERS | | DECADE 2000-2008 | | | | | | | | | TOTAL |
SURNAME	FIRST NAME	00-01	01-02	02-03	03-04	05-06	06-07	07-08	08-09	TOTAL	SEASON
Brisebois	Patrice	77	71	73	71			43	62		6
Poulin	Patrick	52	28								2
Brunet	Benoit	35	16								2
Robidas	Stéphane	65	56								2
Landry	Éric	51	2								2
Bouillon	Francis	29	28	20	73	67	62	74	54		8
Traverse	Patrick	19	25	65							3
Delisle	Xavier	14									1
Chouinard	Éric	13									1
Laflamme	Christian	39									1
Descoteaux	Mathieu	5									1
Odjick	Gino	13	36								2
Bélanger	Francis	10									1
Ciccone	Enrico	3									1
Bertrand	Éric	3									1
Ribeiro	Mike	2	43	52	81	79					5
Théodore	José	59	67	57	67	38					5
Garon	Mathieu	11	5	8	19						4
Fichaud	Éric	2									1
Perreault	Yanic		82	73	69						3
Juneau	Joey		82	72	70						3
Quintal	Stéphane		75	67	73						3
Dykhuis	Karl		80								1
Audette	Donald		13	54	23						3
Gratton	Benoit		8		4						2
Fiset	Stéphane		2								1
Michaud	Olivier		1								1
Blouin	Sylvain			17							1
Beauchemin	François			1							1
Dagenais	Pierre				50	32					2
Bégin	Steve				52	76	52	44	42		5
Dandenault	Mathieu					82	68	61	41		4
Ferland	Jonathan					7					1
Côté	Jean-François					8					1
Lapierre	Maxim					1	46	53	79		4
Danis	Yann					6					1
Latendresse	Guillaume						80	73	56		3
Tanguay	Alex								50		1
Laracque	Georges								33		1
Denis	Marc								1		1
TOTAL: FRENCH-SPEAKING QUEBECERS		19	19	12	12	10	5	6	9	92	11.5
TOTAL PLAYERS USED		46	40	32	34	32	29	30	34	277	34.6
YEARLY AVERAGE		41%	48%	38%	35%	31%	17%	20%	26%	33%	33%

List of Tables and list of Abbreviations

List of Tables

Table 2.1	French-speaking Quebec hockey players drafted (1970-2009)	33
Table 2.2	English-speaking Quebec hockey players drafted (1970-2009)	33
Table 2.3	Comparison of Quebecers drafted (1970-2009)	33
Table 2.4	Hockey background of all Quebec hockey players drafted (1970-2009)	33
Table 2.5	Percentage of English-speaking hockey players drafted per decade	34
Table 2.6	Comparison of Quebec hockey players drafted by decade	34
Table 2.7	Comparison of Quebec hockey players drafted (1970- 2005)	35
Table 2.8	Comparison of Quebec hockey players who were drafted and who played (by decade)	38
Table 2.9	Comparison of Quebec hockey players who were drafted and who played between 1970 and 2005	38
Table 2.10	The number of French-speaking Quebec hockey players drafted (by rank, 1970-2005)	39
Table 2.11	The number of players who played one or more games (by rank, 1970-2005)	40
Table 2.12	Summary table (1970-2005)	40
Table 2.13	French-speaking Quebec players not drafted (by decade)	42
Table 2.14	English-speaking Quebec players not drafted (1970 to 2009)	44
Table 2.15	Midget by year (1970- 2009)	46
Table 2.16	Ranking of NHL teams by the number of French-speaking Quebec hockey players drafted	48
Table 2.17	Draft of French-speaking Quebecers 1970-2009	51

Table 2.18   Draft results for French-speaking Quebecers
1970-2009   70

Table 2.19   Draft of English-speaking Quebecers 1970-2009   71

Table 2.20   Draft results for English-speaking Quebecers
1970-2009   76

Table 3.1   Quebecers drafted by team 1970 to 2009   96

Table 3.2   Quebecers who played in the NHL by team 1970
to 2009   120

Table 4.1   Comparison by position of French-speaking
Quebec hockey players who played more than
two hundred games (1970-2009)   162

Table 4.2   Comparison of the Quebecers who participated
by year   163

Table 4.3   Comparison of the Quebecers who participated
by decade   164

Table 4.4   Participation of Quebec Hockey Players in NHL
All-Star Games   165

Table 4.5   Centres 1970 to 2009   172

Table 4.6   Centres whose careers began before the 1970-71
season   175

Table 4.7   Wingers 1970 to 2009   177

Table 4.8   Wingers whose careers began before the season
1970-71   183

Table 4.9   Goalies 1970 to 2009   186

Table 4.10   Goalies whose careers began before the season
1970-71   189

Table 4.11   Defencemen 1970 to 2009   190

Table 4.12   Defencemen whose careers began before
the season 1970-71   194

Table 5.1   Quebec coaches in the NHL   197

Table 6.1   Comparison of the average height and weight
of Canadian major junior hockey league players
according to their positions (1984-88)   201

Table 6.2   Average number of goals per season and per team
in the Canadian major junior hockey leagues
(1979-97)   203

Table 6.3   Results of NHL player draft by nation between
1994 and 2009   207

Table 6.4   Registered Minor Hockey Players by Nation
and Presence in the NHL (2009-10)   215

Appendix

Table 1   Quebecers who played for the Montreal Canadiens
Number of games played per season   217

Abbreviations

A	Assists
CU	Canadian universities
PIM	Penalties in minutes
W	Wingers (position played)
C	Centres
D	Defencemen
P	Position played
T	Ties (for goalies)
AV.	Goals against average
G	Goals
GP	Games played
W	Wins (for goalies)
L	Losses
PTS	Points
LHJMQ	Ligue de hockey junior majeur du Québec

 Recycled
Supporting responsible use
of forest resources
www.fsc.org Cert no. SGS-COC-003153
© 1996 Forest Stewardship Council

MARQUIS

Marquis Book Printing Inc.

Québec, Canada
2010

Printed on Silva Enviro 100% post-consumer EcoLogo certified paper,
processed chlorine free and manufactured using biogas energy.